INSCRIBED ACROSS THE LANDSCAPE
THE CURSUS ENIGMA

INSCRIBED ACROSS THE LANDSCAPE
THE CURSUS ENIGMA

ROY LOVEDAY

TEMPUS

FOR DEREK BARKER
*without whose questioning enthusiasm for the past my research
would never have begun*

First published 2006

Tempus Publishing Limited
The Mill, Brimscombe Port,
Stroud, Gloucestershire, GL5 2QG
www.tempus-publishing.com

© Roy Loveday, 2006

The right of Roy Loveday to be identified as the Author
of this work has been asserted in accordance with the
Copyrights, Designs and Patents Act 1988.

All rights reserved. No part of this book may be reprinted
or reproduced or utilised in any form or by any electronic,
mechanical or other means, now known or hereafter invented,
including photocopying and recording, or in any information
storage or retrieval system, without the permission in writing
from the Publishers.

British Library Cataloguing in Publication Data.
A catalogue record for this book is available from the British Library.

ISBN 0 7524 3652 X

Typesetting and origination by Tempus Publishing Limited
Printed in Great Britain

CONTENTS

	Acknowledgements	6
	Preface	7
	Background – the British Neolithic	9
1	Introduction – the nature of the enigma	11
2	'A new unobserv'd curiosity'	14
3	Variations on a theme – the cursus continuum	20
4	'Difficult to see on the ground' – non-monumental monuments	35
5	'Reeking bone yards'? – long mortuary enclosures	45
6	Pattern and purpose – long enclosures in the landscape	59
7	'Monsters of degeneracy' – bank barrows	88
8	'A solemne walke' – avenues	103
9	Inscribing the landscape – layout and its implications	114
10	Rivers, hills, sun, moon and stars – cursuses in the landscape	131
11	Sacred landscapes	143
12	Sacred sites and power – transformation in the north	162
13	Sacred sites and power – emulation in the south?	182
14	Cursus afterglow	192
	Appendices	203
	Endnotes	208
	Bibliography	213
	Index	221

ACKNOWLEDGEMENTS

I owe a great debt of gratitude to the very many people who assisted me with my initial research into cursuses so many years ago, amongst whom I should particularly thank Gavin Maxwell and Richard Bradley. I am also extremely grateful to the following people and organisations that have generously permitted me to use their material to illustrate points made here: Martin Green, David Hogg, Gordon Barclay, Kenneth Brophy, Alistair Barclay, Stuart Palmer, Candy Stevens, Owen Bedwin, Roger Massey-Ryan, Arnold Baker, the Society of Antiquaries of Scotland, the Prehistoric Society, Yale University Press, the Ashmolean Museum (Oxford), English Heritage, RCAHM Scotland, and the Bodleian Library, University of Oxford. I have also benefitted from time generously given by numerous people to discuss points or share information. Particular thanks are due to Gill Hey, Chris Ellis, Mike Allen, Kenneth Brophy, Clive Ruggles, Alistair Barclay, Jan Harding, Terry Manby, Philip Abramson and Dave McOmish.

I am hugely grateful to John Litchfield for accomplishing computer miracles with my data and then uncomplainingly re-working it, to Kate Morgan for endlessly saving me from computer tangles and to Derek Barker for reading and commenting on the text. I owe a great debt of gratitude to my family – the puzzled observers of an obsession – for their patience and to Lynn for her unswerving support, encouragement and ideas.

PREFACE

Cursus monuments are too important to inhabit just specialist journals and air-photograph libraries. These 'British Nasca lines' – staggering and frustrating by turns – encode the beliefs of a rapidly changing Neolithic society and record the point at which it took off on a trajectory that would lead ultimately to the great structure at Stonehenge. This book explores that story in a manner that it is hoped will be accessible to all interested readers, although some may wish to skip the more detailed evidence on origins set out in chapter 6. Those with a deeper interest may seek the sources of the evidence (largely academic journals) through the footnotes.

Only calibrated radiocarbon dates have been used and are quoted at 2 sigma, the highest level of probability. They have been rounded to the nearest 50 years to avoid a false impression of precision.

The author's full survey of cursus and related monuments containing details of sites and plans at a common scale can be consulted through Archaeological Data Services on:
http://ads.ahds.ac.uk/catalogue/reources.html?cursus_phd_2006

BACKGROUND – THE BRITISH NEOLITHIC

4000–3400 BC EARLY NEOLITHIC

This was the period that witnessed the advent of agriculture in the British Isles. In the lowland zone earthen long barrows were constructed covering small wooden structures that contained collections of disarticulated bones from partial human skeletons.

Causewayed enclosures defined by segmented ditches were built amongst the long barrows on the southern chalk. They are also detectable as cropmarks in the valleys, but typical, flanking ditch long barrows are not. The enclosures appear to have been used for activities ranging from feasting to the exposure of corpses to judge from the ashy midden material and cattle, sheep and human bones that their ditches contain. Some were redefined by a continuous defendable ditch at a late stage in their use, and a few display evidence of attack. In the highland zone, long or round cairns with stone chambers contained comparable collections of disarticulated bone to those in the wooden structures of the lowlands. Causewayed enclosures, however, are an extreme rarity north and west of the Trent. Pottery in all areas was of plain, round bowl type along with finer carinated forms. Regional styles developed later in the period.

c.3600–2800 BC MIDDLE NEOLITHIC

This is a shadowy period during which causewayed enclosures and long mounds were no longer built. In eastern Yorkshire it is marked by the appearance of intact burials with prestige artefacts under round barrows; in southern England by similar but less well-furnished burials under small long barrows. In northern

Scotland construction of chambered tombs continued, as it did in Ireland where the Great Boyne passage tombs were built. Radiocarbon dates indicate that most English cursuses were built during this period; some in Scotland belong in the earlier period. The decorated tradition of Peterborough Ware now covers much of lowland England, with allied regional impressed styles in southern Scotland. Grooved Ware makes an early appearance in Orkney.

2800–2200 BC   LATE NEOLITHIC

This period is marked by the spread of Grooved Ware – decorated, flat-based, tub-like pottery – apparently from northern Scotland. The users of this pottery built a new type of ceremonial monument – the henge. These were circular to oval ditched monuments with external banks and often internal post or stone settings. In Wessex they were expanded to form huge enclosures like that at Avebury; elsewhere large post enclosures may have fulfilled the same purpose. Burials are absent during this period except for cremations placed at major ceremonial sites. Cursuses may still have been respected.

c.2400–1600 BC   EARLY BRONZE AGE

With the advent of Beakers (finely made drinking pots) and the first copper artefacts (daggers), individual burial under round barrows reappears. These monuments were constructed in increasing profusion as bronze became a familiar prestige item.

I

INTRODUCTION – THE NATURE OF THE ENIGMA

The word enigma could have been coined for cursus monuments. Alone amongst the many seemingly empty sites of British prehistory the size, form and layout of cursuses defy logical hypothesising. The greatest of them (actually two cursuses butted onto each other) runs for nearly 10km across Cranborne Chase in Dorset, crossing four valleys and enclosing within its parallel ditches over 100ha – equivalent to 122 football pitches, 72 Aveburys or 4 Amun-Re precincts at Karnak. In fact the whole of the latter vast temple complex – often held to be the largest in the world – took less land than each arm of the Dorset Cursus. It has been estimated that digging its ditches involved nearly half a million worker-hours (say 500 people working for 100 days). Yet this vast double enclosure appears to enclose *nothing*; nothing that is beyond a long barrow about a quarter of the way along its length. Even this seems unlikely to furnish any clue to purpose since it is set *across* the line of the southern (Gussage) cursus, making processional access to the probable burial area at the end of the barrow awkward and ungainly. Four kilometres further north the Pentridge arm of the cursus is deliberately aligned on another long barrow, but not to lead people to it: this barrow was buried in one of the monument's side banks. In both cases funerary processions along the cursus to the barrows are excluded. Nor are causeways to allow access obvious, except about a kilometre from the northern end of the Pentridge arm where opposed gaps may have been left.

As we follow cursus sites down their huge linear scale from 10km to just 100m (no more then the width of the great Dorset site) the same picture presents itself. Parallel lines, marking ditches that often seem to be ruler drawn, leap out from the usual tangle of prehistoric and Roman farm and field ditches on aerial photographs, yet enigmatically seem to lead nowhere and enclose nothing. To add to the problem the huge surface areas of even the smaller sites inhibits total excavation, and this is further discouraged by their reputation for barren ditches and interiors (72m of ditch were fully excavated on the site at Maxey in Cambridgeshire without producing a single find!).

They can of course be viewed as just one further manifestation of the drive that leads mankind to create huge structures to honour its gods. Certainly any mundane role is excluded by their size, layout and lack of domestic rubbish. Yet cursuses also obstinately fail all the obvious tests that can be applied to ritual structures: in essence to accommodate the celebrants (inside or out), to focus and lead them to the sacred area and to impress them. Comparison with another gigantic monument, the great mosque at Cordoba, is illuminating. In order to accommodate an ever-growing Muslim population, this amazing edifice was extended to record-breaking proportions – 178m x 125m (22,250 sq m). The Dorset Cursus was also extended, doubling its size to 10,000m x 100m (1,000,000 sq m). It beggars belief that the population of Neolithic Wessex so vastly exceeded that of Cordoba, the greatest city in Europe in the tenth century AD, that a structure 45 times larger was needed. So huge in fact were cursuses that the longest cathedral in Europe (St Peter's, Rome: 187m) would only just fail to fit inside one of the very *smallest* cursus – Barford in Warwickshire (185m). Of course internal accommodation of worshippers was probably the exception rather than the rule in antiquity. Yet should we envisage the opposite – that those attending activities at a cursus gathered outside its confines - problems of visibility and audibility arise. Those orchestrating events at the centre of the monument may be as much as 50m distant from those outside.

1 The avenue of sphinxes at Luxor, Egypt – marking the route of the great Opet festival procession

INTRODUCTION – THE NATURE OF THE ENIGMA

2 The Greater Stonehenge Cursus looking from the eastern end. Its sides are marked in the foreground by the trees on the right and the fence on the left; in the distance by the gap cleared in the woodland. Compare with figure 1

Cursuses equally fail to impress in that role most often ascribed to them – as processional avenues. These are cross-cultural features of great ritual sites, occurring at points as diverse as Teotihuacan, Karnak and Stonehenge. They have a common purpose: to overawe worshippers through a combination of flanking monumental structures and a highly charged focus. Dimension and proportion are vital to the achievement of this end (*1*). Thus a person walking along the Stonehenge avenue is aware of its restricting side ditches and is progressively drawn to the stones that emerge powerfully on the skyline in front. By contrast a person walking along the centre of the adjacent Greater Stonehenge Cursus apparently sees nothing ahead and would be hard pressed to be aware of its parameters let alone be impressed by them (*2*). Today the swathe cut by the National Trust through the wood covering its western end furnishes a measure of three-dimensional focus but environmental evidence makes it clear that this was not a feature of the site during the Neolithic – the landscape then was cleared and open. Cursuses rarely terminate at another monument, and when they do it never appears monumentally significant.

This then is the nature of the challenge – to explain vast empty enclosures, often laid out with striking precision, that cut swathes across the countryside. Nothing like them had been witnessed before, and with their passing nothing like them was to be seen again. The structures that followed – Avebury, Silbury Hill, Stonehenge – were monumental in the strict sense of the word and far more readily explicable within the 'grammar' of ritual architecture.

2

'A NEW UNOBSERV'D CURIOSITY'

On 6 August 1723 a 36-year-old Lincolnshire doctor with strong antiquarian interests and acute observational skills honed by 13 years of annual horseback expeditions across the length and breadth of the country, discovered the first cursus. He was William Stukeley, and it lay about half a mile from the subject of his obsessive interest – Stonehenge. He had also been the first to record the ditched avenue running to Stonehenge but that only required a half-observant fieldworker. Recognition of the cursus was of a quite different order: it was set apart, on a quite different alignment and defined by barely visible ditches. Perhaps he noted the first ditch while selecting one of the adjacent round barrows to excavate the next day; an exercise he recorded by detailed notes and even a drawn section, the earliest in British archaeology and well over a century ahead of its time.[1] But he had to move 100m away to discover its parallel twin. This was a separation without precedent amongst linear monuments. Other observers might have dismissed it as an ancient field ditch but he traced the full 2700m of its course and appreciated its distinctive, square-ended enclosure form. So struck was he that he returned three weeks later to complete another simple field sketch. These primary records are invaluable, not only because a great deal of the site was subsequently obliterated by ploughing, but because Stukeley himself was later to falsify his observations (*3* and *4*).

By 1740, when he published his findings in *Stonehenge, a Temple Restor'd to the British Druids*, he had satisfied himself as to the purpose of this huge elongated enclosure. It was a chariot race track – a cursus. To accommodate this interpretation he blatantly changed his drawings (*5*). Now he confidently stated that: 'The west end of the cursus is curved into an arch, like the end of the Roman circus. And there probably the chariots ran round in order to turn again.' As convex terminals were later to emerge as features of cursuses elsewhere,

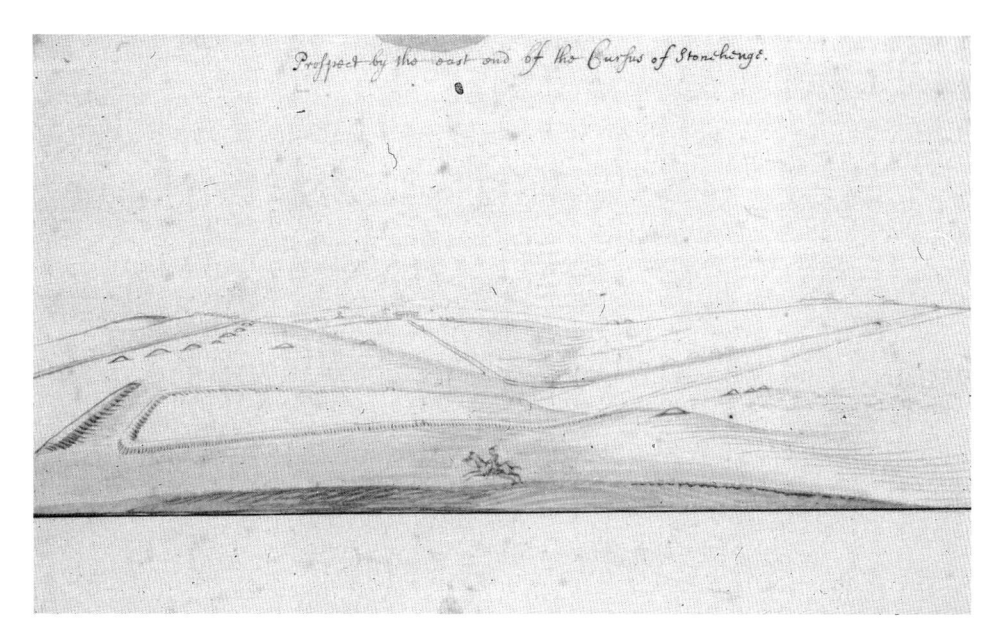

3 Stukeley's field sketch of the eastern end of the Greater Cursus showing he knew it was not joined to the long barrow. *Bodleian Library: Gough Maps 229, fol 122*

4 Stukeley's field sketch of the western terminal. *Bodleian Library: Gough Maps 229, fol 125*

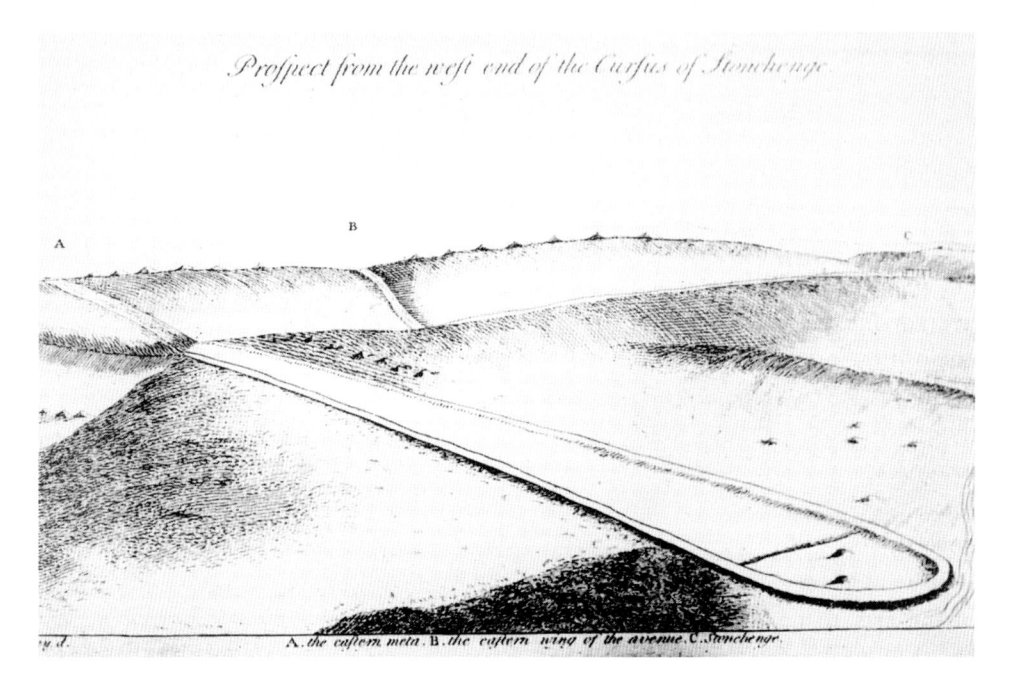

5 Stukeley's published drawing of the western terminal – now curved for turning chariots!

this piece of adaption was less damaging to future study than that which he perpetrated at the eastern end of the monument.

There he decided to totally ignore his own observation that the cursus terminated 40m before a long barrow set across its alignment. Instead he described the long barrow *as* the terminal ('The east end of the cursus is composed of a huge body of earth, a bank or long barrow.'). This adjustment was vital to his case since the barrow had been conscripted as the seat of the judges, who could hardly have pronounced on races finishing 40m away! Despite the clearly contrary evidence of Colt Hoare's plan at the front of *Ancient Wiltshire* published 70 years later, and of aerial photographs, that single fabrication dominated thinking about cursuses for more than two centuries – judges vanished along with chariots as an Iron Age date was dismissed but that fictitious junction remained, demanding a functional link between the two types of monument. Thus cursuses popularly became avenues along which the dead were taken to their final resting places in long barrows.

Sadly, then, Stukeley stands both as discoverer and distorter of the cursus. Significantly it was only when he attempted to interpret his findings that his judgement erred – a timely warning in a modern age of interpretative, phenomenological archaeology. This flaw led him to ignore the Lesser Stonehenge Cursus since it was too short for a chariot course and possessed a cross bank halfway along its length. Instead he added the Dyke Hills at Dorchester upon Thames and the Raw Dykes at Leicester, both heavily elongated, parallel-sided earthworks: in fact, as we now know, respectively the spaced banks of a Late Iron Age oppidum and a Roman aqueduct.[2] The problem remains. Isolated lengths of trackway or Roman road adjacent to ring ditches are often claimed as cursuses while elongated enclosures, akin to the Lesser Stonehenge Cursus, pass unnoticed. Had Stukeley stuck to his dispassionate field sketch evidence this might have been avoided but what would we then be calling these monuments – elongated enclosures, long enclosures or just enclosures? More accurate perhaps, but scarcely doing justice to these most singular monuments. Stukeley the gifted fieldworker then bequeathed a new type of monument, while Stukeley the first new age mystic 'rediscovering the roots of "true religion"' bequeathed us (in addition to some spurious conceptual baggage) an archaic, and totally anachronistic title that nevertheless still serves to evoke something of their mystery.

It was left to Sir Richard Colt Hoare of Stourhead, wealthy banker and patron of the arts, to recognise the Lesser Cursus, a double enclosure just 600m away from Stukeley's 'most noble work', and to publicise in 1819 William Cunnington's recognition of two surviving miles of the Dorset Cursus on Cranborne Chase.[3] These three were to remain as the sole representatives of cursus for the next 124 years, once quite different explanations had disposed of the Dyke Hills and Raw Dykes sites. And, with the incomplete Dorset site appearing perhaps as a 'British trackway' leading to the impressive Iron Age settlement on Gussage Hill, cursuses came to be viewed as yet another unique feature of Stonehenge: the monument overlooked the midpoint of the Greater Cursus and afforded ideal views of its course ('A delightful prospect from the temple, when this vast plain was crowded with chariots, horseman and foot, attending theses solemnities with innumerable multitudes').

In fact other small sections had been recorded as earthworks. On Thickthorn Down in Dorset a strangely monumental three-sided enclosure occasioned interest but there was nothing to link it to the earthworks of Cunnington's cursus across the valley on Gussage Hill. On a similar chalkland ridge top, nearly 2km south of the great monolith at Rudston in the East Riding of Yorkshire, there was another monumentally constructed three-sided enclosure. This one had, however, been excavated by Canon Greenwell in the belief that it represented a unique arrangement of linked long barrows.[4] In each case the earthworks represented hilltop islands of preservation separated by cultivated land where nothing remained visible above ground. It would require a new invention to enable the buried cursus ditches that ran from the Thickthorn and Rudston 'enclosures' to be detected – the aeroplane.

AERIAL PHOTOGRAPHY

When in 1922 Air Commodore Clark Hall noted strange marks that proved to be Celtic fields on RAF aerial photographs of the downs near Winchester archaeology broke free from the spade and the vagaries of historical land use. Nevertheless it required an interested and intelligent observer to realise the potential of the new knowledge that crops might parch and ripen earlier over buried foundations and banks, and later over the damper, richer fill of buried ditches. Archaeology found that person in Major Allen, and luckily for our study, he was based in the Upper Thames Valley. In the years before 1934 he had brought 'more than one instance of a remarkable type of rectangular enclosure in the valley of the Thames below Oxford' to the notice of E.T. Leeds of the Ashmolean Museum.[5] Many of these 'mysterious lines and enclosures revealed by aerial photography' possessed a ruler-drawn and right-angled precision that suggested the hand of Roman surveyors (6). Leeds, however, noticed that the cropmarks of one such ditch extended the line of a ditch that he had been excavating, along with Anglo Saxon houses, as it was exposed in a gravel pit at Sutton Courtenay – Drayton. In its upper fill he had found a hearth with 14

6 Major Allen's photograph of the Benson cursus, 1933. Allen145: Ashmolean Museum, Oxford

scrapers, sufficient to demonstrate that it had been dug '… in the Bronze Age – presumably Early – or even in the Neolithic period.' The implications were not lost on the redoubtable fieldworker O.G.S. Crawford. In the very next copy of the *Antiquaries Journal* he responded by suggesting that Major Allen's rectangular enclosures were in fact cursuses and incidentally placed in print for the first time the anglised plural of the latin cursūs, a form that has precisely the same validity as circuses.[6]

From this point there was no looking back: from just two certain sites up to 1934; to 15 by 1960 when the Royal Commission published 'A Matter of Time'; to 19 in 1964 when Webster and Hobley identified the small sites of the Warwickshire Avon; to 29 when Gordon Maxwell realised that pit-defined sites in Scotland belonged in this class; to 45 in 1984 when I completed a nationwide trawl; to over 100 possible sites in Britain and Ireland today. No class of monument it seems has grown at such speed.[7]

There can, of course, never be a definitive list and distribution map for these, or any other, archaeological sites. Heavy, moisture retentive soils and areas of forest and pasture act as blankets obscuring large areas. In more responsive locations the variables of drought, fields brought into cultivation after years (even centuries) under grass and the chance presence of an archaeological flier overhead at the right time, all operate on cropmark production and recognition. Even in the Upper Thames Valley, intensively observed since the 1930s, another cursus turned up in 1986 at Stadhampton just 5km from the great Dorchester upon Thames complex carefully mapped by Major Allen 50 years earlier.[8] Nevertheless, sufficient sites are now known to be able to recognise common characteristics, establish a dateable context and so approach the vexed question of their use. Before we attempt that, however, we must face the problem of definition: with ditches of the same basic plan ranging in length from nearly 10,000m to just 65m, and being defined by ditches or pits, with banks or in some cases a central mound, can we be certain that they all merit the title Stukeley bequeathed us?

3

VARIATIONS ON A THEME – THE CURSUS CONTINUUM

If we are to begin to understand these monuments – whether the monsters of the Wessex and Yorkshire chalk or the midgets of the Warwickshire Avon valley – we must be certain that we are comparing like with like. If partial sections of trackways, roads and fields are included through misinterpretation (e.g. Ufton Nervet: RCHM 1960), these will inevitably distort potentially critical conclusions about the proportions, alignment and associations of the group. It is often comparatively straightforward to recognise and remove these. But there are other sites that present greater problems, appearing to be neither 'fish nor fowl'. Such uncertain sites inevitably raise the question of definition: can we justify drawing distinctions based on our perceptions of plan?

Since definition and classification are based on plan views of monuments that were never seen by their builders, it is increasingly argued that this is a spurious exercise – a pseudo-scientific attempt to impose taxonomic order on the many and varied manifestations of mankind's religious activity. Exemplifying this position is the statement that:

> all Neolithic monuments have their origins in attempts to mediate difficult social relationships (such as between the living and the dead) by controlling areas of space within the landscape. Their meaning will not be resolved merely by formal classification because there is increasing evidence that Neolithic people did not think in terms of these categories…. (Since) cursus sites are primarily concerned with alignments and linear paths rather than complex divisions of internal space, attention should be focused on their role in structuring people's movement within the landscape, particularly in relation to adjacent monuments[1]

This approach has the great virtue of forcing us to view sites as their builders did, on the ground, and of placing them in their immediate, local context; its weakness

7 Holywood North – emphatically convex (type A). Pits can be seen just within the ditch line. Crown copyright © RCAHMS

lies in placing an *assumed* function, rather than formal plan, at the forefront of site recognition and labelling. How can we be certain that such activities actually took place, let alone furnished the *raison d'être* for the monuments? Plan logic would after all lead us to assume, wrongly, that long barrows were designed to cover a large number of burial structures.

Distinct plans by contrast have the virtue of objectivity and in their repetition we have apparent evidence of contemporary significance (*7* and *8*). Just as 'standardised' Greek temple and Early Christian basilica forms did not result by happy convergence from random local imperatives to provide a covered structure for the cult image or accommodation for worshippers, so commonality in Neolithic ritual structures must not be dismissed in parochial, functional terms.

INSCRIBED ACROSS THE LANDSCAPE: THE CURSUS ENIGMA

8 Above: Holywood South – equally emphatically square (type B). (Note the considerable width of this minor cursus compared to the dual carriageway beside it.) *Crown copyright © RCAHMS*

9 Left: Ritual architecture as message – a modern statement of Roman Catholic identity and primacy

To do so patronises — even insults — the builders of monuments that were replicated with such sophistication. Equally the laying out of cursuses with precisely rectangular terminals, or opposed entrance henges with subtle ovate ditch segments, at a range of different sizes is not to be characterised as 'slavish copying'. The fact that these forms did not result from the repetition of simple setting out procedures, and that they were largely invisible to the celebrant on the ground, supports the idea that shared underlying concepts dictated plan. This should not surprise us: ritual is repetitive and formulaic, not merely in its procedures but in the venues set apart for its practice. And it is through the latter that group identity is often proclaimed — witness the common adoption of Early Christian architectural forms by the modern English Roman Catholic Church whose medieval style and structures were usurped at the reformation (9).

There is no apparent functional reason why cursuses from Dumfries to Devon should be closed at each end by terminals of the same convex or rectangular plan; tapered, splayed or oblique forms might equally have been selected to close paths and avenues. So clear in fact is terminal form that Julian Thomas recognised a cursus at Dunragit from no more than this, despite arguing that function rather than plan should form the basis for archaeological explanation.[2]

Definition and classification are neither ends in themselves nor blocks to the recognition of regional or geological variation; they are simply tools to be used in the search for commonality as an initial, secure step towards explanation. We would be foolish to ignore the differing plans of adjacent cursuses as at Holywood in Dumfriesshire. Variation must of course be expected, both across the passage of time, and from peripheral, usurping, 'unorthodox' and even inept groups. Prehistoric monument classification can no more be precise than that of church architecture: we recognise Romanesque or Perpendicular churches by their distinctive stylistic and ritual 'grammar', not because they are identical. It is within this context of a common, observable ritual 'grammar' that individual site histories can be observed.

DEFINITION AND DIVISION

To securely establish what constitutes a cursus it is vital to focus on those sites proven by excavation. Almost without exception, when fully exposed, they prove to have possessed terminals at each end of the same basic plan. Only at the Lesser Stonehenge Cursus and at Hastings Hill, Co. Durham, do we have sites clearly possessing only one.

Two broad terminal types can be recognised: rounded and squared. For ease of reference these can be referred to as types A and B. This carries no implication

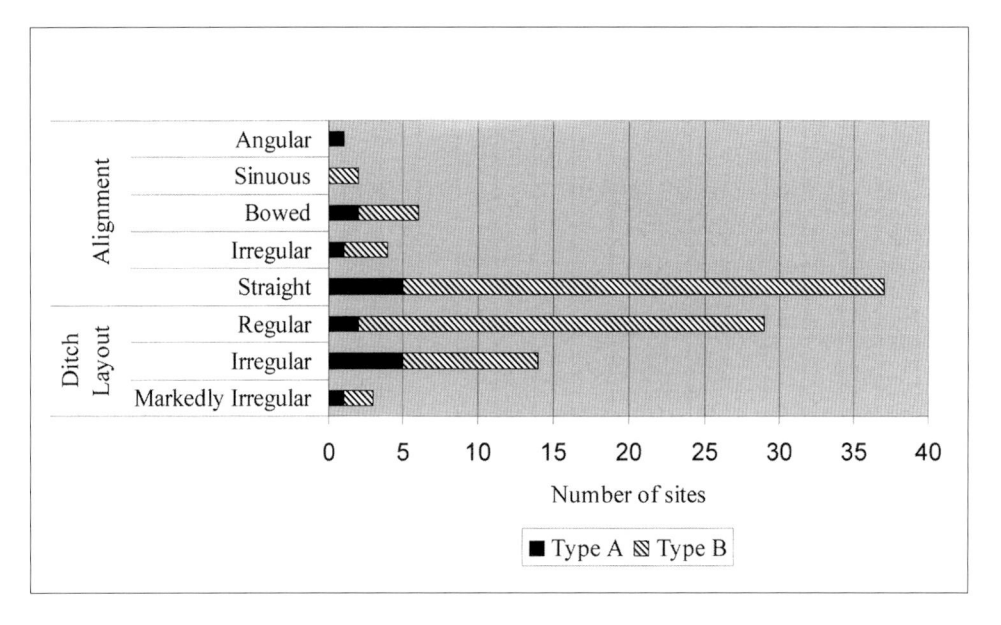

10 Cursus form

of date, cultural affiliation or function. It is simply a record of observable difference that is sufficiently marked as to suggest positive choice on the part of the builders. Variations within these broad types probably indicate little more than lack of accomplishment in layout. A distinctive group of rectangular sites laid out with considerable geometric precision is obvious, however. They can be termed Bi sites.

It is equally clear that the overwhelming majority of sites are straight, or at least approximately so. This highlights the obvious anomalies of Gussage/Pentridge (the Dorset Cursus), Rudston (site A) and Fornham All Saints with their distinctive sinuous or angular sections (*10*).

Structural form is difficult to establish since almost all the sites have been ploughed flat. Nevertheless the limited evidence that we have suggests marked variability; internal banks on the classic earthwork sites in Wessex and Eastern Yorkshire; central mounds at Scorton, North Yorkshire, Cleaven Dyke, Perthshire, and Stanwell, Middlesex; and pits or posts in Lowland Scotland. All coherence it seems breaks down here with some sites appearing to be essentially bank barrows (massively extended long barrows), and others, post-defined long mortuary enclosures (places where bodies are assumed to have been exposed to the elements prior to burial under long barrows). Were it not for similar variation in stone circle and henge architecture, we might conclude that there was indeed no single monument type that we call a cursus. Nevertheless, in both of those cases 'orthodoxy' (or at least broad consistency) seems to centre on perimeter definition. That is equally true amongst cursuses where the pits or posts of Scottish sites exhibit the same convex and rounded-terminal forms as the ditched cursus series. A mixing of traditions and the magnification of certain sites appears evident, that may lead us to an explanation once we are sure of the consistency of our data.

We can then define cursuses as: 'Parallel sided sites closed by at least one terminal and defined by ditches or pits/posts. They may possess either banks or a central mound.'

This allows us to place a question mark over those sites that do not follow the pattern – they may be related to cursuses proper but that needs to be demonstrated by excavation. Unfortunately it does not resolve all the difficulties since sites conforming to these morphological criteria can be traced down from nearly 10km on Cranbourne Chase (the Dorset Cursus) to merely 35m on Normanton Down, adjacent to Stonehenge. What is more, the small sites display exactly the same tendency to possess either banks or a covering mound (e.g. Charlecote).[3] As with henge monuments, a continuum appears to exist from minute to truly massive sites (*11*). Clearly to give the title cursus to sites at the lower end would seriously devalue the name and lead to confusion: on the face of it, it seems improbable that they could have fulfilled the same function. Yet where is the distinction to be made? Functional judgments are as invalid as morphological ones here – if the sites were, for instance, processional routes at what length might these commence? There is nowhere to process within a

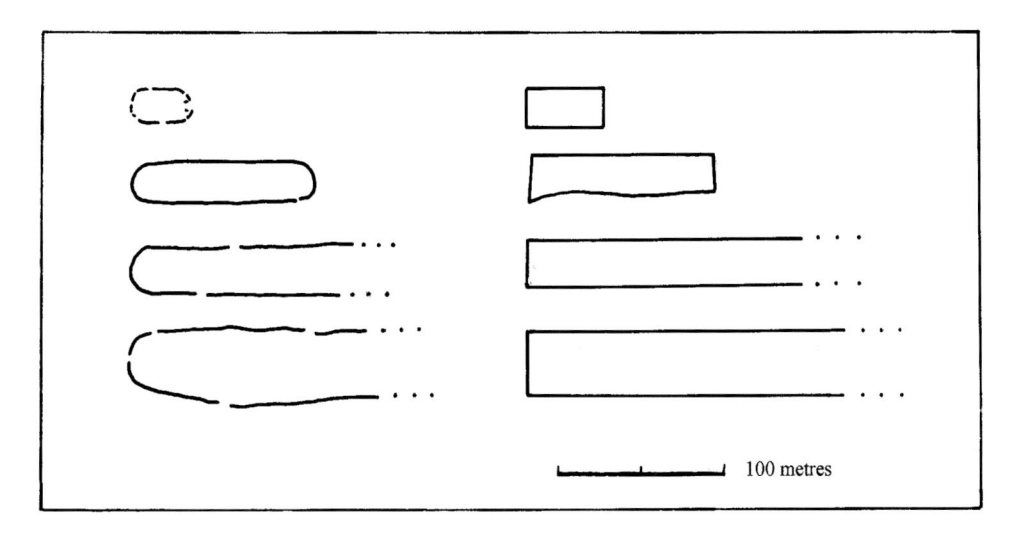

11 The cursus continuum

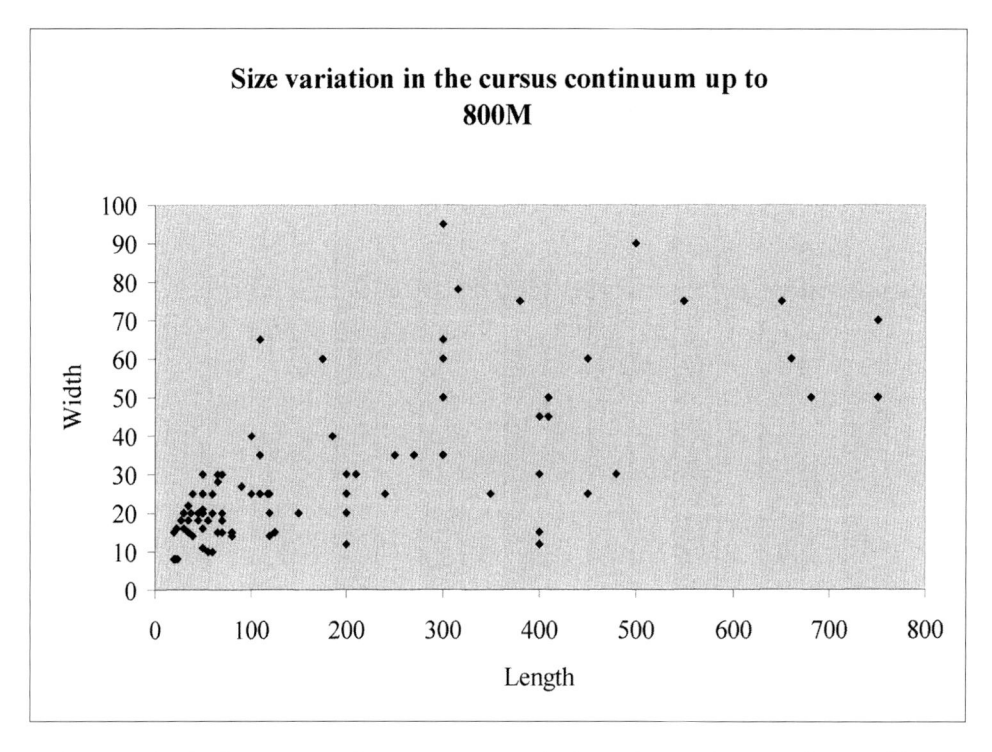

Size variation in the cursus continuum up to 800M

12 Size variation in the cursus continuum up to 800m (major and mega sites extend group 2b)

35m-long site and no logical reason why a 3000m-long one should be blocked at each end by identically formed terminals. The only appropriate divisions are those objectively based on mathematical clustering.

Four broad groupings emerge (see *12*):
1. A tight group that extends to some 150m in length and 25-30m in width. These are normally referred to in the literature as long mortuary enclosures but, since such a use is unproven and the structures may have been mounded (see below), a neutral name akin to ring ditch seems most appropriate. The term oblong ditch[4] is ideally neutral for cropmark classification but is inappropriate when talking of identical sites that were defined by posts instead of ditches. Collectively, therefore, they will be called simply *long enclosures*.
2. A group of sites some 180-800m in proven length that either:
   a) greatly extend the length of group 1 while remaining of similar width – these sites will be termed *cursiform long enclosures*; or
   b) increase in length *and* width. These sites can be referred to as *minor cursuses* after the example of the Lesser Stonehenge Cursus.
3. A dispersed group of classic cursus sites extending from 1000m to 2000m and

achieving widths of 40-100m. These sites can be called *major cursuses*.
4. A very few hugely longer sites (2700-5640m) that demand distinction from the former group and are perhaps best termed *mega cursuses*.

These distinctions carry no implication of date or function – they simply allow us to handle an unwieldy continuum of sites sharing common plan characteristics. The pattern does, however, suggest that small sites of long enclosure type may represent a conceptual baseline from which some were greatly extended in length (2a) while others were expanded to full cursus form (2b, 3 & 4). Nevertheless, this cannot be assumed from plan alone and needs investigating.

An alternative division based on 'use life' has been proposed by Francis Pryor:[5]

1. 'Monumental' or continuously used sites
2. Short-lived, single-period sites
3. Long-lived episodic ditched alignment sites

This has the advantage of greater 'humanity' than the mathematical and morphological divisions just set out but unfortunately does little to help us to get to grips with the relationship between cursus, long enclosure and bank barrow groups. Added to this many 'monumental' sites were only ever substantially built at their terminals; side ditches running from them were modest – very modest in the case of the 'monumental' Greater Stonehenge Cursus. Most importantly perhaps, the episodic nature of sites in the long-lived category is open to question. If, as Pryor suggests, their ditches were not dug and used in parallel but in relatively short lengths of perhaps 500m – each representing a short-lived site, event or episode on a shared alignment – variations in ditch form could be predicted between each 'event' section. This is rarely to be seen. Even at the great complex at Maxey in Cambridgeshire that suggested this 'type', aerial photography reveals ditch form that is totally consistent along each *c*.1km arm of the cursus, but which contrasts with that of the next arm. This is only explicable if each were a distinct monument built as a piece and butted onto another, as happened on Cranborne Chase. Equally, whilst on certain sites causeways exist in some number, that need indicate no more than gang construction: causeways are, after all, the defining characteristic of causewayed enclosures yet have never been advanced to question the *raison d'être* of those sites *as* enclosures.

Shared plan characteristics then suggest that monuments in the cursus continuum record an overriding concept rather than simply random definition of a significant route or alignment. Within this unifying concept there is significant variation.

INSCRIBED ACROSS THE LANDSCAPE: THE CURSUS ENIGMA

VARIATIONS ON A THEME

Lowland Scotland (*13*) is noted for a very distinctive series of sites defined by pits. Excavation has usually, but not always, confirmed that they once held posts. Amongst the smallest sites are those at Balfarg in Fife, where even fence lines contrast with larger, irregularly spaced post holes along the sites' axes. The excavators decided that the internal posts once held up mortuary platforms for the exposure of the dead. Douglasmuir is larger and of emphatically different plan at the ends. The post holes defining the square ends and the central division were larger than those of the sides. This, and the inturn of the side posts, makes it virtually certain that it was originally a one-unit structure that was later almost exactly doubled in size. A very large post stood in the northern of the two units. The site has been radiocarbon dated to 4000-3350 BC, although this may record the heartwood of the large oak posts and thus be too early. Pit-defined sites not far from Douglasmuir, at Milton of Guthrie and Balneaves appear to record different processes of enlargement: the first by multiplication of units of the same size, the second by the addition of a long extension (*13e* & *13g*).

Enclosures with opposing type A and type B terminal plans, situated just 11m apart, were excavated at Bannockburn. The pits of the round-ended (type A) site had been recut several times and contained charcoal but there was no evidence of posts being left in them; the pits of the square-ended (type B) site had held posts. The type A site was dated from 3800 (or possibly even 4000 BC) to 3400 BC, and the type B site to 3400-3000 BC. At Holywood near Dumfries two cursuses of different plan, as at Bannockburn, were defined instead by ditches. Pits were visible on aerial photographs running around the inner edge of the type A cursus, and excavation showed these had held posts.[6]

The Bi series of precisely laid out sites are overwhelmingly concentrated in the Midlands and East Anglia (*14*). The little enclosure at Fengate was so regularly laid out that before excavation it was thought to be of Roman date. No obvious internal features were found that could be related to its use. A ring ditch overlies a similar site at Charlton in Hereford and Worcester, and inside another such site at Yarnton in the Upper Thames Valley a pit containing Late Neolithic Grooved Ware was found, as well as a burial that could not unfortunately be dated. A larger site at Barford in Warwickshire appears to have been abutted against a small long enclosure. Like the Fengate enclosure it lacked obvious evidence for use but within the yet larger cursus at Springfield in Essex a post circle was found. This filled the eastern end of the monument that strangely lacked any evidence of causeways to permit access. Middle Neolithic Peterborough Ware in the Mortlake style came from the lower ditch silts and from the pits of the circle. An even larger site in the same tradition at Aston on Trent in Derbyshire very unusually had ring

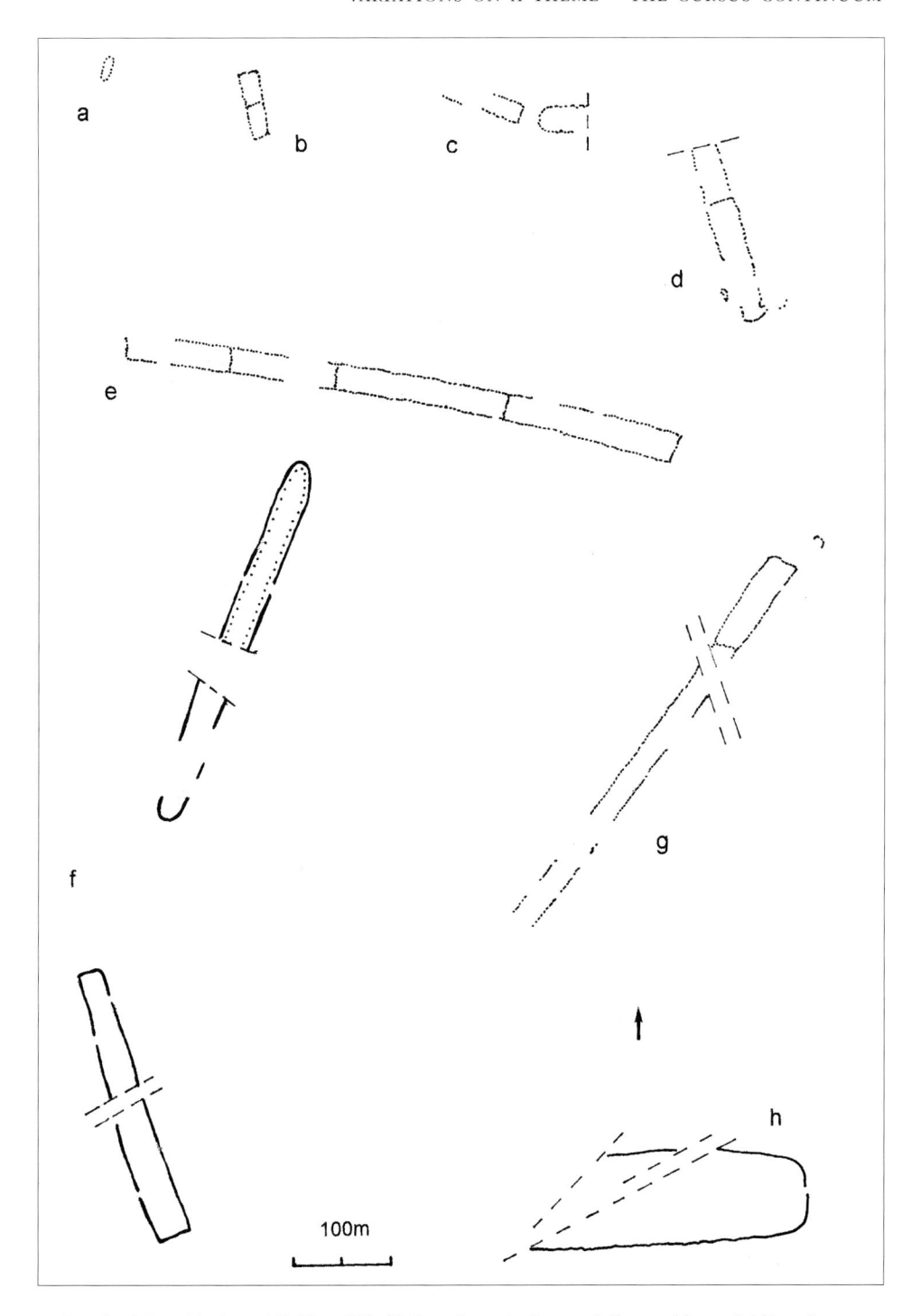

13 Lowland Scottish sites: a) Balfarg, Fife; b) Douglasmuir, Angus; c) Bannockburn, Stirling; d) Kinalty, Angus; e) Milton of Guthrie, Angus; f) Holywood, Dumfries; g) Balneaves, Angus; h) Curriestanes, Dumfries. *After Brophy 1999*

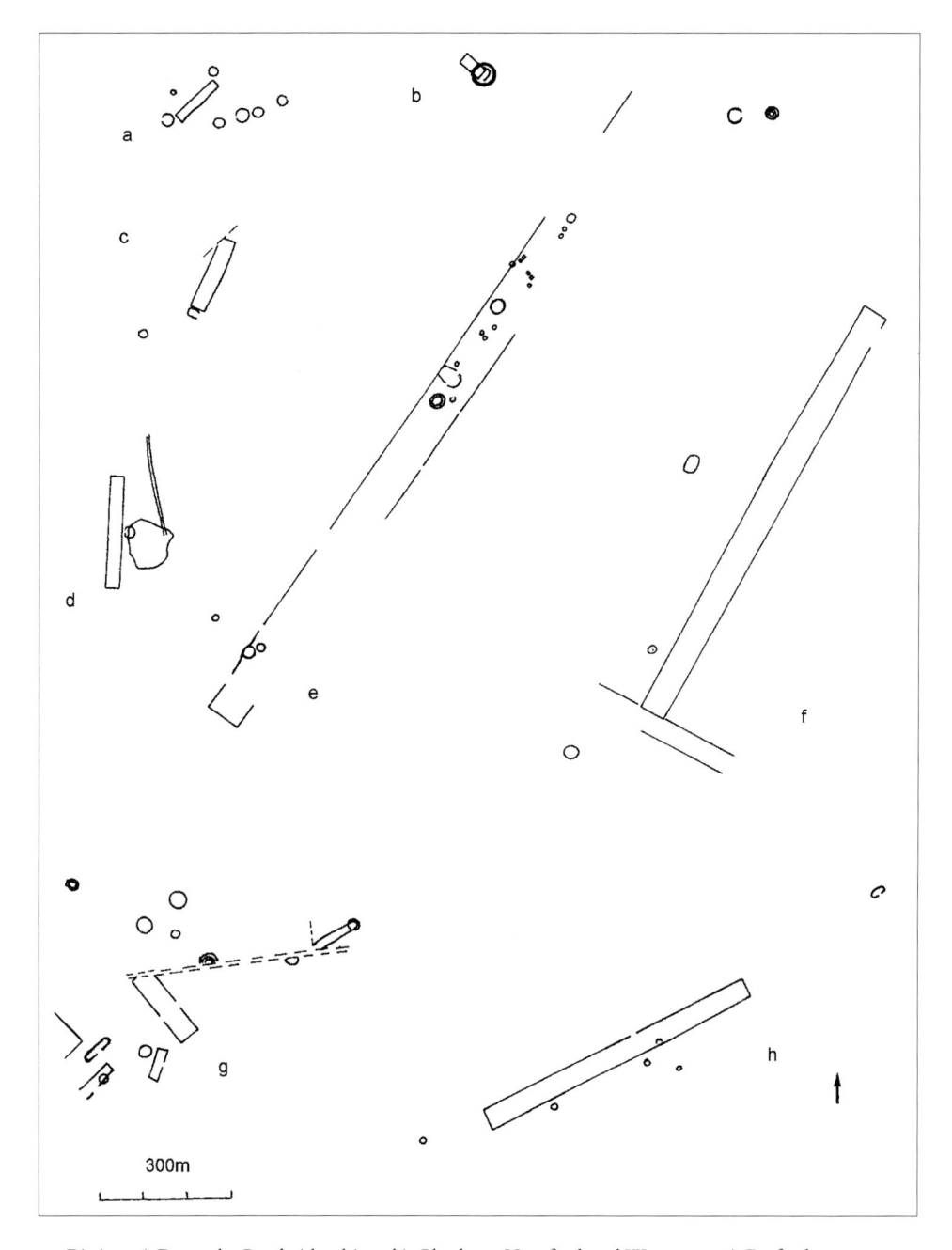

14 Bi sites: a) Barnack, Cambridgeshire; b) Charlton, Hereford and Worcester; c) Barford, Warwickshire; d) Longbridge, Warwickshire; e) Aston, Derbyshire; f) Benson, Oxfordshire; g) Cardington, Bedfordshire; h) Springfield, Essex

ditches/round barrows placed along its axis. One of these covered a hearth with Earlier Neolithic carinated bowl pottery and a substantial quantity of charred wheat that has been dated to about 3600-3400 BC. Similar large Bi sites are found in the Upper Thames Valley. The unexcavated cursus at Benson is a good example. These rarely seem to have attracted many ring ditches.[7]

Major complexes like Dorchester upon Thames are very different to neighbouring Bi sites in terms both of plan and the high number of ring ditches they attracted (15). Small ring ditches with a single causeway, and sometimes defined by pits rather than a continuous ditch, are concentrated around and even *in* the Dorchester cursus. So are irregular ring ditches with multiple circuits. Both are refered to as hengiform sites because of their resemblance to larger henges and both are generally several centuries later in date than cursuses. A post circle was placed along the axis of the Dorchester cursus at about the same time, and close by a great double-ditched henge was constructed. Maxey appears similar to the Dorchester complex but probably comprised three separate cursus sites to judge from differing ditch lines. The henge laid out around a central barrow overlying the cursus has an unusually narrow ditch. The complex attracted more ring ditches than Dorchester. Fornham All Saints has not been excavated but seems certain to have been laid out across the adjacent causewayed enclosure. The precise, angled plan of this cursus appears unique.[8]

Mega complexes hugely exceed the foregoing in size. The Greater Stonehenge Cursus is laid out in the same precise way as the Dorchester cursus but has a deeper terminal ditch at its western end, presumably to furnish material for a now destroyed monumental bank (16). Neighbouring ring ditches are aligned alongside the monument in a way very rarely seen elsewhere. The Rudston complex in Eastern Yorkshire uniquely has four cursuses (A,B,C and D) crossing each other to 'box in' the tallest standing-stone in the British Isles. Although not particularly regular in layout, only one of them shows a distinct change of alignment – cursus A that has a strange dog-leg just before its monumental terminal bank. The great Dorset Cursus on Cranborne Chase stretches for nearly 10km. It is really two monuments joined end to end: the Gussage cursus (SW) and the Pentridge cursus (NE) (17). A long barrow on the top of Gussage Hill is set across the line of the first monument and another one is incorporated in the bank along the side of the second. Several realignments take place along its course. Long barrows are also set around both ends of this greatest of all cursuses and its terminal banks are more massively constructed. This has led to the suggestion that they have been built to imitate long barrows.[9]

In terms of dimensions the differences between the sites are vast yet they have the same range of terminal forms, lack any obvious function and are overwhelmingly straight monuments. Even the smallest – Douglasmuir – has large end posts that

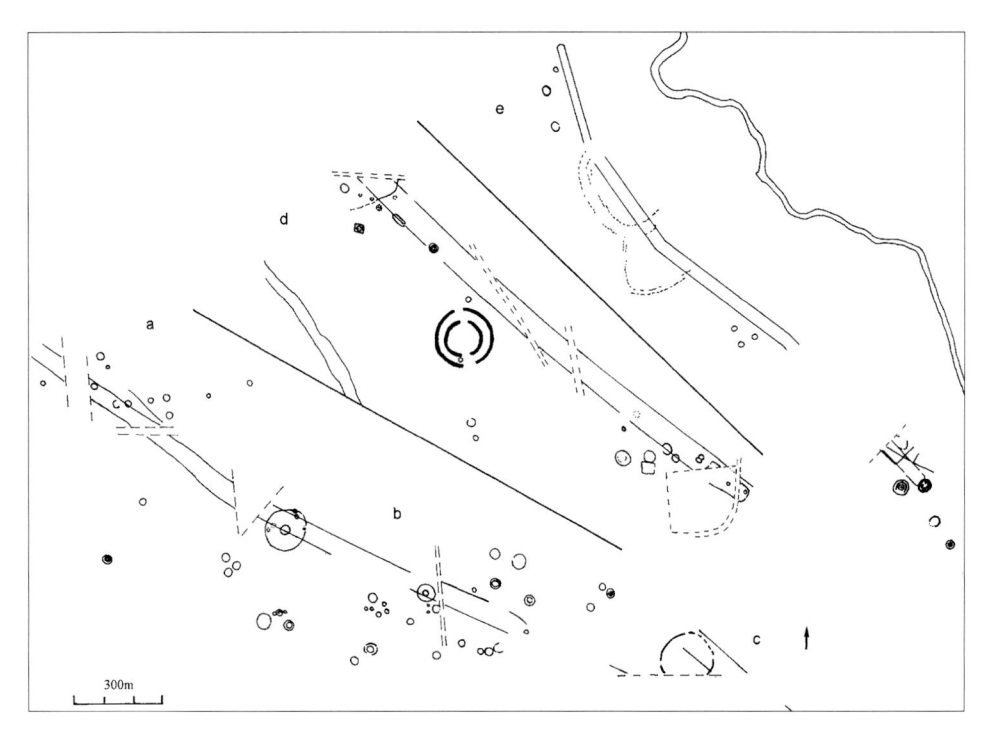

INSCRIBED ACROSS THE LANDSCAPE: THE CURSUS ENIGMA

15 Maxey–Etton, Cambridgeshire (bottom left): a) Maxey NW, b) Maxey SE, c) Etton; Dorchester upon Thames, Oxon: d) (centre); Fornham All Saints: e) (top right)

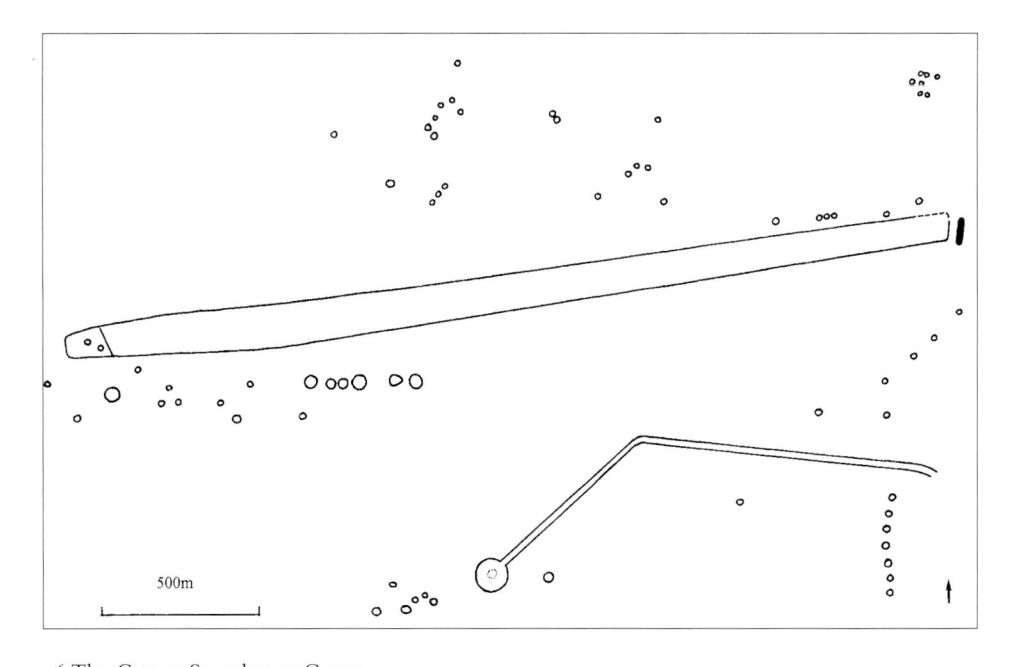

16 The Greater Stonehenge Cursus

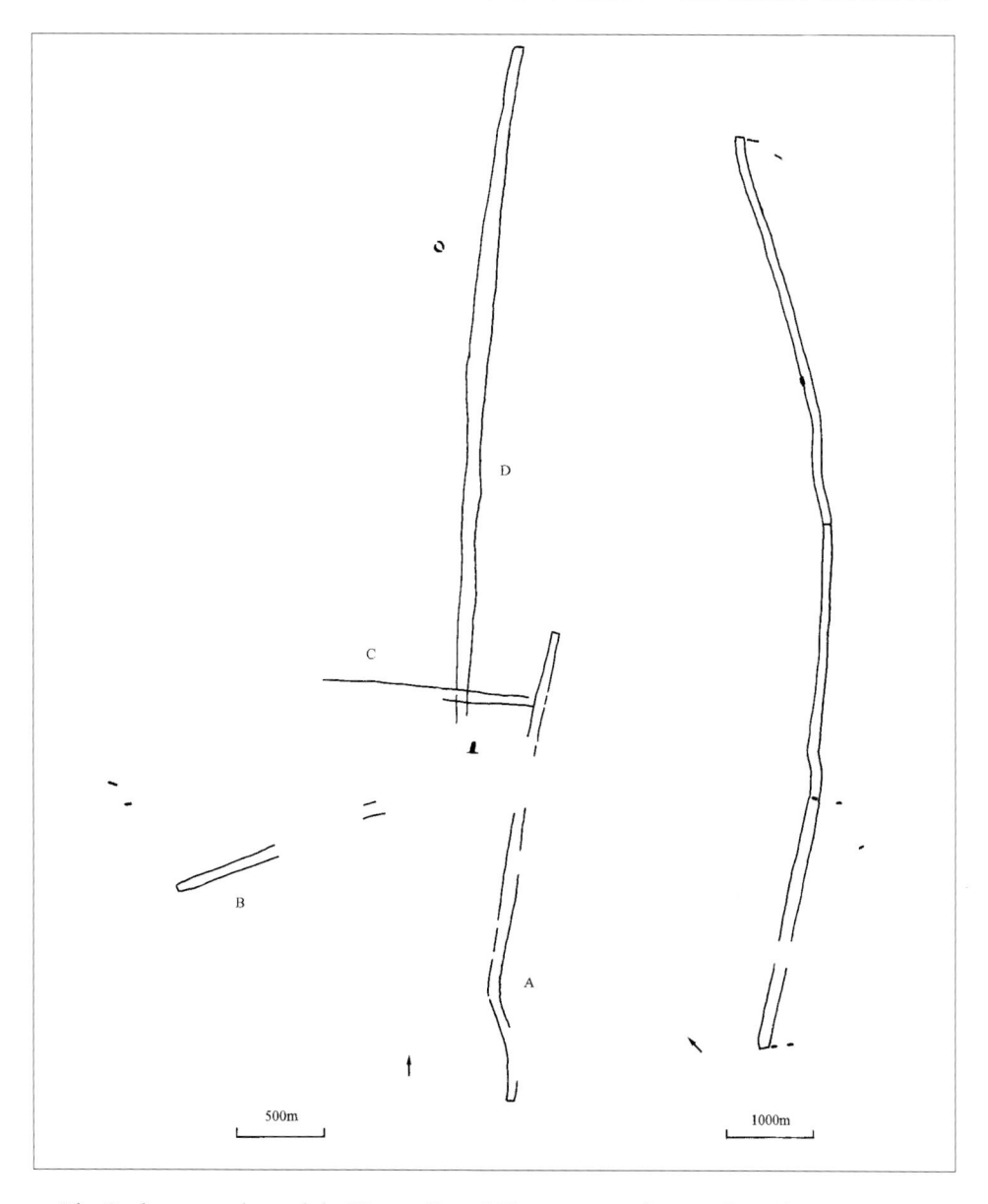

17 The Rudston complex and the 'Dorset Cursus' (Gussage cursus bottom; Pentridge cursus top)

must have emphasised the terminals in the same way that the larger banks did at the mega sites. Late Neolithic ring ditches (hengiform sites) cluster around Dorchester and Maxey, and Early Bronze Age round barrows and ring ditches around the mega sites, but many of the smaller sites have only one or two; the Scottish sites often none at all. In these variations lie the histories of the monuments, but more importantly the histories of the societies that built them (*18*).

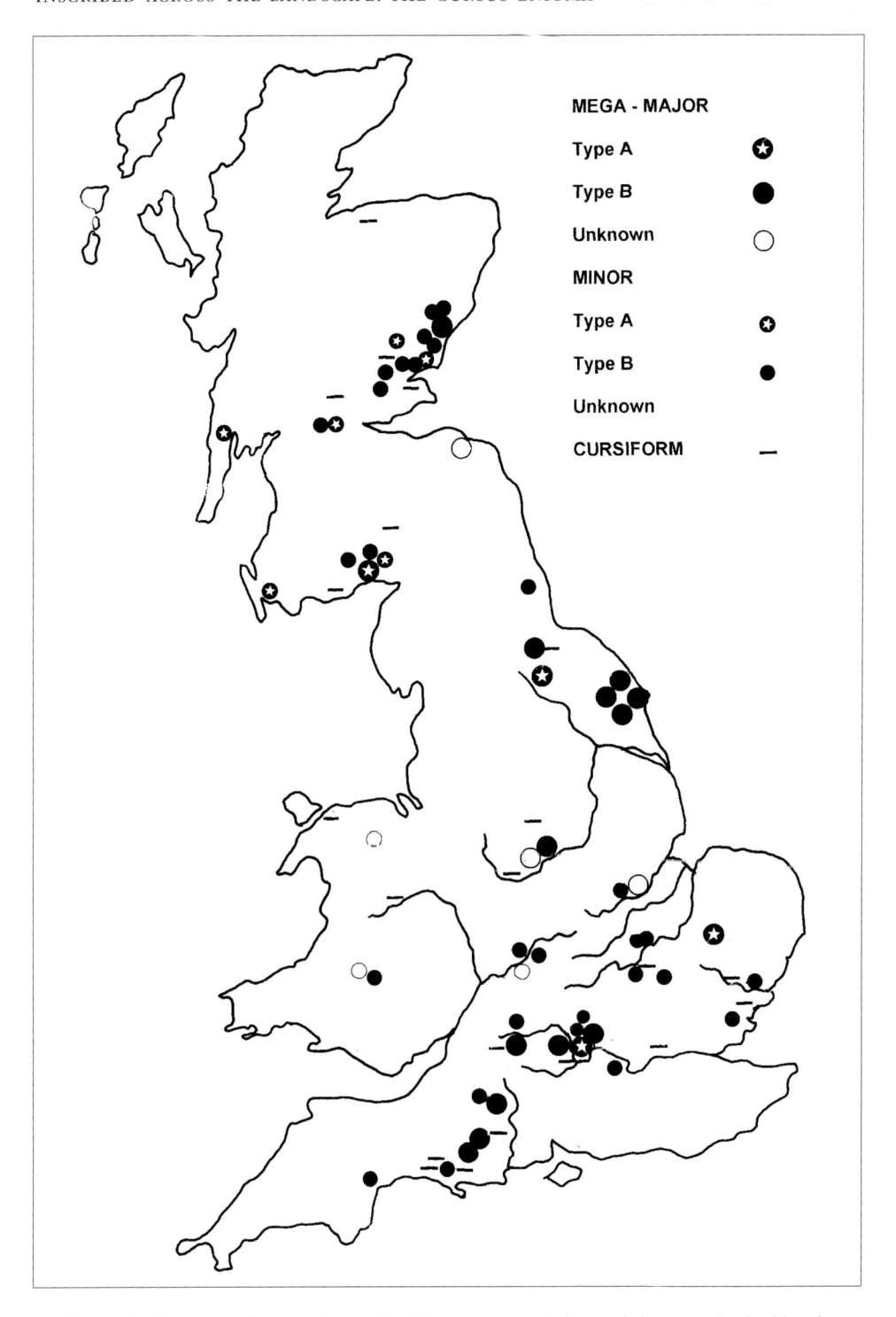

INSCRIBED ACROSS THE LANDSCAPE: THE CURSUS ENIGMA

18 Cursus distribution: well-attested sites. Cursiform group includes bank barrows. *Scotland based on Brophy 1995*

4

'DIFFICULT TO SEE ON THE GROUND' – NON-MONUMENTAL MONUMENTS

Monuments by definition arrest attention: the larger their surface area, the greater their structural mass. Thus mounds such as West Kennet, Duggleby Howe, Maes Howe and Newgrange, or enclosures such as Avebury and Arbor Low still loom large after millennia of decay. Cursuses are the exception. The surface area of all but the smallest dwarf burial mounds and henges yet were structurally very unimpressive. Ditches, even where protected from later plough erosion, could be miniscule: less than 0.3m deep at Maxey, where protected by the mound of a round barrow, and 0.8m at Drayton North where protected by alluvium. Even pit-defined sites appear to have possessed posts of no great height: the pits at Bannockburn were only 0.21m deep that suggests, even allowing for erosion, posts no higher than 1/1.5m. So unimpressive are the earthworks of the Stonehenge cursus that Stone remarked that they were 'difficult to see on the ground' and excavation at points along its course, that were apparently never subject to ploughing, has recorded depths of only 0.6-0.8m.[1] The extent of the contrast with the other great Neolithic enclosure tradition – henges – can be demonstrated by plotting average ditch dimensions against distances across the monuments (*19*).

It is clear that there is a generally close relationship between monument size and ditch size in the henge tradition but absolutely the *opposite* amongst cursuses – ditch size remains almost constant whatever the width or length of the site. This is quite alien to a monumental tradition. It finds its closest parallel in a most unexpected place – fields. Their ditches have a similar size range and likewise remain constant however large or small the area enclosed. Their role is not to impress but to demarcate and to furnish material for a bank on which a barrier (fence or hedge) can be placed. Yet cursuses were clearly not huge fields, however ritualised: fields may have squared ends but not *convex* ones. The demarcating role of fields is, however, significant.

Monument size and ditch width

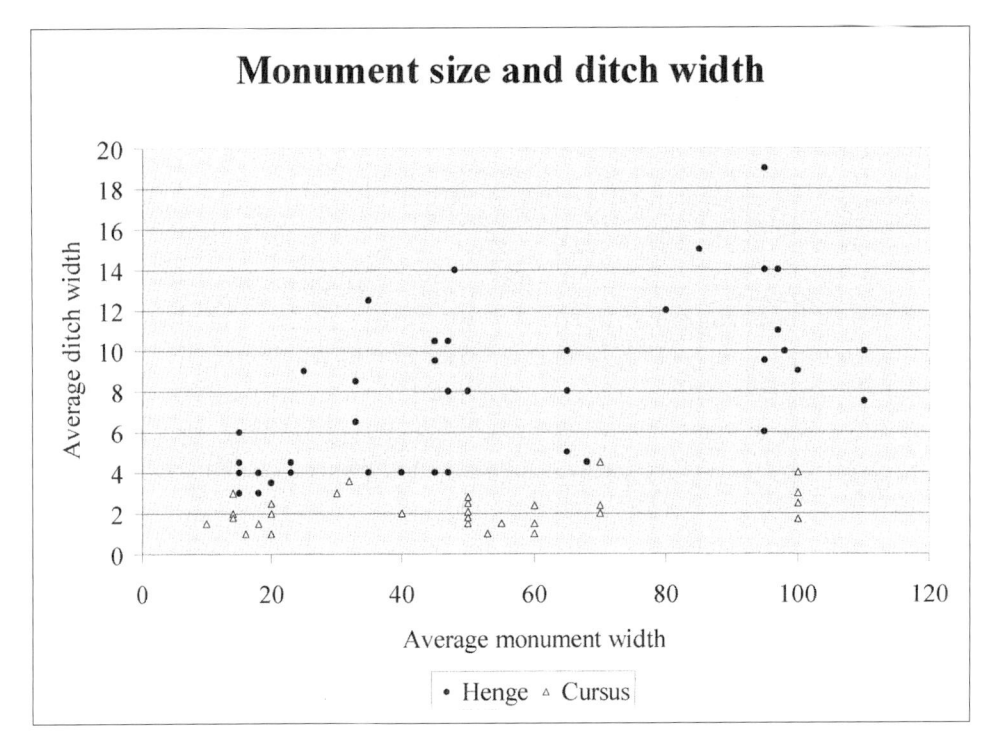

19 Contrasting patterns: variation in henge and cursus ditch width with monument size

Ditches demarcating the temenoi of later Romano-Celtic temples were similarly constant irrespective of the size of the enclosed area. They were neither monumental nor obscurational, their role was simply to define a precinct set apart for 'otherworld' purposes. Here perhaps we have an insight into the purpose of the cursus. Yet even in a purely definitional role a greater three-dimensional component might be expected. Could woodland have provided this?

WOODLAND OR GRASSLAND?

As a linear opening in forest cover a cursus might possess both the impact and liminality ascribed to Celtic groves by classical writers.[2] Early work by I.W. Cornwall at Thornborough in Yorkshire suggested this was the case: a dark layer at the base of the cursus ditch was identified as humus derived from leaf litter. He identified similar material in the ditch fills of the cursus and adjacent hengiform ring ditches at Dorchester upon Thames. As at Thornborough, this very dark fill contrasted markedly with the lighter, non-humic silts of the succeeding great ceremonial henge monument. He considered this reflected vegetation change from fairly close deciduous forest to a more open grassland environment. Unfortunately the clarity of this picture has been undermined by more recent work at the south-eastern end of the Dorchester cursus where no such black humic layer was identified, and by work elsewhere.[3]

At the broadly similar site at Maxey silt in the cursus ditches had a low humus content. It was dominated instead by sand despite a wide, shallow profile that would reduce fill from ditch-side collapse. An open landscape is also indicated at the two Stonehenge cursuses where snail shells reveal a predominance of open country species. Although shell numbers are not great and conclusions are therefore uncertain, the picture is backed up by samples from the buried soil under the adjacent long barrow (Amesbury 42) that indicate it was constructed in pre-existing and well-established grassland. A similar picture of open grassland has emerged from excavations along the length of the great Dorset Cursus, although patches of woodland appear also to have existed.[4] Elsewhere recent excavations have produced less satisfactory results: at Springfield in Essex remains from the western terminal were contaminated from Roman levels and at Drayton in Oxfordshire charcoal was almost entirely absent from the cursus ditch, and snail shells very sparse. Nevertheless, holes left by the roots of fallen trees (tree throw holes) can furnish valuable, if not closely dateable, evidence. Those predating the Drayton North cursus, and the attendant charcoal, pointed to oak-alder woodland that was cleared by the time the monument was constructed (a few *Helicella itala* shells from the cursus ditch indicated at least locally open conditions). Charcoal from succeeding Beaker-period pits reveals a significant reduction in oak and alder with dominance instead by charcoal from woodland edge species such as hawthorn and sloe.[5] This could indicate the proximity of woodland but others conclusions are also possible, as will be discussed below.

Whilst then woodland may have compensated for the monumental limitations of cursuses on a handful of sites, it is clear that comparable sites elsewhere were laid out across open country where their modest ditches could never have been impressive. Whatever these limitations, if their role was definitional then at least some attempt at maintenance of their modest ditches should be evident. That is not apparently the case. The rare cases of ditch recutting appear to result from restructuring: the slight first phase enclosure (or perhaps marking out trench) at the Lesser Stonehenge Cursus was cut almost entirely away by the larger ditch of the extended second phase: at Scorton, North Yorkshire only the very bottom of the V-profiled cursus ditch was visible below the wide, flat ditch that provided gravel for the great internal bank barrow; and at Holywood North recutting may have been associated with the erection of a post setting in the interior. Rather different is the clear recutting recognised in the eastern (but not the western) ditch of cursus A at Rudston. It could represent restructuring of just one side of the monument but two facts advise caution: the fill of the recut includes Iron Age pottery and aerial photographs show boundary ditches of presumed Iron Age/Romano-British date precisely following the eastern side of the cursus. It would have been far easier for those digging the boundary ditches to cut into the soft fill of the cursus ditch than to have dug through solid chalk.[6]

It would appear then that recutting of cursus ditches was rarely considered important and possibly was only undertaken in association with some form of rebuilding. Indeed in some cases the opposite appears to be true: ditches were deliberately backfilled after digging to judge from the very clean, almost rammed nature of the silts (e.g. Lesser Stonehenge Cursus). Not surprisingly this pattern of 'neglect' or closure has led to explanation of the monuments as short-lived event sites. Francis Pryor in particular has argued that this best explains the great Maxey monument with its very shallow, unrecut ditches and disruptive layout 'across the grain' of expected land use (i.e. it does not run at right angles to adjacent rivers). The only way to fully test such a proposition is to check the vertical stratigraphy of ditch silting against the 'horizontal stratigraphy' of adjacent structures. Spatial patterning can furnish vital evidence, and at Maxey it does.

STAKES, POSTS AND BANKS

Ring ditches densely cluster around the Maxey cursuses in a manner that appears quite random at first glance. Closer inspection, however, reveals distinct differences: those around the irregular ditched north-west arm possess no particular pattern, yet those around the precise, straight-ditched south-east arm are laid out broadly parallel to it (15). Since Neolithic ring ditches are comparatively rare (even here where at least two have been recognised), these sites can be safely regarded as predominantly former Early Bronze Age round barrows. They are therefore a millennium later in date than the shallow cursus ditches that 'swiftly vanished as soon as vegetation re-established itself.' That this was the case is confirmed by the fact that the henge ditch cut through the *fully* silted cursus ditch. How then could the cursus possibly have influenced ring ditch layout? Pryor found no evidence of a bank, even where it passed under the protecting cover of the barrow within the henge, nor of post holes. But Gavin Simpson, excavating a length of the site some 20 years earlier, found five small post holes (0.15-0.25m in diameter and 0.10m in depth) spaced 1-2m apart along the outer edge of the ditch. This 6m-long line was clearly related to the cursus. In one direction it stopped short at a pit circle that overlay the cursus ditch and in the other at the edge of the excavated area. It may never have been continuous but it is perhaps significant that in this area the cursus was overlain by a medieval plough headland; further south-east where Pryor excavated no such protection existed along the cursus edge.[7]

This fortuitously surviving evidence may help us to understand how cursuses continued as a feature of the landscape long after their ditches had filled up. It deserves to have received greater attention, since elsewhere on sites where ditches had deeper and less stable profiles, pits set only 0.3m from the ditch edge could be expected to have vanished through collapse. Nevertheless, possible post holes of closely similar size to those at Maxey have been noted some 0.2-0.3m from the inner edge of the Lechlade cursus ditch set nearly 7m apart. A similar slight feature (0.3m diameter) was identified 0.5m outside the cursus ditch in a single trench cut across the Aston on Trent cursus, and another one barely a metre outside the ditch of the nearby Potlock cursus at a causeway.[8] If these were not of natural origin – and there is no question of that in the case of those at Maxey – they are unlikely to have held posts of any size *unless* they were merely the bases of holes cut through now vanished banks.

Aerial photographs revealed much larger pits set back some 2-3m along the inner edge of the Holywood North cursus near Dumfries (7). Excavation has confirmed their size (on average 0.7/0.8m diameter x 0.4m deep) and role as post holes. Some posts had been burnt *in situ*. Julian Thomas, the excavator, suggested that they had been a revetment structure for the cursus bank and that burning had led this to collapse into the ditch, where a very substantial, internally derived layer was found.[9] Given that there is evidence for ditch backfilling on other sites, and for independent structures of spaced posts (e.g. Litteour), it might alternatively be possible to see this as evidence of more than one phase of construction.

A very large ramped post hole (over 1m in diameter and more than 0.5m deep) was found 0.5m outside the ditch of the Scorton cursus; another, similarly located, had been recorded in the side of a quarry nearby. In addition a far smaller post hole was found in the bottom of the recut cursus ditch. Similarly along a 45m length of the Stanwell cursus/bank barrow truncated post holes about 0.5m in diameter and set about 5m apart have been recorded in the ditch floor. They have been interpreted as the remains of an earlier irregular post avenue, later respected and removed by the cursus builders. Other possible post holes were located in the base of the suspiciously deep and narrow ditches of the North Stoke cursus/bank barrow. Although thought at the time to be natural solution holes, there is a possibility that quite different monuments were following each other here as appears to have happened at Stanwell and Scorton.[10] Perhaps significantly those sites with evidence of post holes *in* the ditch appear to have possessed mounds and should therefore strictly be considered as bank barrows.

The very variable evidence for cursus post or stake settings then suggests four types or situations:

1. Definition purely by contiguous, or near contiguous, posts as at Bannockburn, Douglasmuir and other Scottish sites
2. Spaced settings of large posts as at Holywood (internal) and probably Scorton (external)
3. Slight, partial and perhaps later stake/post lines as at Maxey
4. Settings in the base of the ditch as at Stanwell and Scorton

Mixed traditions seem to be evident, with groups 1 and 2 apparently restricted to northern Britain and group 4 to bank-barrow-related sites. Whether the elements making up group 3 are chance survivals of a once universal means of demarcating cursus edges we may never know. They do, however, hint at a missing upstanding component that appears vital to the obvious link with pit-/post-defined cursuses and long enclosures. They may even hold the key to the enigmatic survival of cursuses as long respected landscape features. Research needs therefore be directed as a matter of urgency at the very few surviving cursus banks as posts like those suggested at Lechlade and Aston on Trent could never have stood unaided.

SURVIVAL IN THE LANDSCAPE — AN ENIGMA AND ITS IMPLICATIONS

The most striking example of cursus survival as a landscape feature forces us to think beyond lightly fenced enclosures however. At Drayton in Oxfordshire the northern, and lower, of two quite distinct cursuses separated by a steep terrace edge runs across an island of gravel surrounded by alluvium. Halfway along its length a field ditch from a Roman enclosed settlement dated to the first century AD runs up to its western ditch and then turns to run *exactly* alongside it for 170m (*20*). How was this possible? On very mobile gravel soils ditches fill rapidly and dates for the cursus place it between 3600-3300 BC. The cursus ditch 1-2m wide and 0.4-0.7m deep cannot have been visible some 3500 years later, let alone have represented a significant landscape feature. Preservation of the eastern, and slightly larger, cursus ditch under alluvium at the southern end of the site preserved the ditch and bank profile as it appeared in the Middle Iron Age when flooding began: the ditch then was marked by a dip of only some 0.2m, and the bank by a rise of no more than 0.20m in a 4.4m-wide spread of gravel. Confirmation that the bank was not a significant feature further north comes from the fact that the Roman ditch was cut right along the top of its line — a most improbable thing to do to a raised feature.[11]

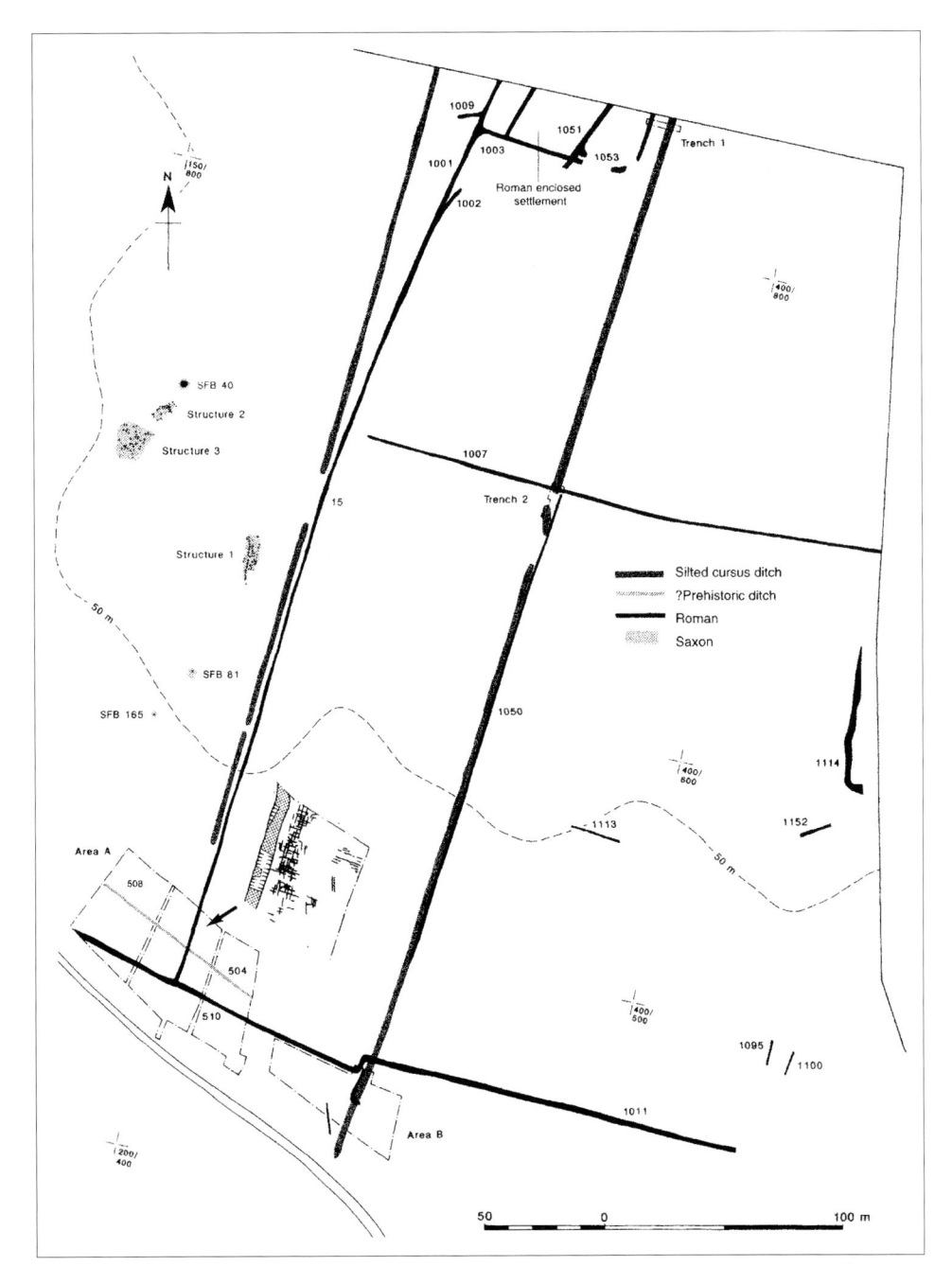

'DIFFICULT TO SEE ON THE GROUND' – NON-MONUMENTAL MONUMENTS

20 Drayton North, Oxfordshire: Roman ditch following the fully silted western cursus ditch. Inset plan: ard marks and the Roman ditch. *From Barclay et al. 2003*

Faced with the seeming impossibility that the cursus earthwork was being respected, yet with clear evidence that its alignment was, and very precisely too, Alistair Barclay has suggested the presence of a long-lived open field boundary. This is a real possibility but there must be doubts that an unmarked boundary would survive so exactly for three and a half millennia. Here the circumstantial evidence furnished by Romano-British agriculture is critically important (*20*: inset plan). Plough marks preserved beneath a gravel spread, and undoubtedly associated with the field established within the cursus, come too close to the Roman field ditch to have let a plough team turn. It is possible therefore that the plough furrows are associated with a phase of agricultural activity prior to the construction of the field ditch and to the gravel spread that preserved them. Were they respecting something, now invisible, that occupied the consistent and inexplicable 0.75m gap left between cursus and Roman field ditch? If there was nothing there why wasn't the field ditch simply cut along the cursus ditch line that established the boundary? An enduring but now invisible feature that could have filled this gap is a hedge. If this had been the boundary before the Romano-British field ditch was dug it would allow the space for plough teams that had created the furrows to turn. Later redefinition of the field by a ditch dug along the side of the old hedge would create the bank upcast that covered and protected the plough marks.

Hedges have the capacity to survive over great periods in the landscape and need not have been deliberately planted. On a low-lying island such as that at Drayton the rooting of stakes and colonization of fence lines would undoubtedly take place more readily than on a dry site. Over long stretches of time results would be variable: rot and collapse of light fencing in places; rooting and colonization by weeds and shrubs to form an *ad hoc* hedge in others. With this in mind it is interesting that charcoal from pits associated with domestic activity on the site is dominated by shrub species (blackthorn, hawthorn, sloe) – all hedge line as well as woodland edge species. Seeds of hawthorn and sloe from a ditch fill at Alcester have furnished evidence for an Iron Age ditch and similar seeds have been recovered from the ditches at North Drayton and Springfield, though admittedly in small numbers.

If this relict hedge hypothesis has validity similar circumstantial evidence should presumably be discernible elsewhere. This does appear to be the case. At Aston on Trent in Derbyshire the cursus is overlain at its midpoint by a tangle of fields and trackways of presumed Iron Age date. As at Drayton there is no reason to suppose the cursus was a visible feature: Beaker pottery has been found at the top of its fully silted ditch.[12] Yet the principal trackway crosses it at right angles and then divides with one branch closely following the outer edge of the cursus ditch for nearly 250m (*21*). There is no topographic explanation for this – the

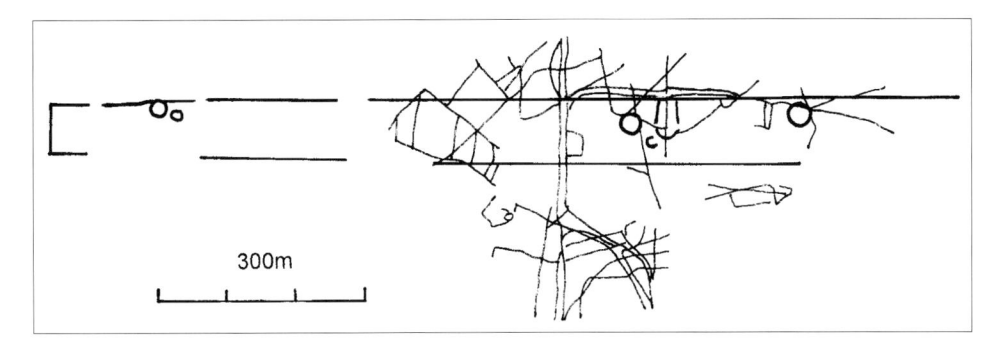

21 Aston cursus, Derbyshire: trackway of later field system respecting silted cursus ditch line

terrain is perfectly flat. Since the only plausible explanation appears to be respect for a relict length of hedge running along the outer edge of the cursus ditch, it is noteworthy that the possible post hole located during excavation 600m further north lay on that side also. Partial survival of this sort is exactly what might be predicted if chance colonization were the mechanism in operation. It may again be evident on similarly flat terrain at Springfield in Essex. There, amongst a number of Late Iron Age/Roman field ditches that randomly cross the body of the cursus, is one that runs suspiciously alongside the western terminal ditch (see *58*). It is unlikely to have been coincidentally aligned yet the cursus ditches are known to have fully silted by that date.[13] Similarly at Eynesbury in Cambridgeshire a very large Late Bronze Age/Early Iron Age pit alignment enclosure (at least 426m long x 180m wide) closely followed the slightly curving ditch line of the northern cursus (running where an inner bank would be predicted) but completely ignored the adjacent southern cursus.[14]

Incorporation of cursus banks, however slight, into later field systems on the chalklands is more understandable since they would have lasted longer as earthworks. Nevertheless their place in the layout of the fields is far from random: cursus C at Rudston appears to have determined the layout of a whole block of field parallel to it, as did the Greater and Lesser Stonehenge Cursuses at their western extremities, and the Dorset Cursus on Gussage Hill.[15] With the exception of the latter, these monuments are unlikely to have presented major obstacles that enforced orientation. Here again it is perhaps not inconceivable that fenced or hedged boundaries survived to guide later farmers.

The capacity of sections of cursus to survive and determine the layout of much later landscape divisions cannot be ignored and on rapidly silting valley soils flies in the face of reason unless an additional structural element is presumed. Coupled with the admittedly slight evidence for stake/post edging, it could point to a method of definition akin to that claimed for long mortuary enclosures (see chapter 5) and exemplified by David Hogg's evocative reconstruction of one of the Balfarg enclosures (*23*). Repair and renewal of these elements at times of assembly may have assured sufficient longevity to permit shrub colonization. If length and the early context raise doubts it is worth noting Wood's report in his *New England Prospect* of 1634:

> Besides their artillery (*the natives*) have other devices to kill their game, as sometimes hedges a mile or two long, being a mile wide at one end and made narrower by degrees, leaving onely a gap sixe foote long, over against which, in the day time they lye lurking to shoot the Deere …

Similar structures for hunting or herding are attested elsewhere and there seems no reason why they should not have been employed by a British Neolithic population utilising wild resources. The skill and experience of laying out ambitious hedge lines may not therefore have been alien to them. Of course cursuses were neither tapered nor hunting traps but the possibility that they were defined by a means familiar over great lengths deserves consideration. In addition to providing a plausible link with pit-/post-defined cursuses and so called long mortuary enclosures, it also points to the possibility of a different structural model for the strangely missing highland zone cursuses – as hedge-banked enclosures. These might conceivably have been masked, like cursus C at Rudston, by inclusion in later field systems.

Whatever the case, it does seem that even the slightest of ditched cursus sites (such as Maxey) may have been defined in ways that both enabled them to endure as landscape features and that linked them conceptually to other traditions. It is to the possible origin of that concept that we now need to turn in order to approach the question of purpose.

5

'REEKING BONE YARDS'? – LONG MORTUARY ENCLOSURES

No monuments sprang up ready made. All had antecedents. In seeking them though we must beware of the simplistic notion that small means early and large means late. Magnification of a monument type may occur at any point in its history in response to local patterns of social cohesion and development. Elsewhere smaller sites may have continued to be built. But it is amongst these smaller sites that the conceptual kernel is likely to lie and, more importantly, be most readily visible. Thus a functional explanation for long enclosures could furnish a model for cursus use.

'LONG MORTUARY ENCLOSURES'

In 1951, whilst excavating part of the great ritual complex planned from aerial photographs by Major Allen at Dorchester upon Thames, Richard Atkinson examined a long enclosure of comparable size to a long barrow (Site VIII: 63m x 22m) (*22*). Dating evidence consisted of no more than a handful of relatively uneroded sherds of a Peterborough Ware bowl from the secondary silts of the ditch and one leaf-shaped and two oblique arrowheads. Inside he found nothing beyond part of an adult human jaw with worn teeth that came up during mechanical stripping of the surface.[1] This, coupled with the fact that the site had been cut from end to end by a ditch of the Dorchester cursus, seemed nonetheless to provide the answer to a problem that had dogged studies of the Neolithic. Like burials in stone chambers, skeletons found under long barrows were almost universally disarticulated and partial, but earthen mounds clearly could not have been re-entered and the burials disturbed. Exposure to scavengers at an open site prior to burial seemed the only answer, but where were such sites? At Dorchester

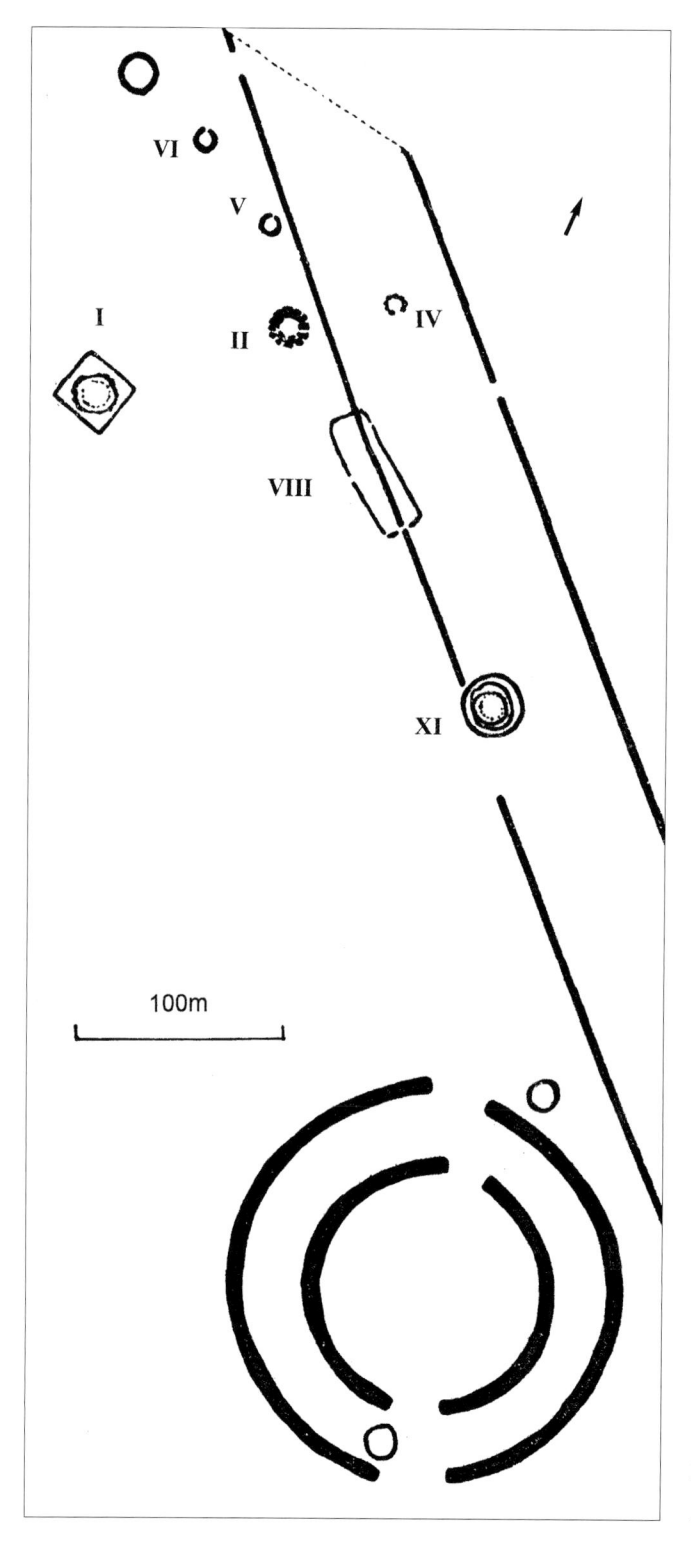

22 The Dorchester upon Thames cursus complex. *After Atkinson 1951*

23 David Hogg's evocative reconstruction of Balfarg as a long mortuary enclosure. Courtesy of David Hogg and Society of Antiquaries of Scotland

it seemed one had survived. Atkinson coined the term 'long mortuary enclosure' to describe it and the others that were assumed to lie hidden beneath long barrows. In so doing he conjured up an enduring, macabre image of an enclosure strewn with partially decomposed bodies and picked bones, and announced in the landscape by wheeling carrion feeders and the reek of decay (*23*).

A site conforming to this picture of the free-standing, open 'long mortuary enclosure' had in fact already been recorded as an embanked earthwork on Normanton Down, just south of Stonehenge. Unfortunately by the time the excavator, Faith Vatcher, arrived on the scene in 1959 it had been levelled. Despite almost total excavation the only features recorded were two short trenches 4m apart lying just within the entrance causeway. They have been interpreted as the remains of a mortuary house but aerial photographs taken by Major Allen 30 years earlier confirm what Faith Vatcher thought on excavation – that they simply provided bank revetment at the entrance (*24*). Evidence for horizontal shuttering and post replacement suggests they fulfilled that role for a prolonged period of time, perhaps supporting a gate marked by a slight gulley

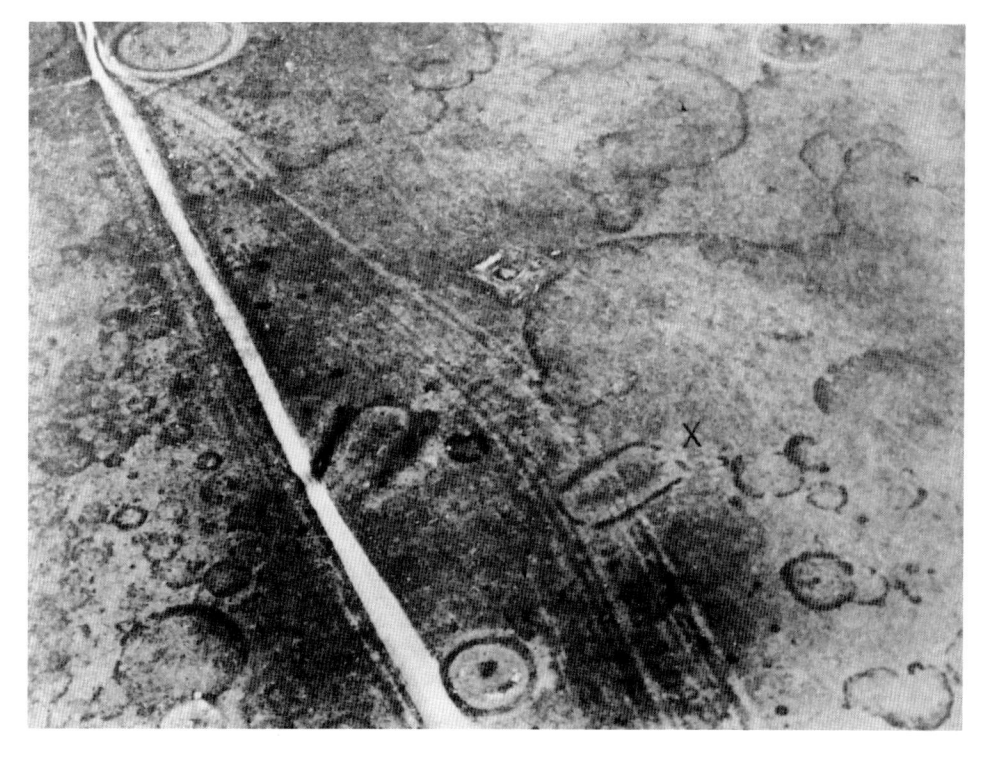

24 Allen photograph of the Normanton Down enclosure showing the bank Allen 851, 1933: Ashmolean Museum, Oxford

running between them. A Neolithic date for the enclosure was confirmed by a radiocarbon date of 3400-3000 BC, from one of the 10 antler picks found mostly on the base of the ditch. It corresponds with the only dateable find, a scrap of Peterborough Ware from the segmented enclosing ditch.[2]

The essential ingredient missing from this excavation was any suggestion of the purpose of the enclosure: beyond the gate structure, neither post holes nor human bone fragments were recovered. As conditions for the preservation of bone on the alkaline soil there were far better than those on the gravels at Dorchester upon Thames that had produced the human jaw bone, this is puzzling. In addition to a pile of three antler picks in the ditch at the entrance the only other possible deliberate deposits were a few cattle bones at a high level.

At this early stage of investigation just one other site of long mortuary enclosure type appeared to have survived – beneath Wor Barrow, a long barrow on Cranborne Chase excavated nearly a century earlier by General Pitt-Rivers. The great quarry ditches of this barrow unusually ran around its ends in the same way as a 'long mortuary enclosure', and visible in their edges were parts of two segments of an earlier, slighter ditch. The centre of the site, covered by the

'REEKING BONE YARDS'? – LONG MORTUARY ENCLOSURES

long barrow, was occupied by a rectangular fenced enclosure within which stood the mortuary house and burials. Here it seemed was an answer to the rarity of 'long mortuary enclosures': they were the *first* stages of long barrows and were usually cut away and covered during later mound construction (*25*). The fact that Pitt-Rivers' pioneered scientific excavation at Wor Barrow – drawing plans and sections, photographing features and even producing excavation models – enabled the site to be reinterpreted. Atkinson pointed out that the posts of the underlying enclosure were set too far apart (10m) to have been roofed as Pitt-Rivers had thought, but too far in from the mound edge (4.5m) to have functioned as revetment. Noting that photographs showed a layer of dark earth running at an angle to the *outside* base of the fenced enclosure, he concluded this was a turf line that had developed over a considerable period of time on top of a low revetment bank intended to support the free-standing enclosure fences. Here it seemed the whole picture was clear: the 'long mortuary enclosure' ditch defined an open precinct and, in this case, provided material to support an inner post-built enclosure that screened the exposure and burial areas. In this way earthen long barrow burials, like those in stone chambers, remained accessible over considerable periods until 'closed' by a great covering mound.[3]

This interpretation was based on three critical assumptions: that the disarticulated nature of Earlier Neolithic burials resulted from exposure within a defined enclosure; that the small revetment bank at Wor Barrow could have acted as fence support; and that its overlying dark layer was a long-developed turf line. Testing these using the records of an excavation undertaken, however scientifically for its time, by labourers with picks and shovels is clearly difficult. Nevertheless Pitt-Rivers was observant and, had bodies been left to decay on the grassland that is recorded beneath this, like other long barrows, small bones should have been found; they are after all missing from the burials themselves. He recorded none. Bones were restricted to the burial structure itself and to a later burial in the great quarry ditch. Nor, as we shall see below, is this unique. Turning to the revetment bank set against the outer foot of the Wor Barrow post enclosure we must ask why, if this was a free-standing fence, there was no evidence of a corresponding inner bank? The principal pressure operating on open downland would be the wind and our common experience with comparably sized fenced enclosures (we call them gardens!) confirms that fences need stressing against *external* wind pressure. In other words the revetment was on the wrong side. Finally, the turf line covering the toe bank was probably not what it seemed. Excavation of the Beckhampton long barrow near Avebury revealed a similar external bank covered by a dark, organic layer. It supported the base of a fence set around the edge of the barrow (*25*). Because this excavation was undertaken in recent years the dark layer was minutely examined. It was confirmed as turf

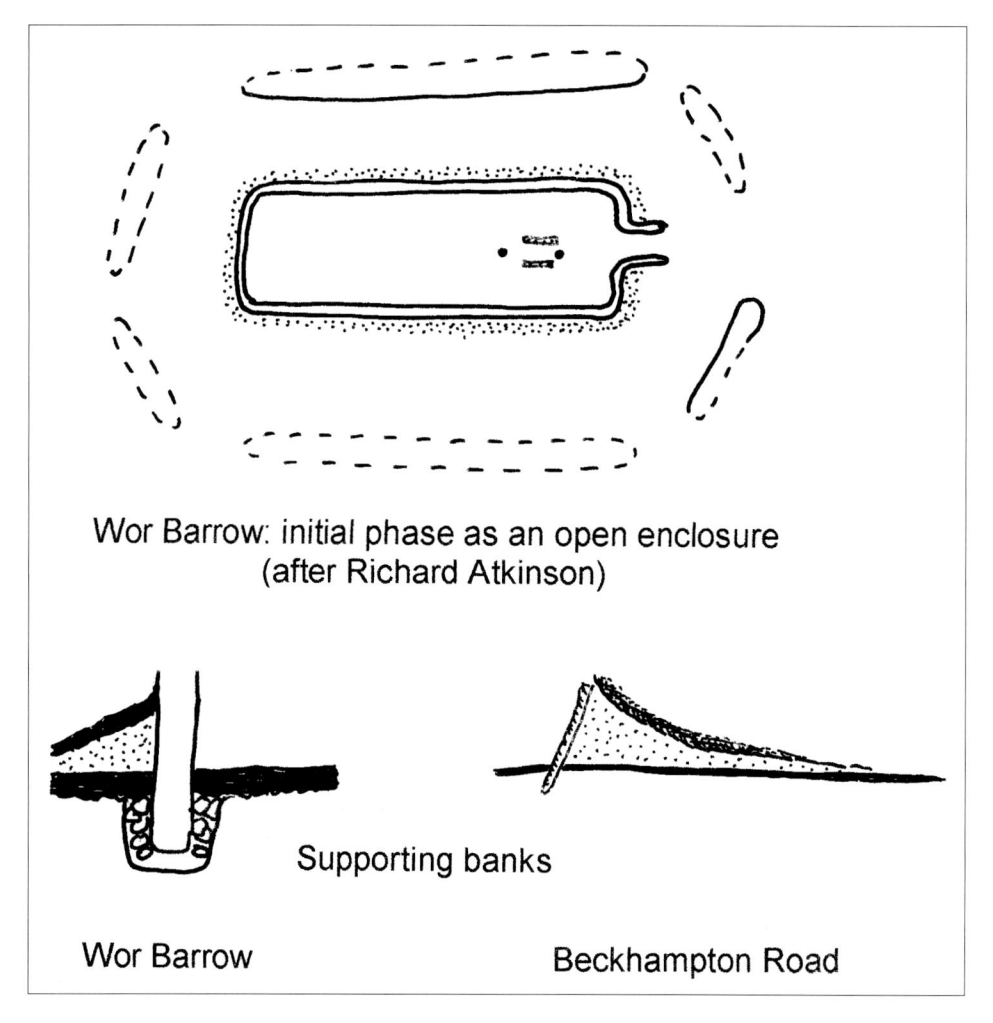

Wor Barrow: initial phase as an open enclosure
(after Richard Atkinson)

Supporting banks

Wor Barrow   Beckhampton Road

25 Wor Barrow as an open enclosure (after Richard Atkinson). Left section: Wor Barrow based on Pitt-Rivers' photograph. *Ashbee 1970, XIII*; right section: Beckhampton Road long barrow. *Ashbee* et al. *1979, fig. 18*

but it was not a natural layer: it comprised cut turves that had been *inverted*. Far from representing a long period of stabilization, the turves had been deliberately placed there, presumably to prevent water run-off from the barrow eroding the underlying revetment bank.[4] Given the lack of internal stressing at Wor Barrow, there seems every reason to suppose that its turf line had the same purpose and that the bank helped to stress mound revetment posts.

Its 'long mortuary enclosure' ditch and fenced enclosure then appear simply to have been the remnants of an early mound that was later covered by the much enlarged barrow. This has been confirmed by Richard Bradley's examination of

Pitt-River's excavation notebooks. These demonstrate that the trench for the posts could alone have provided the necessary material for the toe bank, and that the capacity of the 'long mortuary enclosure' ditches was sufficient to produce a mound some 1.5m high within the wooden enclosure – higher if the area around the mortuary house was initially left open, as can be shown to have been the case within a similar post enclosure under the long barrow at Kilham in Yorkshire.[5]

Misinterpretation of the post enclosure at Wor Barrow as an open site had muddied the waters badly, and in some measure still does. It encouraged the inclusion of wooden palisade structures found under other long earthen barrows to swell 'long mortuary enclosure' site numbers – vital if they were to be accorded a pivotal role in the mortuary process.

PALISADE ENCLOSURES

Palisade enclosures have been recognised beneath a number of earthen long barrows, usually as trenches (Fussell's Lodge, Wiltshire; Kilham, Willerby Wold and East Heslerton, East Yorkshire) but also as spaced posts (Giant's Hill I, Lincolnshire). The posts at the latter site in particular appeared to have no functional role and so were readily conscripted as symbolic edging to a 'long mortuary enclosure' that preceded the mound. Others followed. This simple equation was questioned by Paul Ashbee after he had excavated the great long barrow at Fussell's Lodge, where the considerable size of the posts and their coincidence with the mound edge argued for a simpler explanation – as revetment or embellishment. In retrospect this seemed true of the other sites.[6] The overlapping palisade trenches along the sides of the monstrous East Heslerton barrow were more easily explicable as the results of refurbishment and extension of a collapsing mound than as misaligned mortuary enclosure edges. At Willerby Wold the trench revealed evidence of at least one post and additionally held diagonally stacked chalk slabs that would have aided revetment. Most importantly at Giant's Hills I enthusiastic long mortuary enclosure recognition had ignored the excavator's statement that the posts were '… not set very far into the old ground surface but probably relied for some of their support on being partly buried in the edges of the barrow.'[7] Here, as at the Beckhampton Road long barrow, comparatively slight posts/stakes appear to have embellished the edge of the mound and been additionally support by a low revetment bank.

Confirmation that these palisade enclosures were indeed edging or revetment for barrows, and not pre-existing free-standing enclosures, came with the excavation of the Kilham long barrow. There, Terry Manby found typical palisade enclosure trenches cut into earlier filled ditches of long barrow type:

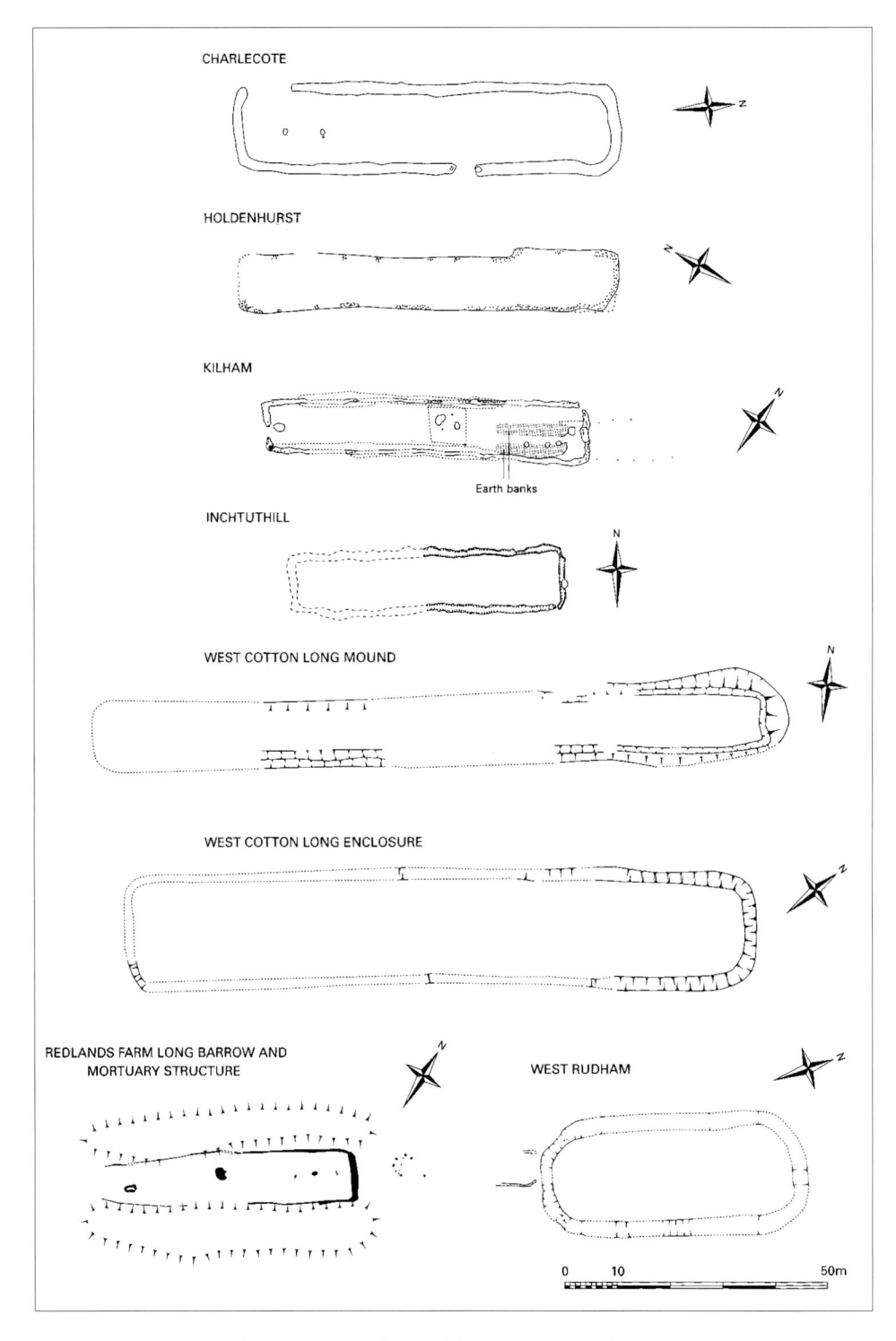

INSCRIBED ACROSS THE LANDSCAPE: THE CURSUS ENIGMA

26 Rectangular excavated sites. *Courtesy of Warwickshire County Council*

the 'enclosure' must have been constructed around a pre-existing mound (*26*). Substantial quarry ditches had then been dug to provide spoil for the larger, second phase barrow that infilled the palisade enclosure but stopped level with the back of the mortuary structure. It was clear that the palisade 'enclosure' revetted a substantial barrow that had, for a period of time, extended only as far as the mortuary structure; that was left open and accessible in front of it.[8]

It appears then that wooden mortuary structures continued to be accessible just as stone chambers were. Some sites, such as Giant's Hills I with a mortuary structure centrally placed in the mound, at first sight appear to challenge the idea but even there scrutiny of the excavation record is revealing. Phillips' invaluable longitudinal section of the 61m barrow shows a near vertical division in the barrow make-up above the structure, and distinctive infilling of this *c.*1.5m wide trench with large chalk blocks. These can only have come from the base of the quarry ditches and been associated with *final* infill. Along with the row of stones leading from the side of the mortuary structure towards the edge of the barrow, this strongly suggests that one of the structural hurdle-fenced bays within the barrow had been left open to permit continued side access to the burial structure. Comparably placed chambers in bays or trenches exist at Hazleton, West Tump and Poles Wood East amongst classic Cotswold-Severn chambered cairns.[9]

This broad homogeneity argues against the notion that palisade enclosures were excarnation areas: identically disarticulated and weathered burials are found under stone and earthen mounds yet the stone sites lack anything that might compare to the palisade enclosure. Nor are there any obvious free-standing enclosures that might have centrally fulfilled the role for a number of chambered cairns. In fact there is a total lack of *prima facie* evidence to suggest that excarnation was ever practised within palisade enclosures. Small bones should have littered their grass-grown interiors yet, despite the most exacting standards of modern excavation, only two small fragments have been found in the top fill of a pit at Kilham. The distribution of skeletal material under long barrows with palisade enclosures and those without is identical and restricted to the burial structure.

There is no good reason it seems to distinguish the post edging of Giant's Hills I from the stone edging of Giant's Hills II, or the palisade 'enclosure' of Kilham from the turf edging of Holdenhurst. They were almost identical in plan yet excavation made it clear that neither stone nor turf structure could have stood independently. The macabre and colourful image of an enclosure reeking of decay and haunted by carrion feeders must, it seems, be put aside; the single jaw fragment from Dorchester VIII is the sole evidence and that came from a site lacking an inner palisade enclosure, as would be expected as it was never covered by a mound. Delayed or disturbed burial was undoubtedly practised but

27 Charlecote long enclosure. Arnold Baker

whether in accessible stone or wooden chambers, or at quite different locales such as causewayed enclosures, remains to be established.

With just two sites (Dorchester VIII and Normanton Down) surviving examination from the 1970 corpus the existence of an open long-enclosure type – even with the 'mortuary' label removed – might be questioned. But, as so often with archaeological research, just as Ashbee's corpus was being published work elsewhere was revealing a whole new series of Neolithic long enclosures.

LONG ENCLOSURES

In 1964 Webster and Hobley had published a remarkable series of aerial photographs taken by Arnold Baker and Jim Pickering along the valley of the Warwickshire Avon. These included a number of sites that appeared to be small versions of the rectangular cursus enclosures already known from the Thames Valley (Bi minor cursus) and two much smaller, elongated sites with partially rounded ends, that fliers graphically labelled 'frankfurter' enclosures. Interestingly they were all termed 'cursus-like enclosures' (itself a major leap of recognition) in

'REEKING BONE YARDS'? – LONG MORTUARY ENCLOSURES

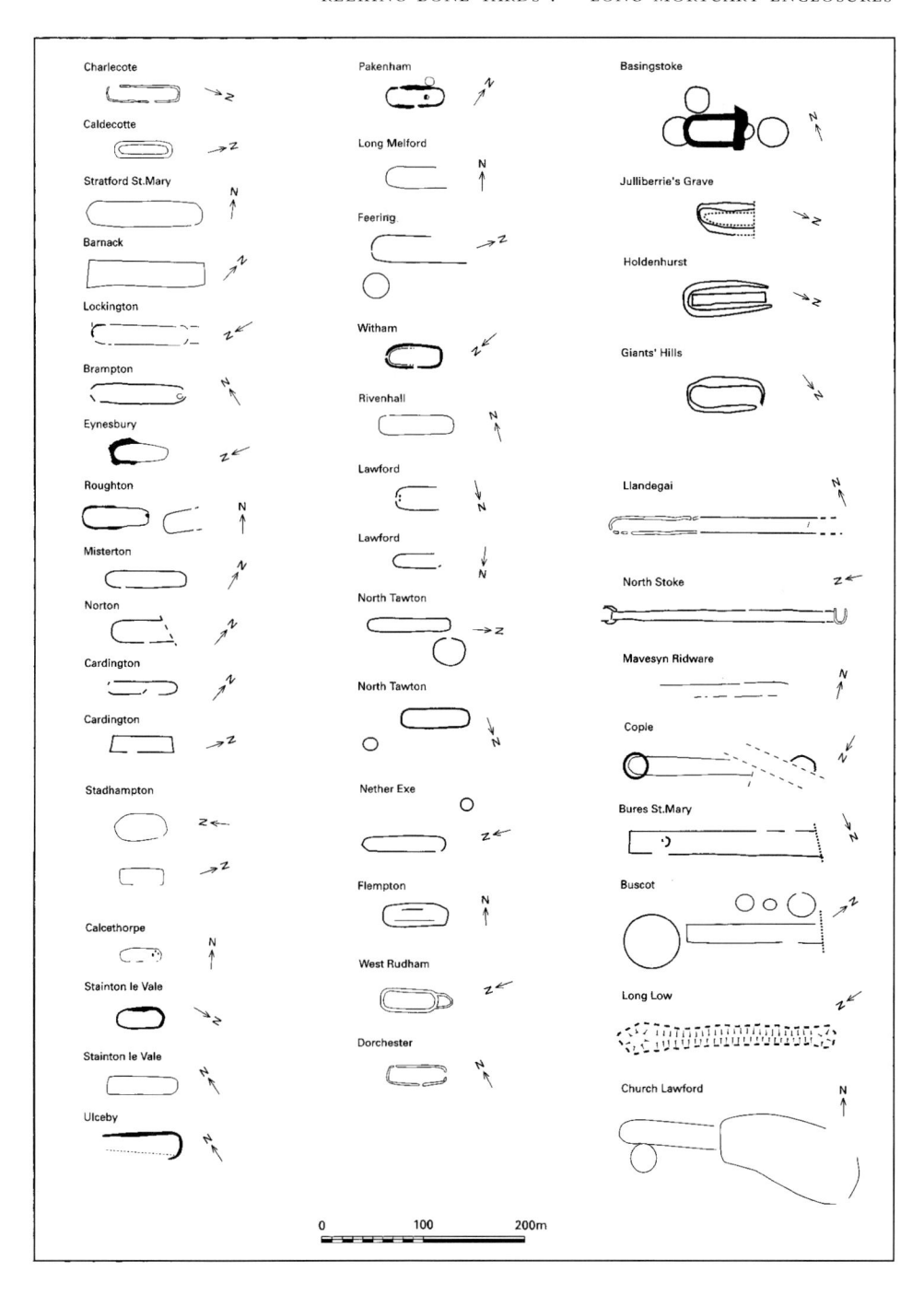

28 Charlecote and comparative sites, mostly cropmark long enclosures from the Midlands and East Anglia. *Courtesy of Warwickshire County Council*

the publication. In 1970 excavation began on one of the 'cursus-like enclosures' – Charlecote site 71 (*27*). Almost immediately evidence emerged that this flattened site had once enclosed a mound. The furrows of open field cultivation, so clear in the surrounding stipped area, were missing across the interior of the enclosure. The only explanation was that ploughshares had been lifted by a former mound as they crossed the site. The excavator, Bill Ford, confirmed this valuable deduction with some experimental archaeology. He had the spoil from a section of emptied ditch heaped up where an internal bank would lie and the result was clear: banks would have covered so much of this narrow enclosure that only an almost unusable 2.5m-wide central area (4.5m if revetted) was left. An initial role for the ditch as an enclosure prior to mound construction could be excluded. So with its Neolithic date confirmed by pottery from the ditch, a new group of sites had emerged – enclosures that were *not* enclosures but barrows.

Simultaneously aerial photography in Essex and Suffolk was picking up almost identical sites and Felix Erith saw a local parallel in the slight enclosing ditch that excavation had revealed around the turf-built long barrow at West Rudham in Norfolk. In 1971 he published a short note in the *Annual Bulletin of the Colchester Archaeological Group* called 'The Levelled Long Barrows'. This and the interim report on Charlecote were of major importance but rather lost in local archaeological group publications. They had, however, begun the process of re-populating the heavily cultivated lowlands with long lost long barrows.[10]

Over the next decade 'frankfurter' enclosures continued to multiply – sometimes referred to as 'cursus-like' because their curved ends resembled that of the cursus at Thornborough; occasionally advanced as possible long barrows, but almost never called 'long mortuary enclosures' since their ditch lines were even and straight (*28*). The little causewayed ditch site at Kettlestone, near Fakenham in Norfolk, was one of the very few to receive the 'long mortuary enclosure' appellation. But this was another case of constrained perception. Excavation had indeed revealed that Dorchester VIII, like Normanton Down, had a broken ditch line but a glance at Allen's aerial photograph of the site (published ironically in Atkinson's excavation report that set out the case for 'long mortuary enclosures') demonstrates that it did *not* appear that way as a cropmark: it appears as a regular – even *precise* – ditch exactly like the other 'frankfurter' enclosures. Causewayed irregularity is not prerequisite for the recognition of an open site therefore, anymore than large, separate flanking quarry ditches are for the recognition of ploughed-out long barrows. Excavation of Dorchester VIII left no doubt that these sites could be open enclosures; excavation of Charlecote equally emphatically confirmed they may once have been barrows.

Clearly neutral geometric labels such as oblong ditch, trapeziform ditch and ovate ditch are ideal given this structural variability, but as comparable oblong

29 A pillow (warren) mound. The name comes from their flat topped appearance that contrasts with the rounded profile of a long barrow

sites in Scotland were defined by posts and not ditches they will all simply be termed long enclosures.

REFINING THE DATA

To conclude that all sites of long enclosure shape are Neolithic would clearly be absurd but equally it would be impossible – and probably pointless – to test them all by excavation: just 26 sherds emerged from the *total* excavation of the 72m x 16m site at Charlecote. Fortunately a series of size criteria enable us to refine the sample.

Perhaps the most common source of confusion comes from pillow mounds. These were constructed in warrens set up in the seventeenth and eighteenth centuries on marginal terrain that was unsuitable to farming. Earth was scraped up, or brought in, to make a mound for rabbits to burrow into, often with pre-prepared gullies. A continuous oblong-shaped ditch was usually dug around the mound to discourage the rabbits from burrowing farther. Such mounds survive in vast numbers on Dartmoor, and on other marginal land such as Charnwood Forest in Leicestershire, and are easily recognised by their low, normally flat-topped mounds (*29*). Once ploughed out, however, they produce a long enclosure cropmark. Luckily, in addition to being sited on terrain generally unattractive to Neolithic settlement, and given away by 'warren' and 'conery' field name evidence, size sets them apart. Long enclosures of proven Neolithic date range in width from 10-25m; pillow mounds overwhelmingly from 2-8m. It seems reasonable to assume therefore that if a long enclosure is narrower than 10m it is probably a pillow mound.[11] Other possible explanations include cropmarks left by drainage trenches dug around root vegetable clamps or the wear gullies of extended horse lunging circuits.

Round barrows were on occasion set close together and enclosed by a continuous ditch. These are comparatively rare but in a ploughed-out state would produce cropmarks of oblong, trapeziform and ovate type if the round barrows inside were simply constructed of turf. Two features aid identification: cropmarks of pits marking tell-tale central graves and the considerable size of most surviving multiple round barrow enclosures (30-50m in width on the Wessex chalk and of comparable size at major sites such as Stanton Harcourt and Radley on the Thames gravels in Oxfordshire). Smaller sites also exist, however. In Micheldever Wood in Hampshire an ovate mound 32m x 24m proved on excavation to comprise two small abutting round mounds covering Bronze Age cremations linked by a central flint cairn. Had this site been ploughed flat only the ovate enclosing ditch would have remained to produce a cropmark. Ovate, trapeziform and short oblong (up to 50m) sites then need to be treated with caution. But, luckily for the 'cursus question', sites above this length appear quite distinct; Grinsell's quadruple multiple round barrow type is long enclosure plan but based on a *single* recorded example near Maiden Castle. Even triples are extremely rare and, along with twin round barrow enclosures, do not exceed 60m in length.[12]

The long enclosure group then appears distinct and, on morphological grounds alone, the case for a continuum with cursuses seems strong. But if these were the lost long barrows of the heavily cultivated lowlands how can they be related to the overwhelmingly open form of cursuses? Was Dorchester VIII the only open site or do any of them reveal evidence of development from an open to a mounded site as the 'long mortuary enclosure' model had predicted? Excavation – undertaken with increased frequency since the potential of the 'type' has been recognised – has revealed a complex picture. This is best illustrated by the examination of regional patterns.

6

PATTERN AND PURPOSE – LONG ENCLOSURES IN THE LANDSCAPE

THE UPPER THAMES VALLEY AND WARWICKSHIRE AVON

Although Dorchester VIII places the Upper Thames Valley centre stage in any consideration of long enclosures, it is atypical of the area. The most common sites here are short and of U-shaped plan. Three have been excavated: North Stoke and Radley in the Upper Thames, and Barford in Warwickshire (*30*).

That at North Stoke was set across the ends of two 225m-long parallel ditches that can now be seen to mark a former bank barrow. Its ditch silting patterns point to recutting probably associated with refurbishment and bank barrow construction. The interior produced only two features: off centre at the rear, a ramped pit that had once held a massive post, and set to one side, a large pit that held a cremation burial with a miniature Early Bronze Age collared urn. The latter might have led to the site being interpreted as a ploughed-out multiple round barrow were it not for the fact that the bank barrow ditches produced a date of 3500-3300 BC and seemed clearly to be later in date than the small enclosure. The collared urn almost certainly accompanied a secondary burial placed at the end of the bank barrow where it overlay the earlier enclosure.[1]

At Barford in the Warwickshire Avon Valley a very similar site to which a minor cursus had been appended contained an almost identically placed large post hole. Two other pits revealed evidence of burning and a central recut pit was large enough to have held a burial etched away by the acidic subsoil.[2]

That burials may have been placed within these small long-enclosure sites was confirmed by Richard Bradley's excavation of an atypically double-ditched site at Radley in the Thames Valley. It lay on the opposite side of a small stream to the Abingdon causewayed enclosure in an area that later attracted a number of Grooved Ware pit deposits and a major Early Bronze Age linear cemetery. The

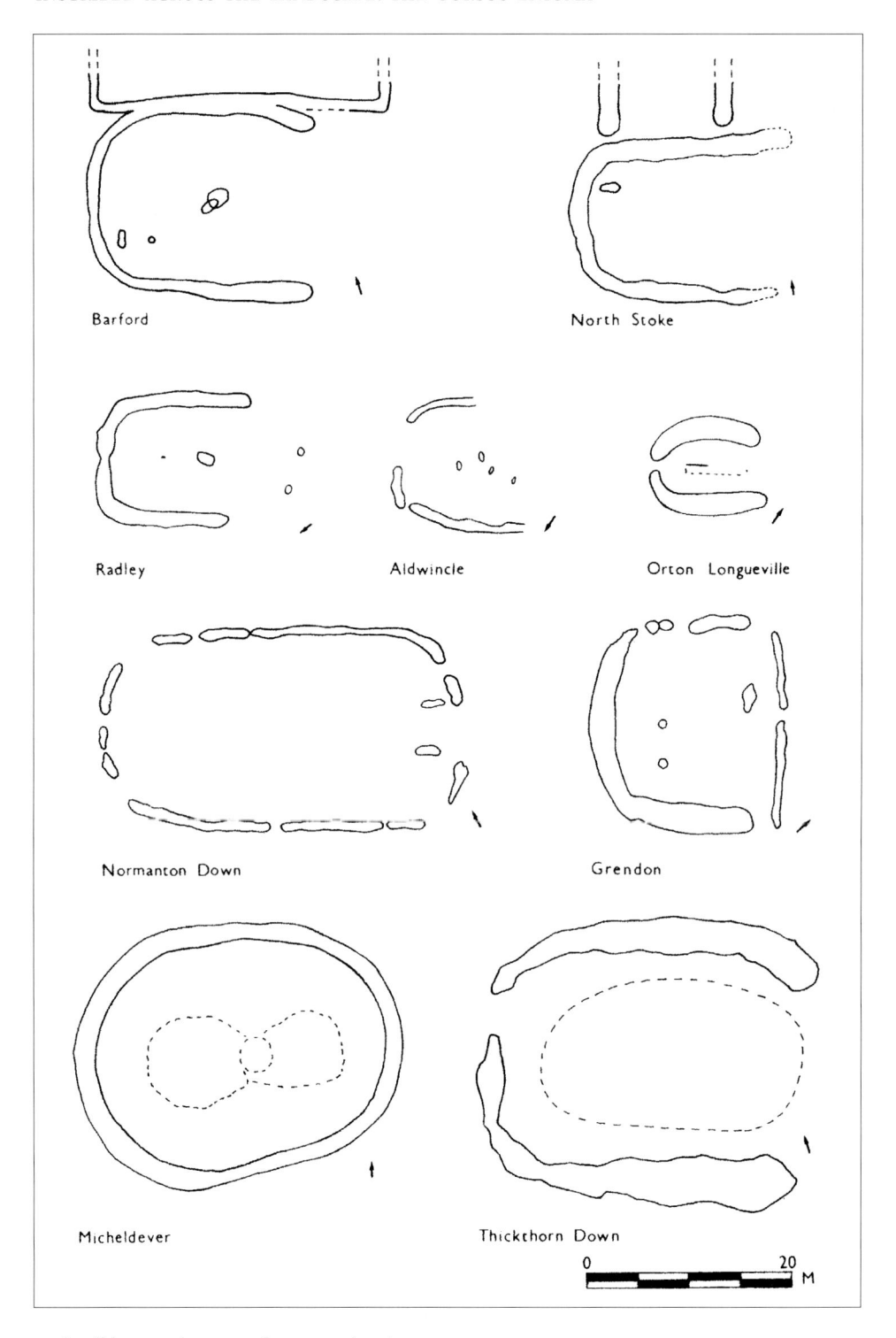

30 Small long enclosures and comparative sites

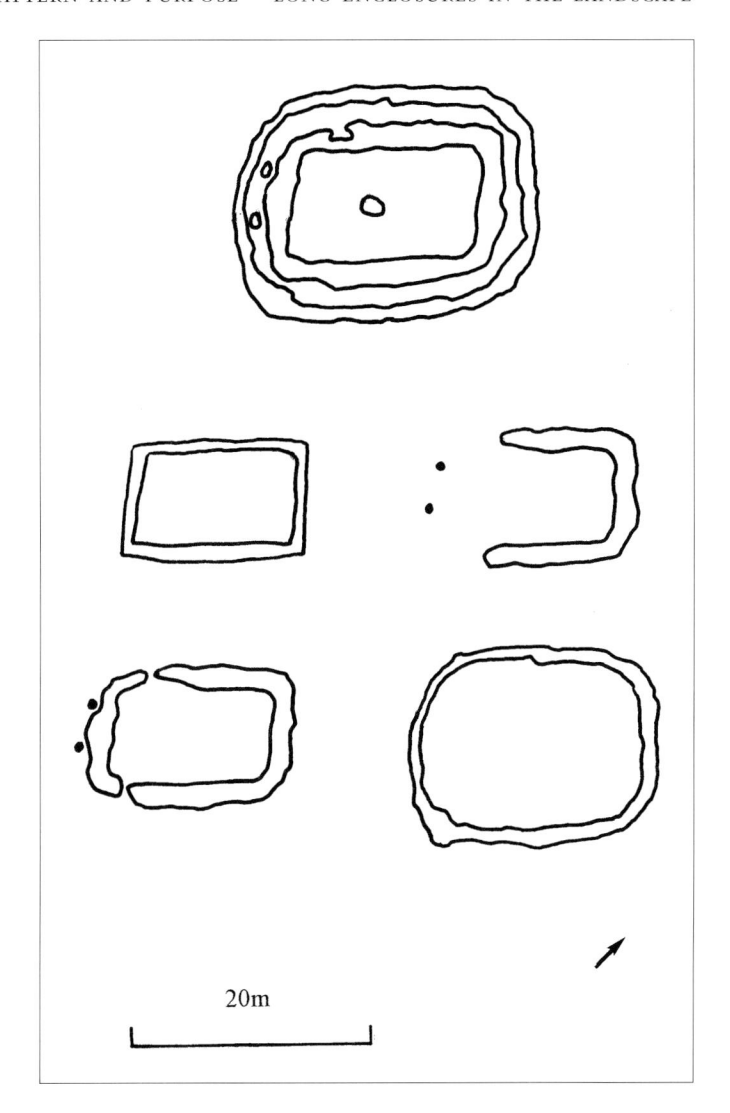

31 Radley: full plan and four suggested phases

inner ditch was of two phases: the first defined a narrow rectangular enclosure with no apparent entrance causeway, and the second saw its re-digging in stages – first to a U plan and later with the addition of a segment blocking the front. The outer ditch was segmented and of rather more bowed plan suggesting it may have been laid out around a spread barrow. Spaced posts were detected in all of the ditches with deposits of antlers placed in both ditches around the south-western end of the monument and deposits of pottery largely on the opposite side. Some small skull fragments occurred in the secondary silts near the antler (*31*).

This small long enclosure has all the characteristics of an Earlier Neolithic long barrow, albeit with posts set in its successive ditches. But the dates obtained from the antlers placed with each modification in the ditches on one side of the open end are surprisingly late: centred between 3400-2800 BC. And the burials were anything but partial. Two fully articulated crouched inhumations were laid out along the axis of the monument, heads towards each end and with legs crossing – a woman with a polished flint knife placed in front of her face and a man with a jet belt slider on his hip. These grave goods are features of the developing Middle Neolithic prestige artefact repertoire. The jet belt slider can be paralleled by one placed on a similarly articulated male burial at Whitegrounds in Eastern Yorkshire that carries a date of 3350-3050 BC, contemporary with the Radley monument. However, radiocarbon determinations on the bones of the Radley skeletons, produced dates several centuries later than those of the monument which could indicate that the burials are intrusive. The grave pit in which they lay was very shallow (only 100mm deep), a fact perhaps explicable in terms of it being dug through a low mound. Such reuse of an earlier site was not unusual at this stage when accompanied individual burial was first being practised – the Whitegrounds round barrow itself had utilised an earlier long mound.[3]

Whatever the case, Radley and North Stoke currently suggest that this small long-enclosure type may have been in use from before 3500-2800 BC or later. Other sites in the region with convex terminals akin to these include examples beside the cursuses at Drayton St Leonard and Benson, and intersecting the cursus at Stadhampton. They are somewhat longer but none achieve the classic 'frankfurter' form that is so suggestive of cursus development.

Classic long enclosures

These are restricted to the Warwickshire Avon catchment, across the Cotswold watershed from the Upper Thames, where closely similar examples are to be found at Misterton, Norton and at Charlecote. As already indicated the latter contained a mound, probably contructed of turf or scraped-up material. Posts were noted in the ditch where they cut into its base beside the central causeway; others may have been undetectable in the loamy silts. In plan the site is strikingly similar to the Kilham and Inchtuthill enclosures (*26*). Like Kilham the enclosure may have been set out around a pre-existing mound and have possessed a two-post mortuary structure at one end; the central clay 'floored' feature advanced for that role is far larger than any known mortuary house and probably represents the base of an infilled mound bay. The internal width of the site (12-13m) is of considerable importance since it corresponds with the fairly consistent 10-14m range of excavated long barrow widths. The conclusion to be drawn from the excavation is that long enclosure sites of that size are likely to have marked mounds and their ditches to have contained palisades or spaced posts used in mound edging (e.g. Lower Luggy, Berriew, Powys). The absence of quarry

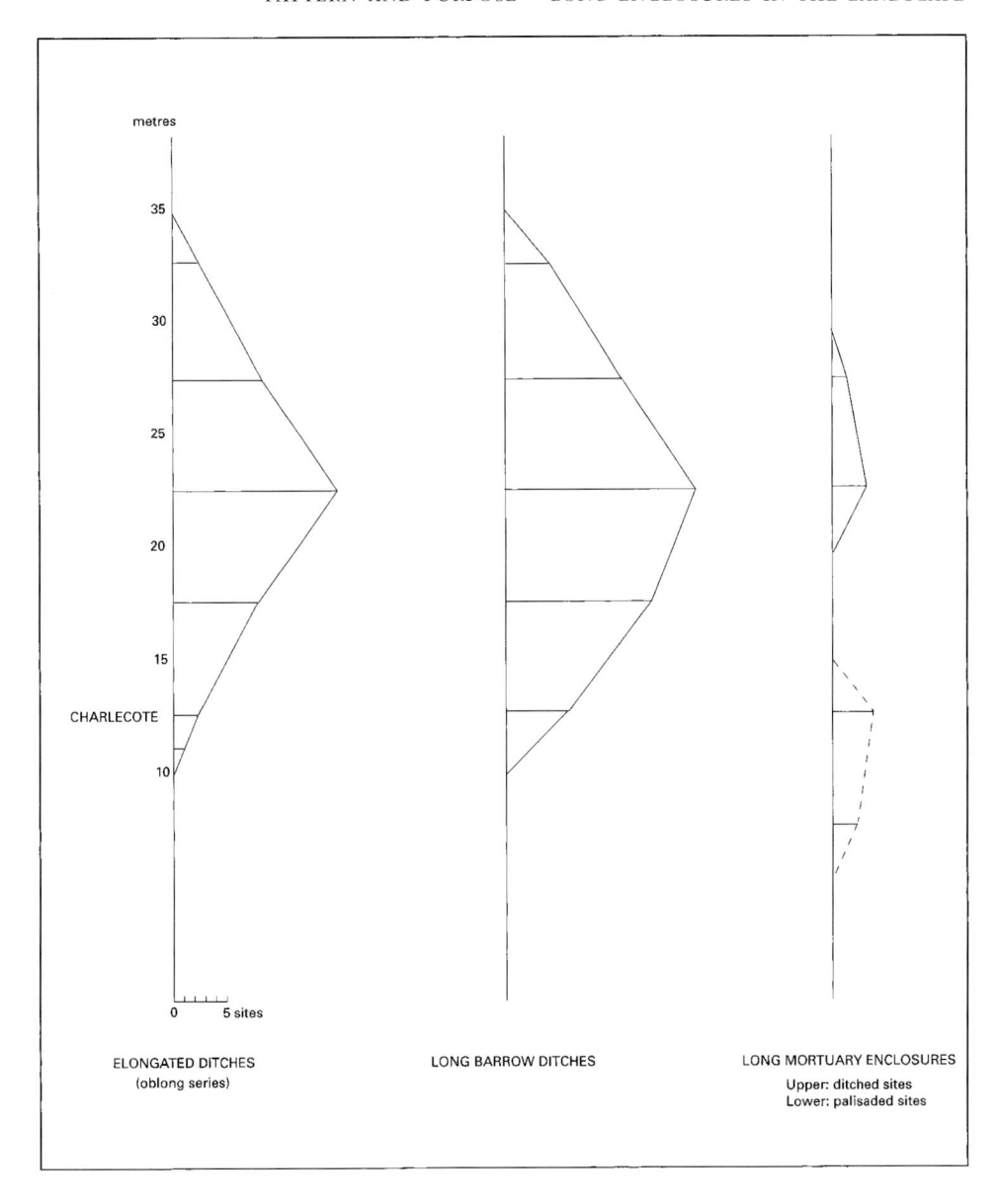

32 Long barrows and oblong ditch (long enclosure) width range. Sites of Charlecote size correspond to palisade enclosures revetting barrows; wider sites to long barrow ditches. Courtesy of Warwickshire County Council

ditches simply points to a different source of material. By contrast the open sites of Dorchester VIII and Normanton Down were almost twice as wide. Their widths correspond to those between the inner edges of the spaced quarry ditches of long barrows (*32*). This hints at a very different demarcating role. We will return to that later when we examine the site at Brampton in Cambridgeshire.

Except for Dorchester VIII, the Thames Valley appears to lack classic long enclosures. Alluvial masking may be responsible. It is now known that water levels were up to a metre lower in the Neolithic than today, and that the present floodplain was fully occupied. It was from just this situation that the enclosure at Yarnton emerged.[4] There, in advance of gravel extraction, Gill Hey's 10-year programme uncovered one of the largest areas of preserved landscape ever investigated. During the Neolithic it was dissected by stream channels. The long enclosure that lay on the edge of one of these was precisely rectangular rather than convex at its extremities. It closely resembled a Bi-type cursus (57a). Nothing dateable came from its initial ditch filling but Fengate-style Peterborough Ware came from recuts either side of the entrance. Much here depends upon the dating of Fengate Ware and estimations of the speed of silting but an Early/Middle Neolithic date seems clear. Post holes and gullies were also located in recuts on the entrance side of the enclosure. Within the site lay a burial with sherds of Peterborough Ware in the backfill of the grave. There were also a number of pits within and around the enclosure that contained apparently selected deposits of fine flintwork and pottery: two with Peterborough Ware, one with Grooved Ware, two with Beaker and nine with Middle Bronze Age pottery. Many contained small amounts of cremated bone. The fact that Middle Bronze Age features focused on the enclosure in the same way as the earlier ones, and that a burial of this date was cut into the filled ditch, appears to preclude the possibility of random respect for a relict element of the landscape; the enclosure seems rather to have retained its sanctity. (I am grateful to Gill Hey for this information in advance of publication.) Ring ditches apparently set over comparable cropmark enclosures at Charlton in Worcestershire and Cardington in Bedfordshire point to similar longevity of use and respect.

Domestic activity, by contrast, was obvious 300m away on either side of the Yarnton enclosure. As well as pits this included a large Neolithic house (20m x 10m). Houses are an extreme rarity on English Neolithic sites and this site, by virtue of its large size (larger in floor area than the great medieval hall at nearby Minster Lovell: 15m x 8m) and lack of domestic rubbish and pottery, raised questions of function in the excavator's mind. Some sort of ceremonial or communal role is not inconceivable. Interestingly its proportions (1:2) are close to those assumed for the long enclosure. A radiocarbon determination places it between 3950 and 3640 cal. BC – probably earlier than the enclosure.

The regional picture
Here, on this remarkably well preserved and meticulously excavated site, we have perhaps the clearest picture of the place of long enclosures in the Neolithic

landscape – set apart from normal domestic activity, perhaps possessing token primary burials but little else, and attracting later burials to their environs. There is nothing to suggest use as an exposure area for corpses. The two cranial fragments from the ditches at Radley and the jaw fragment from Dorchester VIII similarly point to no more than the presence of skulls. These are items known to have been removed from tombs for use in a trophic or relic manner (e.g. deposited in causewayed enclosure ditches) and are thus the *least* likely bones to be casually left on a 'temporary' burial site. Regionally it is clear that spaced posts in ditches gave additional structural impact to several sites but large isolated posts set toward the back of the enclosures were only a feature of the smallest monuments. It is also clear that two, perhaps three, separate traditions existed in these valleys. First 'classic' long enclosures that are largely restricted to the Warwickshire Avon and exhibit no gradation to cursus or cursiform size (the Dorchester upon Thames cursus is of similar plan but hugely larger); they may originally have enclosed mounds but Dorchester VIII demonstrates that was not invariable. Second, small, probably related, sites like Barford that may similarly have been mounded. Third, Bi sites that grade upwards from Yarnton to minor cursus size (major cursus in the case of the Upper Thames) and appear to have been open enclosures. It is possible that the distinction between these groups is one of function rather than date or cultural affiliation.

The Cotswold Hills that separate the Upper Thames and Warwickshire Avon furnish a total contrast with their distinctive chambered tomb tradition. It could reasonably be assumed therefore that the linking influence revealed by Barford-like small open sites and by Bi series monuments came not across them but via the Thame Valley – a reason perhaps for the magnification of the Thame/Isis confluence at Dorchester upon Thames.

THE FEN CATCHMENT

Cropmark evidence suggests that 'classic' long enclosures of are to be found predominantly in East Anglia where, sadly, few have been excavated. The valleys of the rivers running to the Wash act as a bridge with the Warwickshire Avon, however, and sites in these have received considerable attention.

One of the principal concentrations of causewayed enclosures in Britain occurs along the valleys of the Welland, Nene and Great Ouse. The cluster in the Stamford–Peterborough region is only rivalled by those in the Upper Thames and around Avebury, while spacing along the rest of the valleys and onto the headwaters, points to contact with the Thames and Avon catchments. Typical of this region are groupings of minor cursuses and long enclosures with ring

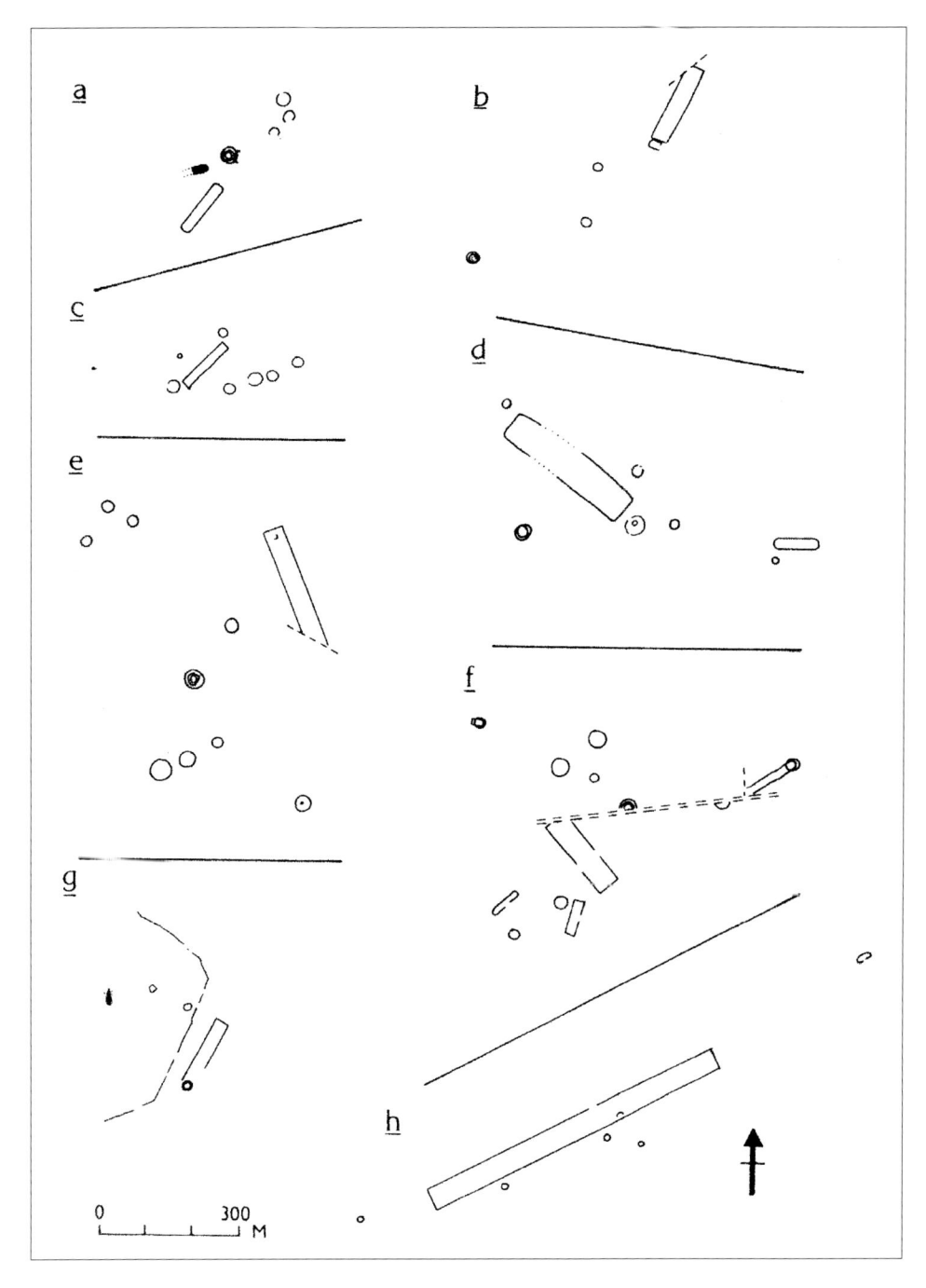

INSCRIBED ACROSS THE LANDSCAPE: THE CURSUS ENIGMA

33 Barford-like complexes: a) West Cotton; b) Barford; c) Barnack; d) Stratford St Mary; e) Lechlade; f) Cardington; g) Drayton St Leonard; h) Springfield

ditches (often including irregular, multi-ringed examples that may represent Later Neolithic hengiform sites). West Cotton on the Nene and Cardington on the Great Ouse are good examples. They appear to represent miniature versions of great complexes like Dorchester upon Thames and can be termed Barford-like complexes since that site in Warwickshire was the first to be extensively excavated[5] (*33*). Other complexes of this same loose type are to be found at Eynesbury and Brampton, both in the Great Ouse Valley and both possessing a long enclosure and a cursus.

Turf-built barrows

The various monuments of the Cardington complex, near Bedford, appear, like Yarnton, to have been situated between ancient stream channels. They lie 1km from a causewayed enclosure set on a higher gravel terrace. The complex comprises a group of long enclosures around a larger, rectangular enclosure (182m x 57m). The latter, at a larger scale, recalls the Yarnton site and clearly belongs in the minor cursus category; the eastern elongated site recalls Llandegai and clearly belongs in the cursiform long enclosure group (*33f*).

A similar complex in the Nene Valley was unexpectedly revealed beneath alluvium during investigation of the deserted medieval village of West Cotton (*33a*). The earliest element of the complex was a long mound (135m x 13/19m) composed of turf and topsoil that ran from the edge of an old channel of the Nene. The mound surprisingly survived to a height of 0.5m (0.8m at its eastern end) and was divided by stake fence lines. It may also have been edged with stakes and was certainly capped by gravel – perhaps derived from the small, shallow scoops located at one point along its length. Subsequently a narrow gulley with spaced stakes was dug around the *top* of the mound, cutting through the gravel capping material. Its purpose was clearly to redefine an eroding mound but deposits of charcoal and fire reddened sand in its fill suggest it was burnt down (*26*). The mound thus defined was some 10m wide – very much the 'national' standard for delimited long barrows but it lacked grave pits, burials or a mortuary structure. Its form appears to have been essentially that of a bank barrow, perhaps more akin to those from northern Europe than those from Wessex. Mildenhall-type sherds in the upper levels of the side scoops correspond with similar pottery from Charlecote-like long enclosures at Cardington and at Rivenhall in Essex. An Early Neolithic context is supported by the earliest of the range of radiocarbon dates returned on the site: 4000 and 3600 BC. This structure dramatically emphasises the very partial nature of our knowledge of long mounds in the heavily cultivated lowlands – in the absence of a ditch there would have been nothing left to record its former presence had it not been fortuitously protected.

Just over 10m away stood a long enclosure 120m long x 20m wide. Although similarly covered by later alluvium, its prehistoric surface had been eroded away before that date. It seems inconceivable, however, that a mound had ever stood within it since the highest surviving point of the long mound lay immediately adjacent. Silting on this site suggested slippage from gravel banks placed along its sides but not apparently at the ends. Finds from the c.25 per cent of ditch excavated were few: 20 pieces of struck flint, two pieces of cattle bone and an antler rake. A radiocarbon determination on the latter that was found near the base of the ditch suggested construction between 3400 and 2900 BC. Significantly, ring ditches at West Cotton appear to ignore the earlier long mound but are strung out in alignment with the extremities of the long enclosure; the two closest are set almost exactly the same distance from each end. This pattern is also to be found at Charlecote in Warwickshire but made more explicable there by a mound marking the site. The presence of a primary burial with a Late Beaker, conical jet button and notched and tanged flint dagger places the northern ring ditch at West Cotton as much as a thousand years later than the slight, open long enclosure that it apparently respected, and that in turn was several centuries later in date than the long mound.[6]

There is considerable time depth to these Barford-like complexes it seems and within this are to be found two different structural traditions: one of open enclosures and the other of turf mounds. The latter may, as at West Cotton, lack any defining ditch or may have an enclosing ditch as suggested at Charlecote and proved at the surviving barrows of West Rudham in Norfolk (level-topped, parallel-sided with a ditch of oblong plan) and Royston in Hertfordshire (trapezoidal, higher at one end and with a ditch of ovate/trapezoidal plan). In each case the ditch was modest and did no more than furnish material to cap the turf mound: gravel at West Rudham; chalk at Royston.[7] In the latter case so complete was this 'disquise' that the excavator was left puzzling over a 'classic' chalkland long barrow 'composed of decayed turves'. He concluded that the monument represented a far flung outlier of the Wessex heartland. Today we might wonder if the reverse was true. What is clear is that quarry ditch construction appeared not to be a feature of barrow building in this region (*34*).

Thus the recently excavated waterlogged long barrow at Haddenham, Cambridgeshire – noted as a gravel patch in the peat of a fenland field that blanketed it – proved to be constructed almost entirely of turf. It was delimited by a modest ditch of trapezoidal plan that provided capping. Here at last a surviving wooden three-posted mortuary structure was found that at a stroke put paid to the endless arguments that had raged over their original form: not tent-like but vertical-sided with flat 'lids' that could be removed. It was linked to a substantial façade of posts at the eastern end of the barrow from which a slighter palisade

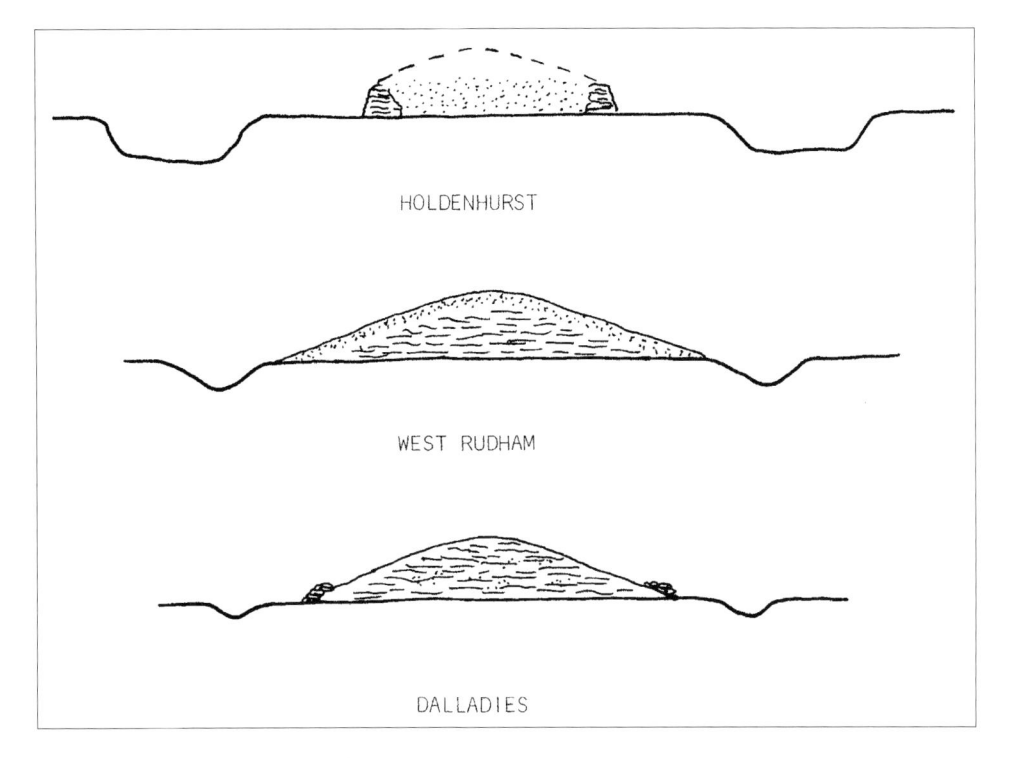

34 Long barrow turf building techniques – Dorset to Grampian

ran back to form a sub-rectangular enclosure delimiting the small phase I barrow. Although partially articulated skeletons were found in the wooden chamber no finds were reported in the interior from beneath the barrow to suggest the exposure of bodies. Early Neolithic Mildenhall pottery was again found here, as at the nearby causewayed enclosure. Dating from the substantial posts suggests construction between 3900-3700 BC (possibly too early), and from the forecourt pavement of 3700-3400 BC (possibly a late feature but broadly contemporary with the causewayed enclosure dates).

Stanwick and Eynesbury

This unified picture of early turf-built long barrows with modest, or no, enclosing ditches has recenty been checked by two excavations – both of long barrows and both possessing quarry ditches. The first was at Stanwick, within 2km of West Cotton. Stripping of alluvium in preparation for gravel extraction at Redlands Farm revealed a 'classic' flanking quarry-ditched long barrow that would have been at home on the Wessex or Yorkshire chalklands (see *26*). Like the West Cotton sites it stood on a gravel island and had been preserved to a maximum height of 0.6m beneath alluvial cover. A trapezoidal timber palisade (50m long and a maximum of 10m wide) constrained the turf and gravel mound; planks preserved in the waterlogged quarry ditches suggest post and panel construction. Radiocarbon determination indicates that the barrow was constructed between 3700-3500. This is the period when similar sites were being built on the Wessex chalk, when the Haddenham long barrow was probably being completed and when the older, and very different, turf long mound at nearby West Cotton was being refurbished with a stake fence.[8]

Stanwick remains the only long mound with separate quarry ditches of chalkland type known in the Midlands and East Anglia but others could, of course, be similarly hidden beneath alluvium. But at Eynesbury in Cambridgeshire a hybrid site has been investigated: a long enclosure of broadly oblong plan that appeared to have been expanded to quarry-like proportions around its northern end where an apparent façade trench stood. Although there was no obvious break in the ditch silts to indicate phased construction at the point of expansion from the regular 2.5m-wide ditch to the ragged 6m-wide quarry, fine grey clay layers found only at the base of the wider ditch perhaps point to some separation. Irregularly placed pit-like recuts and 'structured' deposits were also restricted to this part of the ditch. Recognition of these features in the appalling, flooded conditions on the site is a credit to the excavators and an indication of the value of total excavation: the recuts were unrecognizable until ditch sections dried, and the 'structured' deposits were only located by the sixteenth evaluation trench! Except along the northern 'front', the pits (*c.*1.2m wide x 0.5m deep) only cut the primary levels.

The deposits that were made at the base of the newly dug ditch – or more rarely in the recut pits – mostly comprised animal bones but human bones were also intermingled. One concentration in the ditch in front of the only remaining feature of the barrow – a straight façade trench – comprised at least seven ox skulls, disarticulated sheep/goat bones and five fragments of the arm and leg bones of a young male. The base of the ditch along the sides also revealed spreads of partially articulated human remains. Jacqueline McKinley identified the bone groups from the eastern side (49, 52 and 7 fragments respectively) as those of probably three females – two mature and the other a young adult. Six of the bones from one of the mature women were the only ones completely represented on the site but several of these were broken. In addition, one arm bone had been cut through while it was still green, (probably after death as there was no sign of healing) and polish had been produced around the edges of the cut, either by the process itself or through the use of the cut bone. At the base of the ditch on the other side of the barrow, 17 bone fragments comprised the remains of another mature female. Their condition suggested short-term exposure and trampling, conceivably by cattle since the insect evidence (including a specific dung beetle species) pointed to a high concentration of grazing animals. Human disturbance, on the other hand, is also indicated – two limb bone fragments belonging to this female were found in the fill of an adjacent recut.

Here at last it seems is the elusive evidence for the exposure of bodies in long mortuary enclosures. A macabre picture presents itself of partial articulated limbs, cut bones and the remains of bodies being cleared to the ditch, along with other offerings, when the barrow was built. Certainly the breakages noted all appear to have occurred on dry bone. But it is not quite so simple. There was no sign of the weathering or gnawing to be expected on exposed bone and no apparent selection of body parts as expected in curated (preserved) material. The most common parts were fragments – but only fragments – of frontal vault. The skeletal material was found in the lowest levels of the wide ditch that was undoubtedly dug for barrow construction. If the bone fragments had been in the interior they must have been moved outside until the barrow was built and only then deposited in the quarry ditch. Unlike the remains from causewayed enclosures and other long barrows that point to full population inclusion, there is an absence of infants and juveniles and a reversal of the normal male dominance (4 females to 1 male). Jacqueline McKinley therefore concluded that there was no case for exposure, and little reason to think that bodies had been removed from an original place of burial to a secondary one. The absence of pits for burial within the interior of the site (that had presumably been protected for a considerable period by the presence of a mound) precludes it as such a locus anyway. The fact that the remains were frequently adjacent to animal bone – and that cattle bones in general, and complete skulls in particular (11 in all), dominated that assemblage – points rather to the inclusion of human bone in dedicatory offerings.

The anomalously late radiocarbon date obtained from an antler on the ditch floor (2400-2600 BC) could explain the very real difference from 'classic' long barrow burial practices elsewhere. Human cranial fragments were, very unusually, found in the ditches of the late long barrow at Radley and in another with an interrupted enclosing ditch at Marden, Wiltshire. It might also explain the very unusual near central positioning of the long barrow within a cursus and the fact that it apparently *post*-dated that monument by a very considerable margin. For the moment too much stress should not be laid in this evidence, however, as the antler was the only one of seven selected items that retained sufficient carbon for AMS dating. Waterlogging may similarly have had an adverse effect on this determination, and upon that on a tree trunk that was inverted and set in a pit cutting the lower secondary and primary ditch silts (2200-2000 BC).[9]

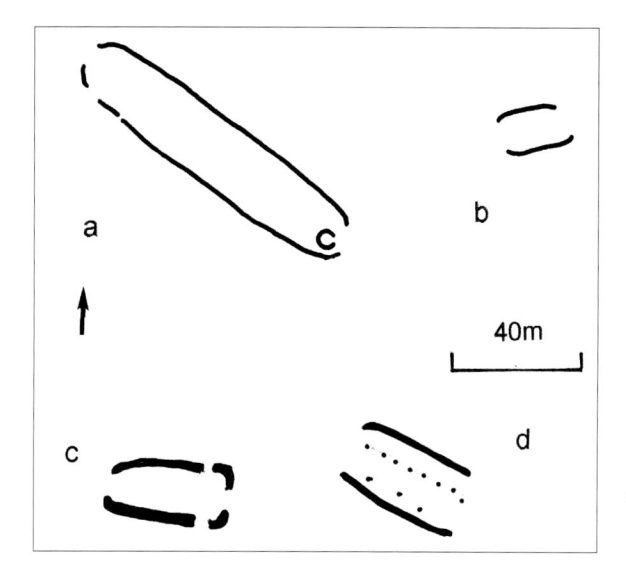

35 Bracketing ditch cropmarks: a) Brampton; b) Sandy; c) Dedham; d) Bures

Parallel ditches

Brampton in the Great Ouse Valley midway between Eynesbury and Haddenham presents yet another long enclosure barrow form (*35*). Like the other sites it lay beside an old river channel on a slight rise in the gravel terrace. Unlike them its ditches were very slight (1m x 0.3m deep) and did *not* form an enclosure; although the flanking ditch lines incurved at each end, gaps were left where terminal ditches would normally be expected. Two post holes were recorded, conceivably the largest and most deeply cut elements of a spaced arrangement invisible in the higher silts. Silting into these shallow ditches was from the exterior but a dark layer at the western end of the interior suggested the presence of a mound – presumably of turf. A shallow horseshoe-shaped ring ditch just within the eastern end of the site resembles sites at Aldwinkle and Orton Longueville that surrounded Earlier Neolithic mortuary structures (see *30*). The ditches and mound may then have been intended to extend and monumentalise a small earlier monument. Dateable material was lacking but pits with evidence of burning in them that cut into the filled ditches returned radiocarbon dates centred on 2500 BC and suggest a Middle/Late Neolithic date for construction.[10]

Brampton has introduced a completely new plan to the discussion. Its separate ditches seem only marginally related to the long enclosure type yet the even incurving of their ends suggests a conceptual link of some kind. It would be easy to dismiss them as revetment trenches for the sides of a turf mound were it not for the fact that they stand some 20m apart, considerably in excess of the width of any preserved mound. They correspond instead to the long enclosure norm (see *32*). They are not alone. Similar sites have been recognised as cropmarks in East Anglia and may provide vital evidence in the vexed long mortuary enclosure debate (*35*).

Narrow palisade enclosures, as we have seen earlier, correspond to the widths of long mounds and are best viewed as revetment/embellishment devices, but what of wider sites like Normanton Down and Dorchester VIII? Their overall width is equivalent to that between the inner edges of long barrow quarry ditches. If they are held to represent the normal first stage of long barrow construction (aborted for some reason) then slight 'long mortuary enclosure' ditches of this sort should be detectable running between the ends of the 'classic' flanking quarry ditches of completed mounds. They are not. Neither excavation nor aerial photography has revealed them. Brampton suggests an alternative explanation – that early ditches did indeed define long barrow sites but that the creation of an enclosure (given such significance because of an assumed exposure role) was not the objective. Instead the concern was to inscribe the plan of the ditches for the next phase (flanking, U-shaped or enclosing) – a statement of group identity and belief, not casual choice. The slight ditch that partially survived along the inner edge of one of the flanking quarry ditches at Amesbury 42 in Wiltshire appears to be one such example, rather than an extension of the cursus.[11] Only in areas such as East Anglia, where mounds were largely constructed of turf rather than quarried material, would such flanking early ditches normally be detectable. There are so few there perhaps because they are not easily recognised; possibly because local tradition favoured early ditches of enclosing plan; or perhaps because early flanking ditches were usually later linked at their ends to create an enclosure form. The latter could explain the gravel silting from bank collapse noted along the sides of the long enclosure at West Cotton but not at its end. It may also lay behind the pattern of straight-ended terminal ditches linked to broadly curved corners.

The regional picture

The Fenland catchment then furnishes a picture of considerable regional complexity with long enclosures and ditchless turf mounds; slight flanking ditches and classic quarry-ditched long barrows; Neolithic round barrows and even small oval barrows as at Maxey. This contrasts with the the homogeneity – even orthodoxy – of areas like the Lincolnshire Wolds and the Cotswolds. But there are indications that these may in turn hide a more complex picture. In the Lincolnshire Wolds Dilwyn Jones has recorded in detail a range of trapeziform and oblong ditch cropmarks that can be linked in size and ditch plan to surviving barrows such as Giant's Hills I and II on the one hand and to river valley long enclosures on the other.[12] Equally in the Cotswolds barrows are often edged with drystone walling of convex plan, copying a turf-building technique.[13] Destroyed turf mounds are a possibility in each region.

Consistent use of turf in the construction of the Stanwick, Haddenham and West Cotton long mounds (all with dates between 3800-3500 BC) points to a common early structural tradition in the Fenland catchment. Although none of them had enclosing ditches of oblong plan, they share with the 'classic' long enclosure sites at Cardington and Rivenhall the presence of Early Neolithic Mildenhall Ware. The single radiocarbon date from the West Cotton long enclosure (3400-2900 BC) does not, therefore, preclude earlier dating of other sites of this type. Importantly it is clear that sites in this region grade convincingly upwards from 'classic' long enclosures of 'frankfurter' type to full blown cursus monuments (Cardington/Cople → Bures St Mary → Stratford St Mary → the narrower northern arm of the Fornham All Saints cursus → the main body of the cursus). It therefore has a stronger claim to be the birthplace of the tradition than the Upper Thames where the Dorchester cursus represents a huge dimensional leap. The fact that many of the smaller sites possessed mounds means that bank barrows must have played a role in the process (see *44d-f*).

No such regional distinction is evident amongst the severely rectangular Bi sites. As in the Upper Thames and Warwickshire Avon region they grade steadily upwards from the small site at Fengate closely resembling Yarnton (50m), to Barnack (125m), Eynesbury (310m) and Springfield (680m). The Bi phenomenon then appears fairly consistent across the Midlands and East Anglia and predominantly associated with small Barford-like complexes. Major sites like Benson and Drayton South are absent from the Fen catchment, however, perhaps because they record seasonal group coalescence in the vicinity of a major sanctuary site at Dorchester upon Thames. Dating remains as uncertain as in the Upper Thames: Beaker sherds from the topmost levels of the ditch of the small Fengate enclosure broadly correspond with Grooved Ware and Early Bronze Age material at the same level in the comparably sized Springfield cursus ditch that had Mortlake-style Peterborough Ware in its lower silts. This conflicts with the exceptionally early dates returned by the optically stimulated luminescence method of silt dating on primary levels within the Eynesbury cursuses (4800-3500 BC).[14] These may yet prove to result from the effects of waterlogging on an experimental technique however, since dates from bank collapse within the secondary fill, just 100mm higher, are far later and fall within the expected bracket (3600-2600 BC). They are also consistent with the presence of Beaker material in the topmost ditch fill. Early dates are, however, a consistent feature of our last focal area.

STRATHMORE AND EASTERN SCOTLAND

The gentle country of Strathmore, cradled between the Grampians and the Sidlaw Hills, with its extension north-east along the coastal strip to Aberdeen, and south-west along Strathallan towards Doune, is the third region in which long enclosures are abundant. Strangely there appear to be few in the 500km that separate it from the Fen catchment but this absence may be more apparent than real. Strathmore has benefited from good soils that encourage cereal farming and hence cropmark production, from perceptive aerial reconnaissance initiated by Gordon Maxwell, and a targeted programme of masterly excavations undertaken by Gordon Barclay and Kenneth Brophy. The results have been striking. Although plan repertoires point to a shared concept, it is clear at a glance that sites here are different from those in the south. First they are defined almost exclusively by pits, and second, cursus development appears to simply take the form of extension to earlier short enclosures.

Mounded sites

The site found beneath barrack blocks of the Roman legionary fort at Inchtuthill in Perthshire was a 'classsic' long enclosure of the type familiar in the two previous regions. It was defined by a ditch within which there was clear evidence for the presence of posts, and has been dated 4200-3700 BC.[15] In size (54m x 10m) and plan (even down to the gap at one corner) the shallow ditch closely paralleled the palisade enclosure around the long barrow at Kilham in East Yorkshire and the long enclosure at Charlecote in Warwickshire (see 26), both of which contained posts and enclosed mounds. Unlike them, this seemed to have been an open palisade enclosure: the last of two phases of spaced posts in the ditch were burned and fell inwards leaving a charcoal layer in the upper ditch silts at an angle of some 40 degrees. A large barrow would certainly have prevented this happening had they been placed at the inner edge of the ditch. They were near the ditch centre, however. From that point they would have collapsed onto an internal barrow (presumably built of turf like that surviving at Dalladies) at about the observed angle. The silts of the partially open ditch support its presence: rain run off from the mound producing a loamy fill on the inner side with natural gravel erosion on the outer side, as at Charlecote where a turf mound is also suspected.[16] The posts it appears, like those at Charlecote and Radley in the south, acted as embellishment rather than revetment.

A similar site at Kintore, just upstream from Aberdeen, raises the possibility of slight rather than monumental barrow construction that would also have enabled posts to have fallen inwards. Like Inchtuthill it was defined by a continuous ditch that had been recut and held a wooden fence. An earlier area of burning that contained Earlier Neolithic bowl pottery lay at one end and had been enclosed by a convex terminal ditch behind which transverse ditches holding screens cut off an area 20m long. A slight mound, no more than a metre at its highest, filled the area between the enclosing ditches that may have provided gravel to cap it. Later a large post had been set up through the mound. Nearby a cremation burial dated 3800-3600 BC was made and an arc of post holes set up around a hollow containing cereal grains and hazelnut shells. Finally pits containing Grooved Ware were dug (one with a cremation covered by sherds) and a 14m-diameter post circle set out.[17]

Nearby, in the Dee Valley, a site still under excavation on the Crathes estate has many points of similarity and may prove to represent the house prototype that was drawn upon by the builders of the mounded site at Kintore. It is a posted structure some 20m x 9m with a possible entrance marked by outlying 'porch' posts at the end of one long wall near the gable end – a noted location for causeways in long enclosures and cursuses. Within the flattened convex ends of the site were large internal pits. Although expected to have held the uprights of a ridge pole, the pit so far excavated proved to have been open. It was lined with alder and hazel branches and contained Earlier Neolithic pottery, flint and Arran pitchstone artefacts, carbonised cereal grains and wood fragments. This has been provisionally interpreted as debris and occupation material falling from the collapsing building as it was burned down. This event, and the destruction of an adjacent pit alignment, have been dated by a series of radiocarbon dates to 4000-3600 BC.[18] The site is therefore contemporary with not only Inchtuthill and Kintore but also the remarkable site at Balbridie that stood less than a mile away on the other bank of the river.

Post enclosures

Balfarg, in Fife, introduces two sites of directly comparable plan to Kintore and Crathes but rather different structure – defined by post holes not trenches (*36a & b*) Except for pits with burnt bone and Earlier Neolithic pottery, they formed the earliest features of a complex that later witnessed construction of a large ceremonial henge, a stone circle and a ring cairn. The two post enclosures lay less than 50m apart on similar north–south alignments and appeared to be all but identical although disturbance prevented the recovery of the full plan of structure 2. Both comprised an outer enclosing fence of light posts and irregular axial lines of larger posts that had, in several instances, been replaced.

The excavator, Gordon Barclay, realised that this precluded the obvious interpretation of the structures as houses: slighter, exterior posts would be the first to weather and require replacement in a roofed structure. It was also impossible to imagine how the ridge poles of a building could be removed

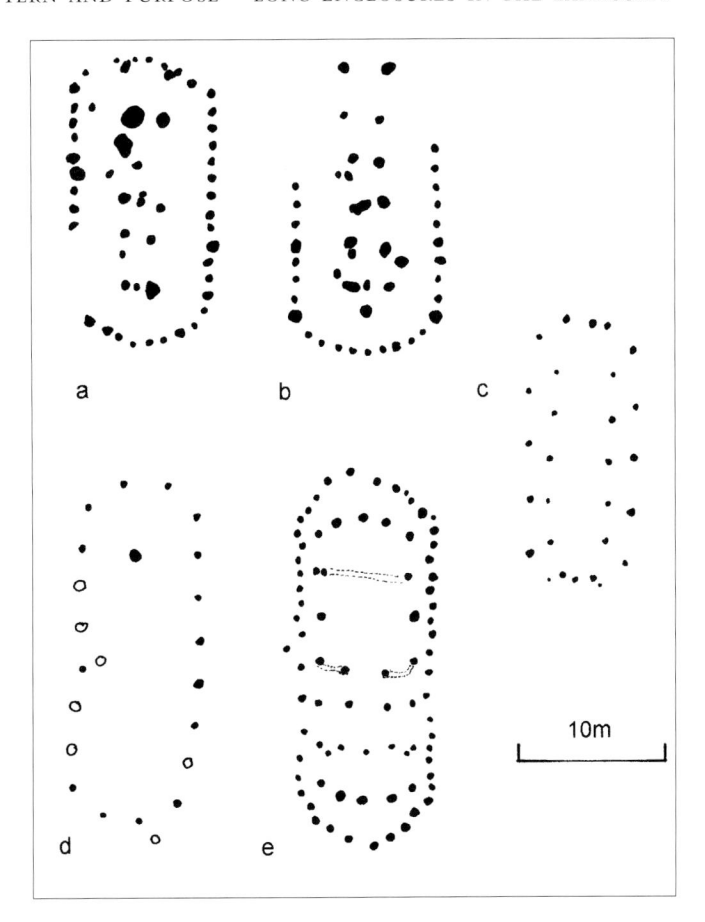

36 Scottish 'halls': a & b) Balfarg; c) Carsie Mains; d) Littleour; e) Claish. *After Brophy 2004*

without disturbing the outer wall posts. David Hogg noted that the irregular layout and close spacing of the inner lines made no structural sense either; despite care taken in structure 2 to oppose the outer wall posts, the inner uprights were so chaotically placed as to make rafter spanning a nightmare. The inner posts were therefore interpreted as lines of 2 and 4 post scaffolds for the exposure of corpses (see *23*), replaced as occasion demanded, around which a fence had been constructed.[19]

Littleour and Carsie Mains lie close to the Inchtuthill 'long mound' structure, and even closer to the great bank barrow known as Cleaven Dyke. They are almost identical in size and plan to the structures at Balfarg but are defined by widely spaced posts and lack irregular axial post settings (*36c* and *36d*). Instead Littleour had a large post set centrally within its northern end. The only other internal feature was a small pit containing Grooved Ware. This recalls the finding of the same material at Balfarg, and, as at that site, probably relates to much later activity. The distinctly bowed nature of the side walls at Littleour, the lack of opposition of side posts and the inferred 7.5m rafter spans all precluded a house interpretation.[20]

At Carsie Mains a plethora of pits left by the roots of fallen trees made it difficult to exactly establish the site plan but may be of considerable importance: they clustered around the perimeter of the structure but only one occurred in the interior – within one convex end, where the large post stood at Littleour and where the only post to show through the covering mound remnant stood at Balfarg 2. Two lines of smaller posts within the interior at Carsie Mains immediately suggested aisle posts for a roofed building but they were spaced at different intervals to the perimeter posts and extended beyond the perimeter post line at one end.[21] To judge from the late radiocarbon date (3350-2900 BC) the inner setting may have been a later structure, perhaps associated with an adjacent, comparably dated, post circle.

The excavators, Kenneth Brophy and Gordon Barclay, have suggested that the Littleour and Carsie Mains structures represent late symbolic renderings of earlier and more complex sites such as that at Claish.

Early halls

At Claish near Callendar a site of identical shape and size to Littleour (24m x 8.5m), but defined by close-set not spaced posts, revealed a whole series of internal linear features that appeared to form partitions (*36e*). This was undoubtedly a house and the consistent series of radiocarbon dates obtained from it were early: 3800-3600 BC. Just within each rounded end of the structure were similarly bowed transverse divisions constructed of posts up to 1m in diameter, set 2m deep and placed so close that they must have formed an impenetrable screen broken only by a central entrance. By contrast other transverse divisions were far slighter and appear to have comprised screens of wattle.[22]

Internal divisions of the same plan occurred at the same points in the closely comparable site at Balbridie, lying just across the river from Crathes but some 150km from Claish. So close indeed is the pattern of internal organisation (although significantly not the outer perimeter) that the excavators discussed the two sites side by side in the Claish report (*37*). At both sites internal partitions appear to delineate a larger open room towards one end of the structure. At Claish this produced evidence of fires lit in two steep-sided pits that produced nearly 600 hazelnut shells and a small number of cereal grains; one was lined with pottery when half full and fires had been lit on top of this layer. These were clearly not normal domestic fires. The other half of both the structures was marked by a considerably increased number of posts. Since more than 20,000 carbonised cereal grains were recovered from this end of the Balbridie site it has been suggested the extra posts held an upper floor intended to keep grain

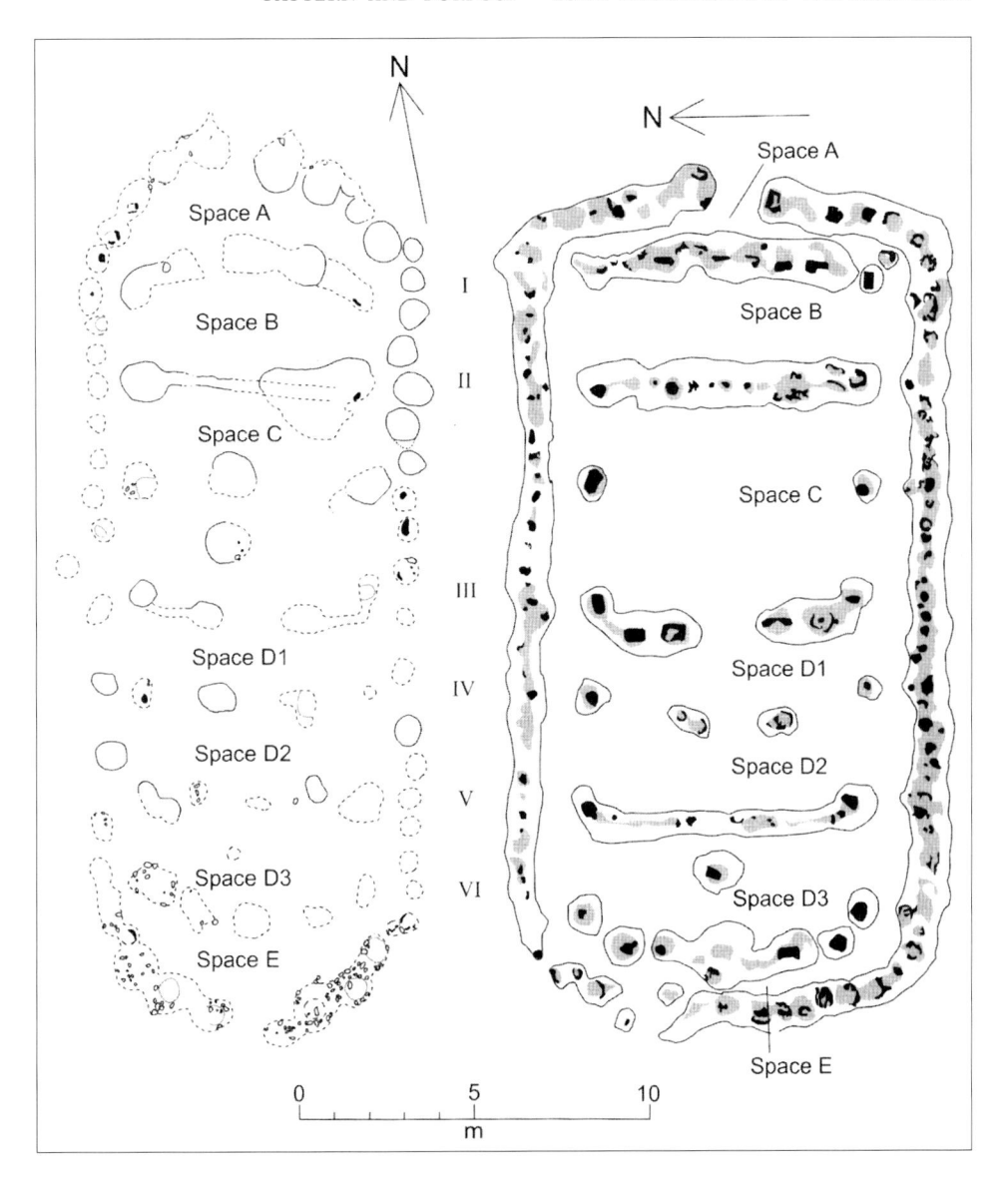

37 Claish and Balbridie. From Barclay, Brophy & MacGregor 2002, courtesy of the Society of Antiquaries of Scotland

dry, as postulated for the similar arrangement found in earlier Danubian long houses.[23]

These two sites then present a strikingly similar picture of internal arrangements and final fate (both burnt down), but externally there are real differences and real problems. That the outer wall at Balbridie was set in a continuous bedding trench may be insignificant, but the fact that it is set so close to the partitions at the extremities as to make access very difficult, is not. The excavators also noted problems with the outer wall at Claish: at one end of the structure posts were far more closely set and appeared to be out of alignment with each other along the wall line. This problem was partly resolved by supposing two phases of construction, and so removing alternate posts in 'crowded' areas. This satisfyingly produces regular wall lines but requires acceptance of total reconstruction of just the northern half of the building; except for a 5m section the southern half was apparently untouched. Such repair is difficult to envisage on a standing building, particularly as there is little evidence for post replacement in the internal partitions.

An alternative approach, as David Hogg suggested, is to view the perimeter walls of both Claish and Balbridie as later, independent elements set around earlier structures comprised simply of the interior posts.[24] This has much to recommend it. It offers an explanation for the use of truly massive posts for the end partitions at Claish (they were the original gable ends); for the very restricted space between partitions and side walls at Claish, and end walls at Balbridie, (movement between them may not have been needed once the buildings were fenced in); and for the piecemeal reconstruction of the 'outer wall' at Claish (simple enough if free-standing). It does, however, pose the question: how were such buildings walled? If internal partitions were marked by earthfast screens surely this would be even more imperative for outer walls. An answer may be indirectly furnished by long barrows that, it is generally agreed, were intended to replicate ancestral houses. That excavated in the region at Dalladies was built entirely of turf as were many, as we have seen, in the southern river valleys. Structural application was not limited to core construction. At Holdenhurst in Dorset[25] we have evidence of its use as walling roughly 1m wide revetting the considerable bulk of a gravel barrow (*34*). Turf walling running between, or beside, the outer partition posts along the sides of Claish and Balbridie houses would aid roof support and explain the limited 1-2m separation from the outer fence.

Reconstruction of these sites as turf-walled buildings surrounded at a later stage by a symbolic demarcating fence also makes explicable the striking similarity of the Balfarg enclosures. As the excavators have shown (*38*) the spacing of the axial post pairs there correspond closely to the positions of the central 'doorway' posts in partitions at Claish. If turf walls are envisaged at Balfarg running where partition end posts are found at Claish, buildings of equivalent width result. In support of the idea it is significant that no pits intrude along these proposed wall lines at Balfarg. This could explain the near identity of the Claish and Balfarg perimeter fences and free the latter sites from the problems posed by multiple post replacement in their interiors. Rather than mortuary scaffolds these can be seen as the result of several phases of reconstruction involving new

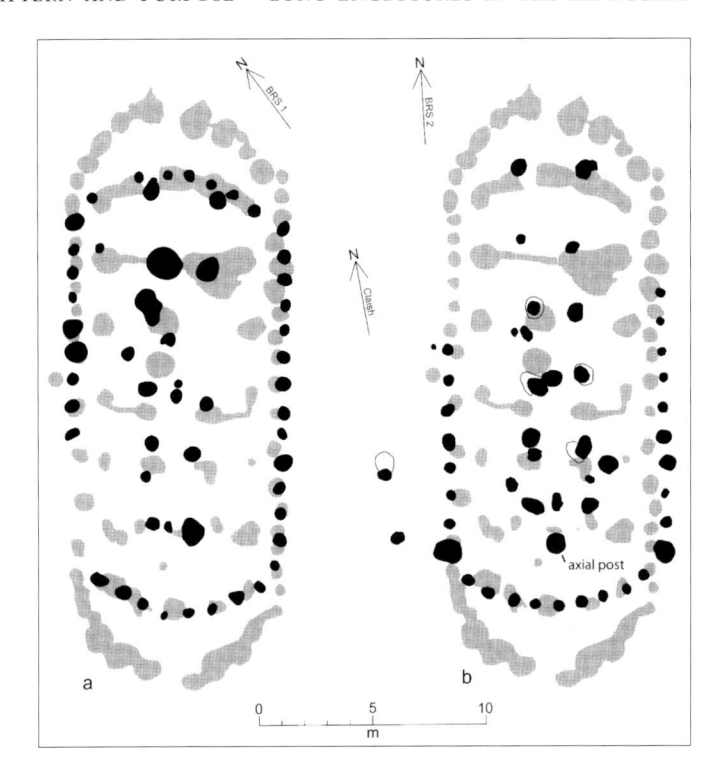

38 The Balfarg structures overlain the Claish 'Hall'. *From Barclay, Brophy & MacGregor 2002, courtesy of the Society of Antiquaries of Scotland*

ridge pole/'doorway' pairs prior to the structures being encased by symbolic enclosures. Such a turf-walled house might also furnish the obstacle that Hogg hypothesised prevented neat axial layout of the convex end of Balfarg 2. Equally the 'aisle posts' at Carsie Mains could be envisaged as supports set inside a somewhat narrower (4m) turf-walled house, later delimited by a symbolic fence of spaced posts.

There is no reason to suppose that turf was restricted in its use to long mounds. Indeed, its use for their construction indicates familiarity and an expectation of structural stability – an expectation that survived from Sutherland to Surrey into the nineteenth century AD.[26] Relative lack of consideration given to its use for Neolithic house structures probably relates as much to a focus on the chalklands (where soil depth and root mat may never have developed sufficiently to encourage its use) as to its vulnerability to erosion and subsequent invisibility. It is a pressing challenge to archaeological science to find a means of identifying its former presence and thus perhaps rendering the random post holes of Neolithic occupation sites intelligible.

That said, it is clear that the Claish and Balbridie structures were in no sense normal houses. Their later enclosure by fences confirms that as much as their rarity, size and lack of occupation debris. Evidence that the main open space at

Claish was kept clean (abundant fire waste from two large pits containing the principal concentration of cereals on the site had not spread into the partition post holes), and that grain was stored in unprecedented abundance at one end of Balbridie, also argues against these being simply high-status residences. All aspects of the sites point to a communal collective role akin to that advanced for the rectangular house at Yarnton in Oxfordshire. This makes more explicable later emergence of the fenced enclosure, symbolically reduced to spaced posts, as a monument form in its own right (see *36d*). The common 'vocabulary' that Barclay and Brophy note links these sites seems certain to be anchored in 'halls' like Claish.

Post-defined long enclosures – cursuses

In Angus, between Inchtuthill and Crathes-Balbridie, lies a concentration of pit-/post-defined cursuses that often appear to have sprung from an earlier, smaller site. The Douglasmuir enclosure (65m x 20m) was defined by pits up to 1m in diameter and 0.6m deep, each holding a post. The square-ended site was divided exactly in half by an oblique line of posts into which the rows on each side appeared to bend (*39*). This suggested multi-phase construction and the fact that the central division, like the terminal lines, was composed of larger posts (0.5m as against 0.3/0.4m along the sides) appears to support the idea. It has been suggested that offset posts in the centre of each of these transverse line could represent blocked or askew entrances.[27] Nothing was found in the post holes, nor in the one internal feature – a very large pit 2m in diameter and 1m deep that had apparently been used to support a post. The fact that this pit was centrally placed within one end of the northern enclosure leaves little doubt that it was the primary focus. Charcoal from the remains of posts burnt *in situ* returned a date of 3900-3400 BC; too unrefined unfortunately to clarify its chronological relationship to Claish and Balbridie but confirming that it pre-dated the Littleour enclosure (3600-3100 BC) that similarly had a large axial post towards its end.

At Bannockburn, 25km from Claish, two other pit-defined enclosures have been excavated with very different convex and rectangular plans. Limited traced lengths and modest widths (35+m x 36m and 98+m x 27m respectively) means they are probably better considered as long enclosures rather than cursuses. The convex-ended site was defined by pits 1-2m in diameter that had been re-dug several times and in some cases stone lined as if to support posts. No traces of these were found however. By contrast the pits of the rectangular site located just 11m away held posts some 0.35m in diameter. Irregular layout on both sites suggested the pits were dug in short lengths of six to eight. Unfortunately nothing on either site gave a clue as to their purpose: burning had taken place

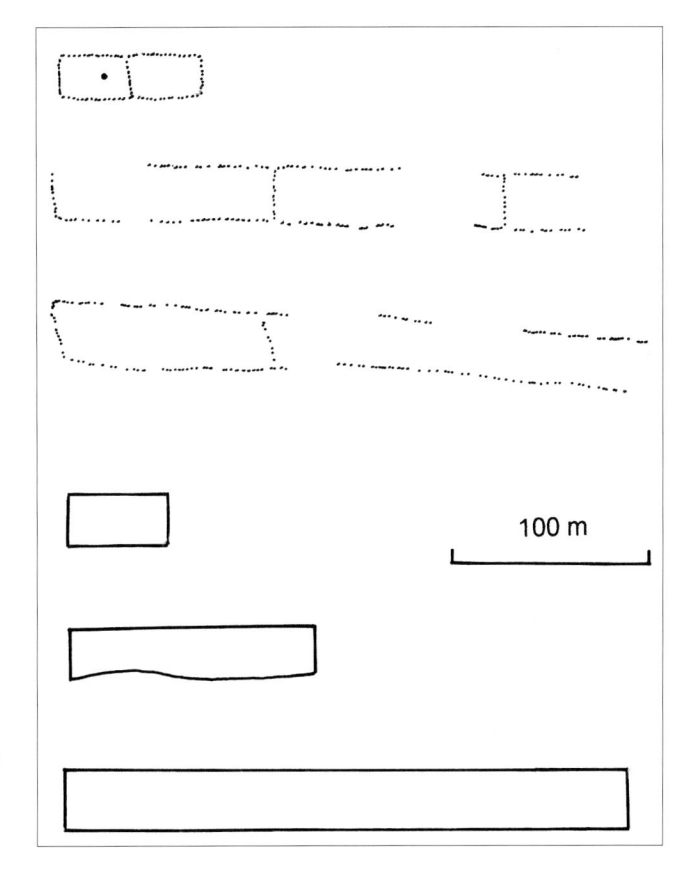

39 Post-defined and Bi sites. Top to bottom: Douglasmuir; Milton of Guthrie (part); Balneaves (part); Fengate; Barnack; Longbridge

in the pits of the convex-ended enclosure but the few sherds of Early Neolithic pottery and chert flakes found in them, and the post holes of the other enclosure, appear to have been accidental inclusions. Radiocarbon dates suggest the convex-ended enclosure was in use between 3800-3400 BC (possibly 4000-3800 BC but these dates come from potentially ancient oak), and that the rectangular enclosure was constructed between 3400-3000 BC. Here at least the convex-ended (type A) monument preceded the rectangular (type B) one, a situation hinted at amongst the sites of the Fen catchment. It does not, however, follow that the older site went out of use; continued activity seems to be indicated. Convex-ended sites at Upper Largie in the Kilmartin Valley and Dunragit in Galloway appear to be related to these Strathmore/Eastern Lowlands sites and similarly have radiocarbon dates of *c.*3800-3600 BC.

The regional picture

The Scottish Lowlands then furnish a picture of as diverse as that of the Fen catchment and Upper Thames/ Warwickshire Avon regions. Three distinctive monument traditions seem to be indicated. One derived from large, possibly turf-walled, 'halls' dated 3800-3600 BC that possessed, besides partition lines, little more than single fire pits along their lengths. These were enclosed by well laid out convex-ended fences, probably shortly after the buildings had gone out of use. Over time (3600-2700 BC) the fence was symbolically reduced to spaced posts and established as a monument type in its own right. The sites were of limited size (20m x 10m) but the form could have been enlarged to represent the inner post setting of the ditched cursus site of Holywood North. The second tradition, represented by enclosures of abutting pits, comprised sites twice as wide as the 'halls' and of far greater length. The Douglasmuir monument records a doubling of enclosure length; that at Balneaves, far greater extension. However, many modules were added the monuments were restricted to a width of about 25m; somewhat wider in the cases of the convex-ended Dunragit and Bannockburn sites distanced from the principal concentration in Angus. A single large pit within the Douglasmuir enclosure resembles that within the Littleour site of the first group. Most current dates suggest the two groups are contemporary but a later determination from the rectangular site at Bannockburn opens up the possibility of a developmental sequence from convex-ended pit enclosures. The third regional group comprises long mound sites. That at Inchtuthill is readily paralleled south of the border but the Kintore monument appears to be related to the local 'hall' tradition.

Evidence for use of these sites is restricted to complex and repeated burning activities in axially placed pits or to large posts set up towards one end of the enclosure. There is no direct evidence of mortuary activity (exposure or burial). Similarly limited evidence of activity might therefore be expected from larger cursus-like monuments that apparently represent the upper end of these traditions (e.g. Claish – Littleour – Holywood North post setting; and Douglasmuir – Milton of Guthrie – Balneaves). Many of the sites had been burned down although this was not evident in the case of the later structures. Grooved Ware placed in an internal pit at Littleour and found in some post holes at Balfarg indicates continued interest in the sites, as do post circles adjacent to Kintore and Carsie Mains, and set over the Upper Largie structure. These small groupings of monuments probably played a local role akin to the Barford-like groupings in the Midlands and East Anglia. A large Grooved Ware associated post enclosure overlying the Dunragit long enclosure/cursus, and adjacent henge monuments and stone circles at Balfarg, point even more clearly to the significance of the locations first marked out by long enclosures. They recall complexes like Dorchester upon Thames and Maxey that unite the two regions previously examined but there are real differences: long enclosures/cursuses here are far smaller and attracted far fewer hengiform/ring ditch sites. Those that are present appear to be related instead to the henge-like sites, quite the opposite to the Midland/East Anglian situation. Large cursuses are a rarity in Scotland. The complex around Dumfries is perhaps the best contender as a Dorchester-like complex. However, the plan of the Curriestanes cursus, and the placing and orientation of the Holywood cursuses suggest it may be an outlier of the southern pattern rather than an aggrandised northern complex. The very large Cumbrian-style stone circle – The Twelve Apostles – laid out adjacent to the Holywood cursuses, and the presence of large numbers of Cumbrian (Group VI) axes in the locality, emphasise the point.

Like the Upper Thames and Fen catchment, Strathmore and the Eastern Lowlands provide evidence of a range of apparently contemporary monuments in addition to those belonging to the long enclosure tradition. Just across the river from Claish lies the longest chambered long cairn in Scotland (Auchenlaich 342m); at Pitnacree a round cairn covered a typical Earlier Neolithic burial structure; and at Dalladies, 25km from Douglasmuir, a similar structure was incorporated in the side of a turf-built long barrow identical in all but material to the long cairns of Caithness. A complex overlay of populations and ideas presumably underlies the pattern but radiocarbon is unfortunately a very blunt instrument for teasing out patterns of change that may have occurred over half centuries rather than half millennia, while the barrenness of most monuments obscures the roots of divergence.

CONCLUSIONS

The three regions examined present contrasting but potentially overlapping evidence. Classic long enclosures in the Fen catchment grade convincingly upward to cursus dimensions but many seem to have contained mounds and to have been later in date than morphologically comparable 'hall' sites in the Strathmore region. For their part, the 'halls' show little sign of straightforward enlargement to cursus proportions; convex-ended post-defined monuments in the region appear to belong in a different, perhaps parallel, tradition exemplified by the rectangular sites at Douglasmuir and Balneaves. It seems virtually certain though that 'halls' and classic long enclosures were drawing on a common concept since convex-ended plan was extremely unusual amongst long barrows. Two possible explanations present themselves.

First, that the early 'hall' concept spread from lowland Scotland. In support of this idea it is notable that classic long enclosures have a dominantly eastern and coastal distribution, with marked concentrations along the Stour and Blackwater Valleys, and along the rivers leading to the Wash; less certain are the sites around

Rudston. Few have been excavated though, so it is by no means certain that they are later in date than the supposed Scottish prototypes.

The second possibility is that just as Scottish 'halls' probably drew on continental prototypes such as Schwarzen Berg in Lower Saxony (*40*), so may the southern long enclosures. In other words, both were products of a common continental pool. An obstacle to the idea is the absence of comparable East Anglian 'halls'. This is probably an inevitable consequence of at least a millennium of intensive cultivation but extensive evidence for the use of turf in barrow building in the region points to another explanation – turf construction. The earlier suggestion that turf walling was used at Balfarg, Claish and Balbridie has wider application. The fact that turf construction lends itself most readily to curved corners (witness the corners of Roman marching camps) has relevance here, if convex-ended East Anglian long enclosures are accepted as deriving from house prototypes. In a region where plough erosion will have removed all but the very deepest of internal post holes there is little hope of locating such houses, but the covering peat of the fenlands holds out the possibility of future discoveries.

Long enclosures in the other tradition isolated in the Midlands/East Anglia – the Bi series – can be distinguished from classic 'frankfurter' type long enclosures by their greater width and shorter proportions. A similar distinction is immediately evident in Lowland Scotland between sites in the 'hall' tradition (e.g. Littleour) and those in the pit-defined tradition (e.g. Douglasmuir). Dating is again uncertain but it does appear that sites of Bi type (with the exception of the Eynesbury sites dated by optically stimulated luminescence) are somewhat later than pit-defined sites like Douglasmuir. Transmission of the elongated enclosure concept south along the eastern seaboard could well have generated the distinctive Bi tradition. Coincidence of enclosure size and proportion is striking (*39*). It seems improbable in view of this that northern and southern traditions were isolated from each other.

A number of features link long enclosures of whatever tradition along the eastern seaboard: single posts set within their interiors (Littleour and Douglasmuir in the north; North Stoke and Barford in the south); single internal pits with deposits of Grooved Ware (Littleour and Yarnton); post line definition (in trenches, free-standing or spaced in the north; spaced in ditches in the south); and, perhaps most importantly, a common cleanliness. There is no evidence to support the idea that corpses were exposed within these enclosures. Absence of bones cannot be wholly explained away in terms of acidic subsoils and, where they have been found, they either fail to fit the pattern expected of this process (e.g. Eynesbury) or comprise fragments from the element least likely to have been lost in such circumstances – the skull (e.g. Dorchester VIII and Radley). It is clear that the term 'long mortuary enclosure' is inappropriate, whether

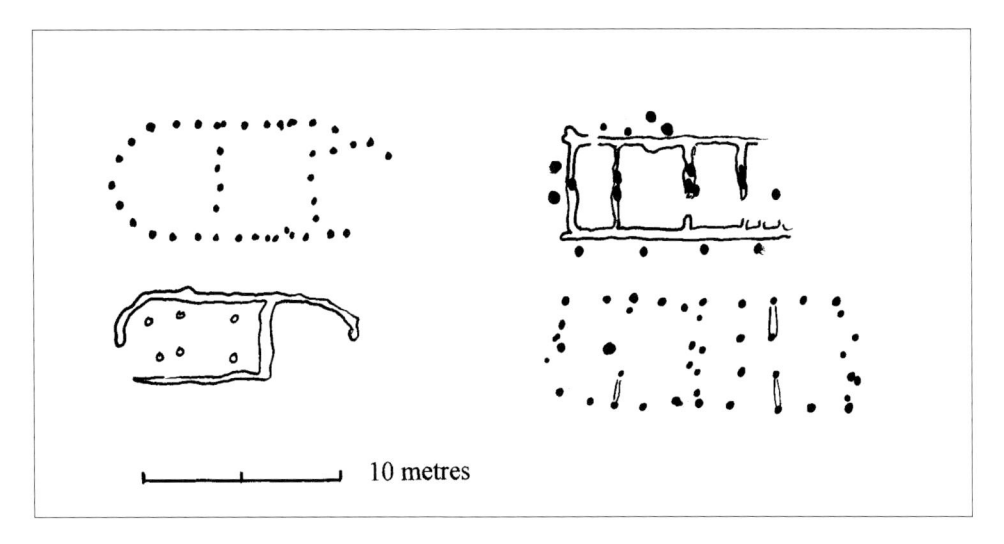

40 Houses – top: Schwarzen Berg (left); Flögen (right); bottom: Ballygalley (left); Lismore Fields (right)

defined as a 'reeking bone yard' for the exposure of bodies or as a place of burial; causewayed enclosures contained vastly more human skeletal material. The idea arose in response to problems perceived in accessing burial chambers under earthen long barrows, and was encouraged by similarity of long enclosure and long barrow plan. The first has been resolved by the recognition of open area or roof access; the latter by recognition of a common origin for *both* enclosures and barrows in symbolic house definition. This poses a vital question however: what motivated the builders to expand these symbolic enclosures to huge dimensions? The fact that mounds lay within many of the classic long enclosure sites in the south suggest an answer may lie in a parallel tradition – bank barrows.

7

'MONSTERS OF DEGENERACY' – BANK BARROWS

In 1935 Nancy Newbiggin spent weeks excavating the great 112m-long cairn of Bellsheil Law on the open moors of Redesdale. Prior to excavation it seemed that the mass of stones at the eastern end marked a forecourt with horns extending from it like those in Caithness. In fact this proved to be no more than a spread of stones from much more recent stone robbing – the end simply bulged outwards. But here at least there was evidence of some attempt to construct proper edging; elsewhere stones had simply been piled up, often chaotically. The excavator's frustration is palpable in her report's conclusions: '… in all its great length, there was not a single find, not a single structural feature of definite type – no cists, no chambers, no ditches, no revetment, no internal structures, no secondary burials, no forecourt, no real horns, no more than the most crude and spasmodic efforts at regular coursing. It is a monster of degeneracy.'[1] Was she, however, missing the point? Was the mound the message – an end in itself, however poorly constructed, rather than a cover for complex burial structures?

As exceptionally long mounds go Bellsheil Law was modest – only a few metres longer than the West and East Kennet barrows near Avebury, and nothing like the size of mounds in Dorset, the Peak District, Stirling and Perthshire that range from twice to five times its length. When Paul Ashbee published 'The Earthen Long Barrow in England' in 1970 he recognised only the sites in Dorset as belonging in this massive bank barrow group (Maiden Castle 546m; Long Bredy 197m; Broadmayne 182m; and Pentridge 2a-b 149m). Subsequent work has located mounds of huge length in Scotland at Auchenlaich, near Callendar (342m), Eskdalemuir (Tom's Knowe and Lamb's Knowe if originally a single site, over 2000m) and Cleaven Dyke (1820m). It has also drawn attention to the inexplicably forgotten site of Long Low in the Peak District excavated in the Victorian period and found to be 201m long. More importantly from the point of view of the cursus question, a number of narrow so called cursus cropmarks seem better interpreted as bank barrows (e.g. North Stoke and Llandegai), and to encourage that conclusion the remnants of bank barrow like mounds have been recorded along the centre of the Scorton cursus in North Yorkshire (2000m +) and the staggeringly long Stanwell cursus at Heathrow (4000m +). Clearly bank barrows can no longer simply be viewed as a product of aberrant Dorset megalomania. Their new found, widespread distribution holds out the possibility of better understanding this obviously cursus-related phenomenon.

First we must be sure that we are comparing like with like: deciding at what point long barrows can be classed as bank barrows is no easy task. All regions exhibit mounds outside the normal 20-70m range[2] but is an extra 20 or 30m enough to consider them something else – a bank barrow? Just as cursuses were first defined by the staggeringly large sites, so were bank barrows. Wheeler's surprise discovery, during his major excavation programme at Maiden Castle from 1934-7, of a barely perceptible mound running for 546m across the hilltop demanded a new classification. He included other Dorset sites whose length was more than twice that of barrows at the top of the normal range. That probably proves the best definition of Wheeler's 'exceptional' length criterion – mounds of 140m or more.

BANK BARROWS AND CAUSEWAYED ENCLOSURES

Maiden Castle deserves pride of place as the first, and by far the most extensively excavated, bank barrow. In plan it comprises three separate segments: a central and higher section just 65m long that was possibly an earlier long barrow, with eastern (155m) and western (225m) arms running from it. These lay just off the crest of the ridge so the monument was skylined when viewed from the Frome Valley, while the eastern arm lay across an earlier causewayed enclosure hidden beneath the hillfort's ramparts. The research programme undertaken in the 1980s to augment Wheeler's findings demonstrated that the enclosure had been built between 3900-3700 BC in woodland that was subsequently cleared. Large amounts of flint waste, Earlier Neolithic South Western style pottery and animal bone had been deposited in charcoal-rich layers in the ditch, probably as result of feasting, ritual and seasonal settlement in the interior. Only a short time after its abandonment – to judge from the insignificant depth of the layer sandwiched between ditch fill and bank barrow mound – the major linear monument was constructed across the site. Radiocarbon dating suggests this occurred between 3500-3200 BC.[3]

Wheeler was struck by the uniformity of the bank barrow ditches. They contrasted with irregular causewayed enclosure and long barrow ditches elsewhere.

Their fill was also remarkably consistent: 'almost everywhere' the rapid fill was followed by hearths and occupation debris in the central dip. Pottery in this 'black hearth layer' was entirely of Earlier Neolithic type but Peterborough Ware followed after no great interval, as was the case 35km away on the Dorset Cursus.

At the eastern end of the barrow four or five cattle skulls were found in the 'black hearth layer', three definitely from wild aurochs – another feature recalling deposits in the ditch of the great cursus. The most striking discovery under the mound at this end was the complete skeleton of a young man from which limbs and head had been roughly hacked and the skull scored by three attempts at trepanning. This became celebrated as proof of sacrifice and cannibalism but over the years its uniqueness became apparent. Disquiet led to examination and to dating. The first demonstrated that the axe used for dismembering must have been a slender metal one; the latter that the body dated to AD 635 and was Saxon. It, and another burial close by, were secondary insertions into the mound. Close by two infants, one accompanied by a small Earlier Neolithic cup, were found in a pit but it is by no means certain that they were primary burials under the mound. The pit lay away from the axial line and here, where the mound overlay the interior of the enclosure, human remains appear to have been plentiful: just 100m away a single trench through the causewayed enclosure ditch produced the bones of two juveniles, a young man and an adult in material apparently backfilled from the interior. Possibly the only intentional feature of the mound was a pit on the axial line rammed with Earlier Neolithic pottery, limpet shells, minute fragments of animal bone and charcoal. It recalls the axial pits at sites like Claish and Kintore but could belong with earlier activity inside the causewayed enclosure.

The mound itself may have been deliberately slighted within a few centuries of its construction – Beaker material was found in chalk rubble that appeared to have been thrown back into the ditch and secondary woodland grew up around the monument. It remained as a low mound (perhaps only 1m high) but was respected during the earlier Iron Age occupation of the site, although perhaps more because of its value as a roadway than for any intangible reason. The length and uniformity of this low monument, marked simply by occasional posts along its sides, recalls cursuses but the similarities do not stop there: cursuses were also laid out across causwayed enclosures.

Layout of the Fornham All Saints cursus immediately recalls the Maiden Castle arrangement (*41*). Unfortunately in the absence of excavation we neither know for certain that the cursus is the later monument nor what form it took – open or mounded? At the similarly relatively narrow cursus at Scorton (*c*.32m) the former presence of an axial mound has been proved. The Maxey–Etton cursus also crosses, or runs adjacent to, a causewayed enclosure but the cropmarks

'MONSTERS OF DEGENERACY' – BANK BARROWS

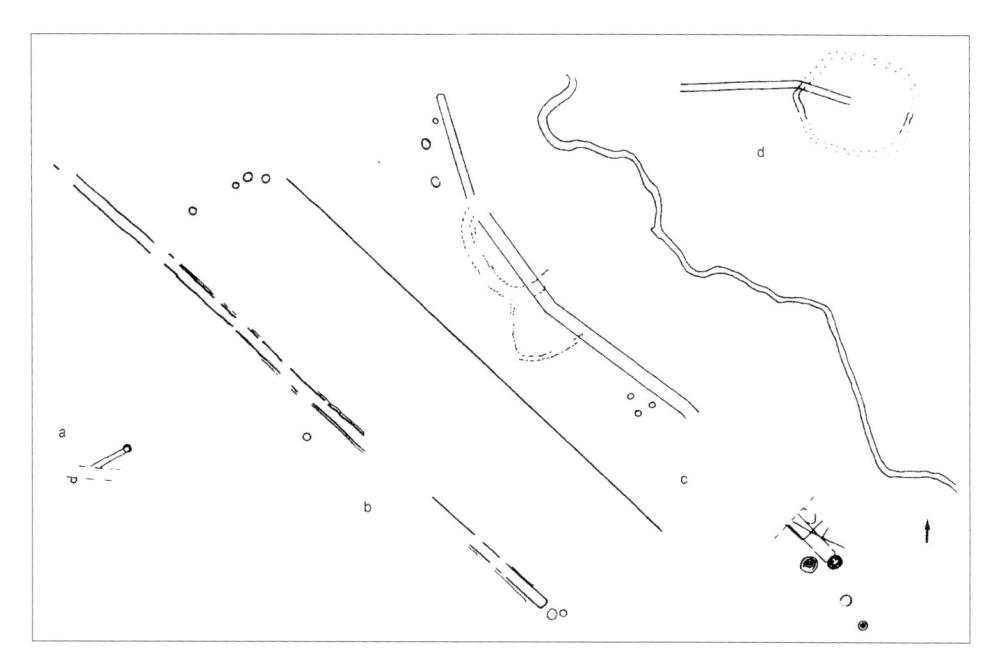

41 Bank barrows and cursuses: a) Cardington-Cople; b) Scorton; c) Fornham All Saints and the River Lark; d) Maiden Castle

42 The Crickley Hill long mound – knee high and only 4m wide

91

are faint and the the plan consequently uncertain (*15*). At Hasting Hill, Offerton, in Tyne and Wear, another cursus is aligned towards an enclosure but here it is the date of the enclosure that is in question.[4]

The clearest picture of bank barrow and causewayed enclosure relationship, after Maiden Castle, appeared to be found at Crickley Hill on the Cotswolds scarp. There an unusually narrow (*c*.4m), knee-high mound was laid out within the confines of an abandoned causewayed enclosure – in this case a site that had been defended and then taken by storm; 400 arrowheads were found in the destruction layers. And, like Maiden Castle, the hill was reoccupied during the Iron Age when a substantial hill fort and settlement were constructed. This presents a problem – how did such a slight barrow, located in the most sheltered location on the hilltop survive that occupation unscathed? In identical circumstances the altogether larger Maiden Castle mound had been all but levelled. The location is also strange for a Neolithic long mound since it is completely hidden; re-positioning by just 15m would have placed it on a dramatic edge where it would have been skylined from the valley below (*42*). An answer appears to lie in the network of trenches found below the mound on excavation, and in the environmentally mixed material that had apparently been brought to the hill to construct it. Both are a feature of pillow (warren) mounds. We have already met these in their ditched form as a possible source of confusion in the recognition of Neolithic long enclosures from aerial photographs. But they were not always ditched, particularly on rocky subsoils as at Crickley. Then they were constructed from material carted in from elsewhere. Such an interpretation of the Crickley mound would explain its siting, survival, form and even its attachment to one end of a round mound – these were frequently employed by warreners.

The same explanation almost certainly applies to a 228m-long bank barrow recorded by Grinsell on Pen Hill above Wells in Somerset. It lies close to a long barrow of considerably greater height, yet whilst its much deeper barrow ditches are all but invisible, those of the much slighter 'bank barrow' are still clear.[5]

FROM LONG ENCLOSURE TO BANK BARROW

We saw that Bill Ford's excavation at Charlecote proved conclusively that long enclosures may once have enclosed mounds. As some – cursiform long enclosures – approach bank barrow proportions can we regard them as the gravel soils equivalents of the upland monsters? Short of the truncated remains of a mound being revealed by excavation, the only approaches open are to seek signs of internal parch marks on aerial photographs and to apply Bill Ford's Charlecote test – dumping excavated ditch spoil along presumed bank lines. The

43 North Stoke: parching between the ditches indicates the former presence of a mound. Allen 869, 1933: Ashmolean Museum, Oxford

first presupposes that any mound was of gravel (turf would leave no such mark); the second that we have excavated ditch profiles from which to calculate volume of spoil and then mathematically apply the test.

A site of comparable width to Charlecote, but of bank barrow proportions, (220m x 12m) exists at North Stoke in the Thames Valley. Excavation by Humphrey Case revealed strangely deep, narrow ditches with hollows on their floors (possible solution holes). The volume of material taken from them would certainly, on the Charlecote test, occupy too much of the interior to make it useable in any normal sense unless revetted against the ditch edge. Three pieces of evidence suggest it was not. First there was no evidence of directional silting into the ditch that would be expected from the eventual collapse of close set banks. Second, parch marks can be seen on early aerial photographs along the spine of the site towards the northern end (*43*). Third, disconnected arcs of ditch at its northern extremity only make sense if we assume they comprise parts of a ring ditch that failed to score the subsoil (and hence produce a cropmark) where they passed over the interior mound (*44c*). A round barrow had been placed in the same way over a terminal of the Broadmayne bank barrow in Dorset. At Cople on the edge of the Cardington complex in Bedfordshire a long enclosure similarly appears to have had ring ditches placed over each end. It is unexcavated

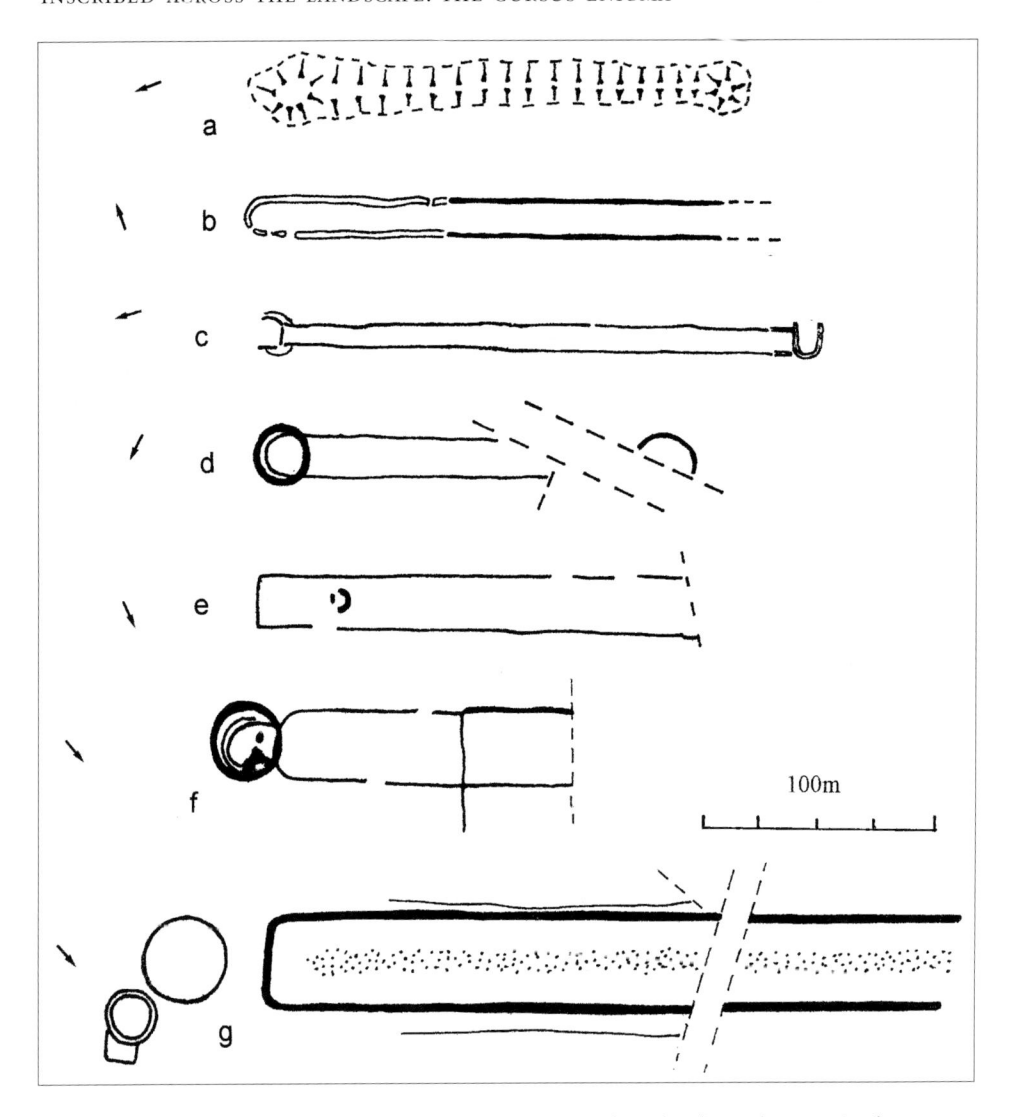

44 Bank barrow to cursus: a) Long Low; b) Llandegai; c) North Stoke; d) Cardington-Cople; e) Bures St Mary; f) Fornham All Saints – south-east end; g) Scorton – south-east end

but its close similarity to Charlecote and North Stoke strongly suggests that it too was a mounded site (*44*).

Narrow unexcavated cropmark sites of this type have also been recorded at Bures St Mary in the Stour Valley of Suffolk, Maesyn Ridware in the Trent Valley, Buscot (site A) in the Upper Thames Valley and Kilmany in Fife. A considerably longer example at Welshpool (380m x 10m), however, furnished a quite different structural type on excavation – ditch silting pointed to *external* banks. This need not of course preclude the former presence of a turf mound, perhaps inhibiting internal erosion as noted at Charlecote and Inchtuthill. Charcoal from this site has been dated to 3900-3600 BC, well in advance of the dates from North Stoke (3600-3300 BC) and Maiden Castle (3500-3200 BC); it may relate to earlier material that had eroded into the ditch. An opposing picture is presented by the date from another site of this type at Llandegai in Gwnyedd. This 170m x 12m long 'cursus' has been dated to *c*.2700-2500 BC from a single charcoal sample low in the ditch silts. Such a late date presents major problems that will be returned to in the final chapter. Total excavation of about half of this site produced neither finds nor features but they did reveal ditches 2.5-3.0m wide and 0.65-1.0m deep. Adding their additional depth from the original land surface (estimated as another 0.3m), and applying the Charlecote test, suggests little more than 5m would have been left clear in the interior. This required the banks to be placed close to the ditch edges yet the ditch showed only 'a slight increase in silt on the inner side.' An axial mound set back from the ditch edges seems plausible.[6]

FROM BURIAL MOUND TO BANK BARROW

Sites examined so far have mostly been the products of a unified plan, or perhaps more accurately ongoing projects with a single extravagant objective. North Stoke introduced a different process, however – an additive, adaptive one. There the bank barrow covered an earlier site at one end (gravel from its mound lay in the upper ditch silts of the small long enclosure), and had in turn been covered at the other end by a ring ditch. An older monument had been reorientated and absorbed possibly as a result of new beliefs, and certainly through the operation of new social imperatives. It was not alone.

A remarkably similar site known as Long Low lies near Wetton in the Peak District. Under a large cairn at its northern end was a 1.5m square slabbed chamber (lacking a cap stone) containing 'a confused mass of the relics of humanity: the skeletons of 13 individuals of all ages and both sexes laid across each other, along with three beautiful thin leaf-shaped instruments, calcinated flakes and animal bones.' A bank runs from this cairn some 210m to another, but rather smaller, cairn raised on its southern end. The bank barrow was roughly constructed with slabs laid against an axial drystone wall built out from the northern cairn. It narrowed from 21m to just 12m and in its best-preserved section is about 1.5m high. Secondary cremations were found in the bank and in the southern cairn (*45*).

As well as the almost identically sized site at North Stoke, Long Low recalls a number of sites farther north. At Auchenlaich, Callendar, on the opposing bank of the River Teith to the Claish 'hall', a low cairn (0.5m) appears to have extended

INSCRIBED ACROSS THE LANDSCAPE: THE CURSUS ENIGMA

45 Long Low, Staffordshire, viewed from the northern chambered mound. It extends to the trees

a trapezoidal chambered cairn to some 342m. It varied from 11-15m in width and possessed a small side chamber or cist near its midpoint. At Eskdalemuir in Dumfries two similarly low banks run from terminal mounds on opposing sides of the valley. They may represent a single 2km-long monument destroyed by the river in the intervening valley or two separate monuments deliberately sited to run to false crest mounds. Either way Tom's Knowe (280m) and Lamb's Knowe (640m) are clearly bank barrows. Interestingly in both cases they have ditches that run continuously around the terminal in the manner of long enclosures. A striking feature of all these sites is their regional isolation within their region, and their north–south orientation.[7]

FROM BANK BARROW TO CURSUS

A very few sites represent an ultimate magnification. The 2km-long Scorton bank barrow/cursus has already been mentioned. Although producing a clear parch mark its bank was so spread that it could only be recognised on the ground following excavation (46). That was also true of the remarkably long Stanwell cursus. This site, striking across land so flat that it has been selected for Heathrow airport, extends for some 4km, crosses two rivers and stops by a stream – originally perhaps a more major river. So straight and apparently narrow is it (20m) that it was originally taken to be a Roman road. Early excavation seemed to support the idea: vestigial areas of gravel between the ditches were scored by shallow gullies resembling cart ruts. Later excavation, however, demonstrated that the ditches of a Late Bronze Age field system cut across it and several scraps of Peterborough Ware were recovered from its ditches. Evidence also emerged of a short (50m) ragged, double row of posts, removed before the ditches were dug on the same alignment. That this was a bank barrow was hinted at by the Charlecote test and by reduction in the depth of field ditches as they crossed the central area. Digital analysis of Air Ministry photographs taken prior to the construction of Heathrow Airport confirmed that a central bank had survived to a height of 0.4m in 1943 and experimental reconstruction following excavation confirmed that ditch spoil would produce a bank 4m wide and 1.6m high.[8]

This bank barrow/cursus then was seven times longer than the bank barrow at Maiden Castle, three times longer than that at Scorton and only exceeded in length by the two linked monuments of the Dorset Cursus and cursus D at Rudston. As with all bank barrows its function remains enigmatic but may have involved signalling across to the areas of slightly lower land to the west from where it formed a skyline feature. Processions along its top would have been clearly visible and it would certainly have formed a barrier to movement.

INSCRIBED ACROSS THE LANDSCAPE: THE CURSUS ENIGMA

46 Scorton showing parching caused by the central mound. Cambridge University Collection of Air Photographs

Remarkably a site comparable to the Stanwell cursus appears to have survived as an earthwork to the present day near Meikelour in Perthshire – the Cleaven Dyke. Its two ditches, set 40m apart with an axial bank 5m wide and nearly 2m high, stretch for nearly 2km. So crisp and clear is the bank that it was until recently regarded as a Roman boundary earthwork associated with the nearby legionary fort of Inchtuthill and akin to the Vallum alongside Hadrian's Wall. Its shallow ditches confirmed a non-defensive role but aerial photography where the monument was ploughed out showed them to be uncharacteristically ragged for Roman work. Since there was no historical context for such a structure, the possibility arose that it was prehistoric. Investigation demonstrated that an oval mound on a slightly different alignment to the rest of the dyke formed its north-western end and that a mound some 80m long had been added to it. Thereafter the mound was extended with cursus-like spaced ditches. This took the form of a number of segments; terminations of successive sections were marked by rounded off, turf-revetted ends and corresponding causeways in the ditches.[9]

Dating remains a problem however. A hearth below the bank returned a radiocarbon date of 4700-4000 BC but the rotten, heartwood nature of the oak charcoal suggests this is considerably earlier than the date of its burning. An unknown period of time also separated the hearth from bank construction. Added to this, excavation at various points has confirmed the consistently shallow profile of the ditches (*c*.5m wide x 1m deep) and an incredibly slow rate of silting: only some 500mm after at least 5000 years. This seems inconceivably slow for a mobile gravel subsoil and, along with the fact that the ditches remain clearly visibile, must leave the date of the structure in doubt.

PLACE, PURPOSE AND ORIGIN

Just 20 years ago discussion of the origins of bank barrows would have been easy. They were a Dorset aberration. Seven of the 10 long barrows over 90m long on the Wessex chalk are to be found in the county and there is clear field evidence that the Maiden Castle, Long Bredy and Pentridge 2a/b mounds were extended. Added to this the Broadmayne and Long Bredy bank barrows lie at opposite ends of the great Dorset Ridgeway cluster. Here then was a clear picture of local aggrandisement and territorial definition. A similar situation was evident in Caithness, although the long mounds added to round cairns there never achieved bank barrow length. Recognition of sites elsewhere has, however, severely undermined the explanatory potential of these local sequences. The new sites are isolated. Rather than tales of progressive regional development they appear to attest sudden, centralised and potentially imposed change. Shape and orientation link sites as far flung as North Stoke and Long Low, Eskdalemuir and Auchenlaich, Cleaven Dyke, Scorton and Stanwell. Constructing individual site histories and phenomenological *raison d'être* for monuments so patently originating from a shared concept is to undermine their potential to illuminate the society constructing them; akin to concluding that rare cruciform and round churches in medieval Britain arose from the demands of central foci or circular procession rather than symbolism and cult site paradigms.

What then might long-distance bank barrow identities proclaim? A concept expressed within common ground rules seems virtually certain, whether the mounds were built afresh or added to earlier monuments. It is tempting to regard the long house as the ultimate conceptual source – house (monument) length equating to group/lineage prestige. Yet there was no such long house tradition in Britain. Perhaps then it is to the continent that we should look for the spur to extravagant monumentalisation. Although construction of the great Danubian long houses there had passed more than half a millennium before the bank

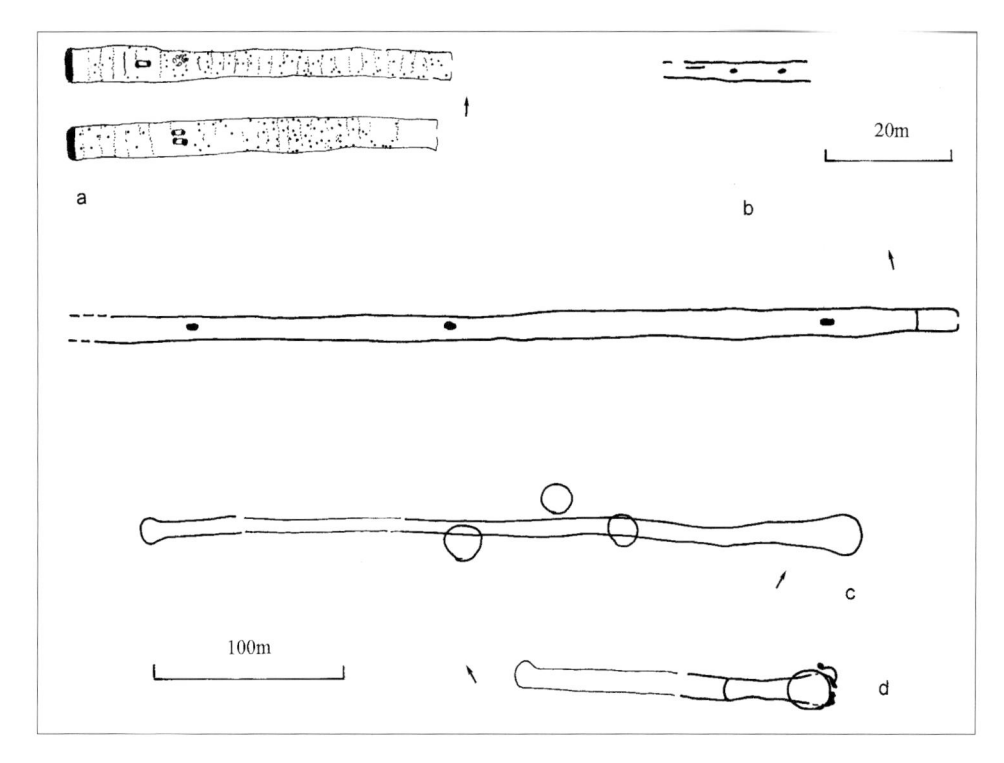

47 Examples of continental bank barrows: a) Barkaer, Jutland; b) Březno, Bohemia; c) Passy 5; d) Passy 15, Normandy

barrow was heaped up at Maiden Castle, the process that had often magnified one house, presumably as a communal or cult house, may have established enduring cosmological roots. Transmission of the concept via successor European communities may have been delayed. Why if sea crossings had been achieved once should they suddenly cease? Alternatively the drive to monumentalisation may have been latent in the long barrow concept from the outset.

Magdelena Midgley has recently reviewed the evidence from north-west Europe that has grown hugely since Crawford's note in 1938 first drew attention to the existence of three long barrows in excess of 400m in length in northern Germany. For a long time the existence of earthen long barrows in those areas possessing megalithic sites was doubted but a combination of aerial photography and meticulous excavation has transformed the picture.[10]

Barrows of triangular form dominate in Poland, trapezoidal in most other north-western areas and ovate with long (sometimes hugely long) tails in the Paris basin and Normandy. Amongst them are to be found a number of rectangular examples that closely resemble British bank barrows and cursiform long enclosures. Common denominators in most cases are an enclosing palisade ditch (often convex-ended in France) and evidence, where it survives, that the mounds were modest affairs. The latter does not seem to have been peculiar to the greatly elongated sites: the few well-preserved earthen long barrows in Denmark only range from 0.7-1m in height and the stone-kerbed mounds are little higher.[11]

There was also an obvious common tendency to elongation. Several north European sites approach 100m in length, of which the parallel pair of mounds at Barkaer in Jutland are the most fully investigated (*47a*). They were defined purely by parallel stake lines and subdivided by bays that had been infilled with sandy material up to 0.5m thick. So unusual was this that for many years they were interpreted as Danubian long houses filled with windblown sand. They do not appear to have to have been planned as hugely long mounds from the outset; the northern barrow had been extended at least once and the southern one, twice. Each of the resulting mounds – nearly 90m long and 6-8m wide – covered just two simple graves set 1m and 5m apart respectively. In common with other north European long barrows each grave had probably only contained a single articulated inhumation. Monument size was clearly not related to the demands of burial.[12]

The Barkaer mounds were not the largest. Examples noted by Crawford around the village of Kochendorf near Schleswig reached lengths of 380m, 450m and 600m. He did not record their form but, like mounds in nearby Mecklenburg and Lower Saxony, they are likely to have been rectangular. In this latter region north–south orientation of mounds was favoured in complete contrast to the east–west pattern that dominated elsewhere in northern Europe.[13] Interestingly we have seen that north–south orientation was common amongst British long enclosures, and bank barrows away from Dorset, but otherwise uncommon.

A site that appears to have much in common with the North German sites is to be found at Březno in Bohemia.[14] There, continuous bedding trenches for 'wooden walls' almost certainly marked the outlines of two levelled long barrows, closely resembling the Barkaer sites in form, parallel layout and orientation (*47b*). One was 143.5m long, the other just 24m but neither was more than 5m wide. Individual burials were placed along the axis of each mound – up to 60m apart in the longest site. It seems certain that their parallel layout, like the Barkaer mounds, was intended to represent the common pattern of houses in Danubian settlements. In Poland where elongated, near triangular mounds were constructed, they similarly exaggerated earlier Lengyl trapezoidal house form and together replicated village layout. A symbolic statement was clearly being made regardless of the house/mound form that was employed.

The same pattern of cemetery agglomeration of exaggerated long mounds has recently been recognised in north-west France.[15] Enigmatic linear cropmarks, first thought to have been geological, have proved to be the palisade bedding trenches of levelled long mound sites. At Passy in Burgundy 25 such sites – 20-250m in length – were rather irregularly grouped in similar fashion to the Polish cemeteries (*47c & d*). Here, however, there appears to be no interval between Danubian occupation and mound construction. At Balloy the evidence is even clearer. At least three long mounds in a cluster of 11 lay directly and exactly over individual houses of an abandoned Late Danubian settlement; the orientation and size of the structures was the same, and those houses covered by mounds were much better preserved. As Midgley points out, this leaves no doubt that the houses abandoned about 4700 BC were still visible to guide barrow construction centuries later and that they really were the symbolic heart of the long mound tradition. The mounds at Balloy were mostly trapezoidal in form, with causewayed enclosing ditches akin to, but at least 500 years earlier than, British trapeziform cropmarks. None were of bank barrow proportions, but those at Passy most decidedly were, several reaching lengths of up to 400m. Like the Danish long mounds they were apparently low structures with single graves spaced along their axes, particularly towards their eastern ends where larger round mounds had been raised. They bear more than a passing resemblance to sites such as Cople and North Stoke (*44*).

Further west very similar elongated ditched enclosures have been found at Rots near Caen. There narrow, parallel-sided sites defined by shallow ditches with one or both ends rounded, ranged up to 350m in length. They possessed just one or two axially placed graves along their length (at this site principally at the western end), and probably originally contained low covering mounds. Like the Barkaer and Březno barrows these were clearly symbolically exaggerated structures monumentalising a cosmology rooted in the Danubian long house. Along with monumental mounds like La Motte des Justices à Thouars in Deux-Sèvres (180m long, 13m wide and 2.70m high with an enclosing ditch and a date of 4600-4000 BC) they leave little doubt that the bank barrow phenomenon in Britain was a conceptual import, whether latent from the outset of the insular Neolithic or the result of subsequent re-invigoration. They also suggest that it is unlikely that significant structures will be found within British examples. Their role was essentially symbolic. That symbolism may have been the decisive influence in cursus development, linking readily to the 'hall' origins of long enclosures/long mounds and encouraging their massive exaggeration. The centralising tendency revealed by bank barrows may have similarly encouraged the magnification of widely distanced complexes like Fornham All Saints and Dorchester upon Thames that possessed cursuses of long mound rather than enclosure proportions. Cleaven Dyke, whatever its date, furnishes the clearest picture we have of probable bank barrow/cursus appearance during this formative phase. Development of contrasting open enclosure form may have resulted from contact with the pit-defined enclosures of the north that seem to owe little to house or mound antecedents. It could, however, equally owe much to another tradition – avenues.

8

'A SOLEMNE WALKE' – AVENUES

Bank barrows are a feature of both highlands and lowlands; cursuses are not. Those located in Wales either lie at the interface of highland and lowland, as at Llandegai and Welshpool, or in basins of flat land within the hills, as at Walton and Corwen (Tyn y Cefn). Cropmarks sites are not, of course, produced on upland pasture but rows of small stones trickling into the Dartmoor mist, great sarsens striding across the downland and gaunt giants guarding the circle at Callanish speak of another tradition. Are these the true highland zone cursuses?

The existence of post-defined cursuses in lowland Scotland, and the suggestion of stake fences defining some of the southern monuments gives strength to the idea. The presence of great stone avenues at Avebury – a centre oddly lacking any sign of a cursus – seems to confirm it. But is it really that simple? Avenues come in multifarious forms and appear, as their name suggests, to be primarily entrance directing and enhancing features, whether for the living or the dead.[1] Cursuses, it will be recalled, never appear to have had this role; even that associated with the highly atypical open-ended structure at Godmanchester was attached to its emphatically *closed* rear end. But before generalising the argument we need to examine the various forms that avenues take, their dimensions and their dates.

EARLY AVENUES

A number of the small mortuary 'houses' found under long barrows have settings of posts at their entrances. These are invariably short (3-10m) and splayed in towards the terminal post or entrance. Only at Kilham in Eastern Yorkshire is the avenue wider (*c.*7m) and parallel sided, extending the sides of the mortuary structure on for a traced distance of 22m. The splayed avenue running from the outer ends of the façade at Kemp Howe, in the same region, was wider (15-20m) and has a known length of 40m.[2] Not only are these sizes – even the largest – insignificant compared to cursuses, their shape and positioning in relationship to long barrows are quite different. They all serve to emphasise the approach to mortuary structures, either directly or via the façade. Cursuses never do.

Until recently these appeared to be the only avenue sites of earlier, or comparable, date to cursuses. Julian Thomas' excavation of pit alignments at Holm just a kilometre to the east of the Holywood cursus complex changed this.[3] What on aerial photographs appeared to be a post-defined cursus of irregular layout proved on excavation to be the spaced posts of three alignments c.14m apart leading north-north-west/south-south-east to a ring ditch that was preceded by a post circle. Rather than a finished monument, individual posts seem to have been erected, burned down and then re-erected several times. To add to the complexity of the site, a later, narrower avenue of pits that had never held posts cut across the post alignments. This pit avenue has produced a conflicting range of dates but could be contemporary with the Holywood cursus complex c.3500-3300 BC. This places the post alignments yet earlier. At Upper Largie in the Kilmartin Valley another pit avenue has produced an early date that suggests it pre-dates the adjacent terminal of a possible post-defined cursus that underlay a post circle.

It does appear then that in lowland Scotland at least there were avenues of comparable date and form to the Kilham long barrow avenue. Although the posts and pits of cursuses in the region are rarely spaced out in the same way such alignments may have furnished a model for the extension of small unit sites.

It is possible that post alignments have even earlier antecedents. Excavation in advance of car park construction at Stonehenge in 1966 revealed three (possibly four) large post holes over a metre deep running in an east–west line. The 0.75m-diameter posts set in them were, to judge from the accompanying charcoal, of pine, a wood that should not have been present on the southern chalklands in the Neolithic. Radiocarbon provided the reason – they were of Mesolithic date: 8000-7000 BC. Subsequently another pit, offset from the previous line, was excavated near the ticket office; it was similarly dated and similarly contained pine charcoal.[4] Whether these posts were carved in North American totem pole fashion or were more generally symbolic, they were clearly neither casually erected nor set out. Alignment was clearly crucial and, perhaps coincidentally, later to be followed by the Greater Stonehenge Cursus 500m away.

Nevertheless a minimum of 3,000 years and 500km separates these unique Mesolithic structures at Stonehenge and the remarkably early, but far less substantial post alignments at Holm. Future discoveries may fill the blank but for the moment it is clear that early post sites, whether avenues or post-defined cursuses, are concentrated in northern Britain. Unless we include the multifarious stone avenues of Brittany — that are in any case almost exclusively multiple lines not avenues — the next time we encounter avenues is over a millennium later.

LATE NEOLITHIC AVENUES

By the Late Neolithic (*c*.2800 BC) cursuses were passing out of use and being replaced by post and stone circles and henges, while round-based pottery was being replaced by tub-like Grooved Ware. This new world certainly drew on the old: the new monuments were often superimposed on cursuses or, like the post circle at Dorchester, placed centrally inside them. That active engagement with the past may have encouraged the range of structures that now appeared. Fairly short avenues (*c*.5m) led into great post-defined enclosures like Dunragit in Galloway or up to smaller post circles like Durrington Walls North. A similar pattern appears in stone with short portal settings at some stone circles and henges (e.g. Swinside and Mayburgh). As becomes entrances, they are not wide: 2-5m in most cases extending to a maximum of 10m.[5] A very few are different, however. In these cases entrance features are elongated, sometimes vastly, to link the monuments to rivers, other sites or just to the wider landscape.

Avebury
Most famous of these is of course Avebury. There the reconstructed Kennet Avenue, and the recently rediscovered Beckhampton Avenue, strike out across the landscape from south and west entrances through the great henge bank. Both follow valleys and both are followed by present-day roads. This is unlikely to be coincidental. It seems highly probable that avenues formalised routes to and between monuments and that inertia ensured that these continued in use long after the monuments had been forgotten. Stukeley traced the wrecked Kennet Avenue south to the top of Overton Hill where holes marked the sockets of stones in a double circle that had recently been wrenched out and destroyed. Garnering information from locals, he additionally suggested another avenue had once led west for an almost equal distance to the vicinity of the Beckhampton long barrow. He was right, but not about its extent. Following their recent re-discovery of the Beckhampton Avenue Mark Gillings and Joshua Pollard traced its termination to one of two great stones that today stand marooned in a cornfield. It formed one side of a cove — a spaced box-like setting of huge stones; the other stone was the sole upright of the avenue to be left standing. The cove had been preceded by three stones set in a line across the avenue's course, and they in turn had been preceded by an adjacent enclosure over 100m in diameter

INSCRIBED ACROSS THE LANDSCAPE: THE CURSUS ENIGMA

48 The Kennet Avenue

with a causewayed ditch. It was this enclosure, dated slightly earlier than the main Avebury enclosure, that the avenue had initially been aimed towards. It did not stop at its periphery, however. Instead it ran through the enclosure's eastern entrance and straight across the south-eastern part of its interior, slighting it banks en route.

At the end of the Kennet Avenue there was similarly an older monument – in this case a post circle of five concentric rings that appear to have been removed and replaced several times. Unlike the enclosure near the end of the Beckhampton Avenue, this monument – romantically named 'The Sanctuary' by Stukeley – was respected. Gilling and Pollard describe the stones of the avenue running up to and 'lassoing' the circle with a large outer ring of stones; an inner one was placed between post sockets.[6]

The avenue stretched for 2.5km following the natural sweep down Overton Hill and along the valley side to Avebury. The last 600m or so as it approached the great henge monument were oddly different, however. An occupation site encroached on the western side of the 14-17m-wide course of the avenue and was respected by the omission of a stone in its area (*48*). The site looked out across the avenue towards the now destroyed Faulkner's stone circle some 200m away in the dry valley. Beyond these features the avenue builders appear inexplicably to have drifted away from the entrance to the henge. For 200m they wilfully directed the avenue on an almost tangential course. Only in the last 100m did they turn the course sharply right in a dog-leg that brought the stones to the monument's entrance. This has been explained in terms of a change of plan, as a deliberately orchestrated surprise for those moving along the avenue and as a product of confused archaeology in an area of recent allotment gardens. These stones had certainly been removed before Stukeley arrived to record the remains. Intriguingly though, as Aubrey Burl has noted, John Aubrey recorded the same dog-leg arrangement amongst the stones, still existing in his day, at the other end of the avenue on Overton Hill.[7] The bizarre plan was clearly intentional then, yet it makes no sense. Builders involved in erecting hundreds of stones might easily have re-positioned a dozen or so pairs to create an effective entrance to the great henge, whilst an open avenue hardly seems a likely vehicle for a visual surprise. Strikingly, a very similar dog-leg occurs along the line of the Gussage cursus but the Kennet Avenue is as much as half a millennium later in date, to judge from the Grooved Ware sherds incorporated in one of its stone holes. Added to that, the cursus is seven times wider. The Kennet Avenue is nevertheless much closer to a cursus than any avenue so far examined. The possibility exists that it was either an earlier free-standing element, perhaps associated with the great Obelisk and with the Peterborough Ware occupation site along its length, or that its builders deliberately referenced the great Dorset Cursus in their plan.

Stonehenge

It is tempting to couple the Avebury avenues with that at Stonehenge, particularly as subsoil anomalies picked up by geophysical survey allow for the possibility that spaced posts or stones stood within the straight final section of the ditched avenue as it approached the monument. Lengths are certainly comparable (2.8km Stonehenge; 2.5km Kennet) but it appears otherwise to have been rather different. Unlike the awkward dog-leg at Avebury, the Stonehenge avenue ditches approach the monument from the bottom of the dry valley with ruler-drawn precision. Before that point the avenue had followed a sweeping course from the River Avon along which it was far more irregular in layout. Questionable bulked radiocarbon samples appeared to indicate that these irregular further reaches were later in date but recent re-dating suggests the whole structure may have constructed over a prolonged period contemporary with the great sarsen structure *c*.2500-1900 BC.[8]

Although far longer, the very well-engineered straight section of avenue rising up to the monument appears to belong alongside other entrance settings such as those at Dunragit, and Meldon Bridge in the Borders and Walton in Wales. It was clearly an adjunct to the monument rather than a feature in its own right. Equally its extension to the Avon has more in common with a trackway than a cursus.

INSCRIBED ACROSS THE LANDSCAPE: THE CURSUS ENIGMA

Milfield and its northern context

The only other known ditched avenue lies in the Milfield basin in Northumberland. It runs north–south for 1726m constricting to pass en route through a large double entrance henge monument at Coupland. In addition to this centrally placed henge monument, there are seven others within the immediate vicinity and the 'avenue' curves around two of them. This leaves little doubt that it is later in date than the henges, and therefore considerably later than a cursus. Its length and irregularity do recall the Thornborough cursus but on that site the henge lay *across* the linear site and at right angles to its course (*49*).[9]

The closest parallel for the Milfield avenue appears to lie not in a cursus but in the remnants of a stone avenue at Broomend of Crichie in Aberdeenshire. They were recorded in the 1920s approaching the southern causeway of a double-entrance henge, smaller but of comparable plan to that at Coupland. Only three stones survive and they are widely separated but the claimed length

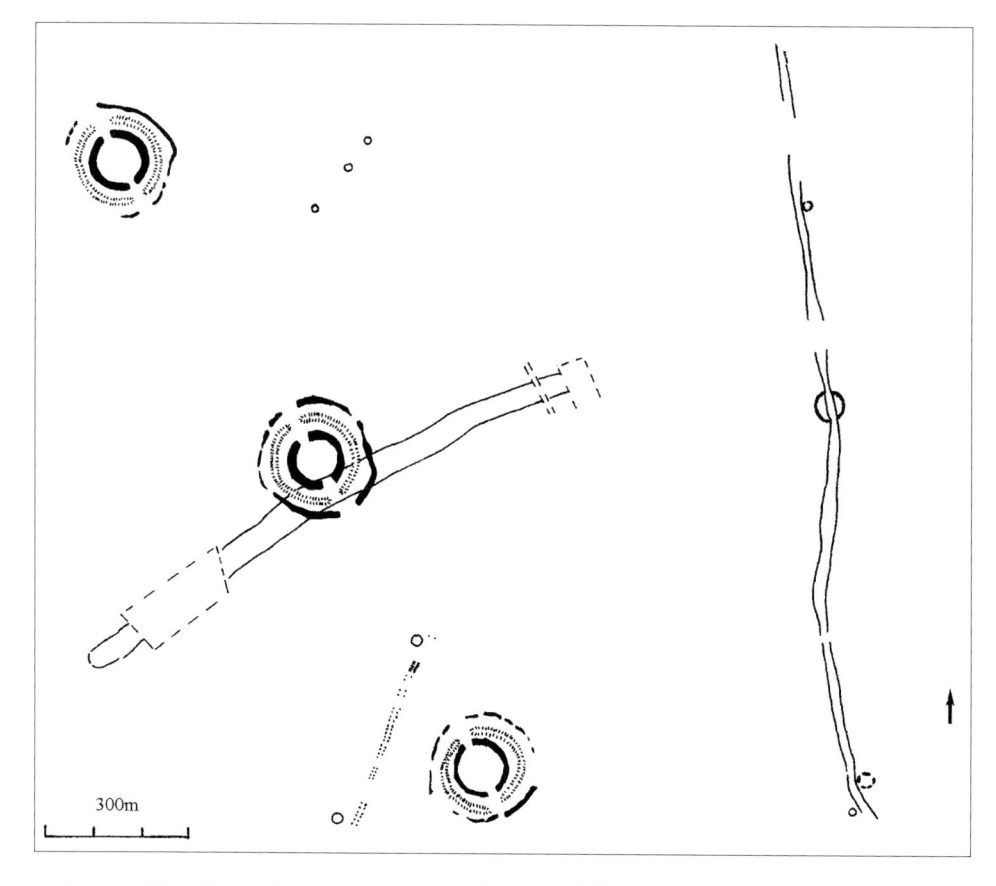

49 Avenues: Thornborough pit avenue, cursus and henges (left); Milfield (right)

50 Callanish. View along the avenue. Note the right side lines up with the centre stone of the circle while the left side has a tangential alignment

of the avenue, as it ran north–south from near the River Don to the circle-henge, was 410m. But this 18m-wide avenue may have been longer; a description of 1757 talks of it crossing the lesser circle (henge) and continuing a short distance to a larger, now destroyed, circle.[10] A programme of excavation currently being directed by Richard Bradley should clarify the evidence. Although the site is far smaller than that at Milfield, the arrangement of features and the north–south alignment of the avenue at once draw attention.

Farther north again, an 82m-long avenue of gaunt stones flanks the northern approach to the gnarled pillars of the celebrated Callanish circle (*50*). From the other cardinal points rows of stones similarly project outwards, but these are single rows. Astronomical interpretations have been advanced for these alignments, with the north-north-east avenue being considered to mark, for a viewer looking across the circle, the setting of the midsummer moon at it major southern extreme along the slope of Mount Clisham.[11] Whatever its function there is no doubting the unusual nature of the avenue. The stones on its western side are aligned, like those of the single alignments, at the centre of the circle; the stones of its eastern side on the other hand would be tangential to the circle but for a final inturned stone. This is quite unlike avenue approaches elsewhere that run radially and always restrict access to a corridor much narrower than the focal monument. It seems probable then that the off-centre eastern side of

51 Lady Lowther's drawing (1775) of the south end of the Shap Avenue before destruction

the Callanish avenue is a later addition, transforming the single alignment into a double. Why this might have been done is not clear but simple emulation of monuments encountered at Milfield or Broomend of Crichie is a possibility.

Shap - 'a singular piece of antiquity'

Today the great avenue at Shap is so totally wrecked that it is all but invisible, both on the ground and in the literature. Yet it occasioned intense interest amongst early antiquarians who happened upon it. Camden in the sixteenth century referred to 'large stones in the form of pyramids ... set almost in a direct line, and at equal distances, for a mile together' and Colt Hoare recorded 'on the left of the great road leading to Kendall over the moors is a most curious, singular piece of antiquity. It consists of a long avenue of large stones, placed at different intervals and extending nearly two miles. One end (south) seems to have terminated ... with a row of stones placed in a semi circular form.' The stones were already being blown up to clear land for agriculture, or being used as the foundations for houses in the town of Shap that lay along its course, when Stukeley passed this way in 1725. Enclosure of the common in 1815 and the ready availability of gunpowder in a quarry community sealed the fate of the rest. Of 3.2km of stones just a handful survive scattered amongst field walls.[12] In its day, however, it was clearly a striking monument. It is interesting that the road runs alongside it, as is the case at Milfield, Broomend of Crichie and Avebury. Topographic inevitability perhaps, but an association of routes with henges – particularly the double entrance form – is recurrent.[13] The same pattern can be discerned amongst cursuses, where roads run inexplicably alongside (not *inside*) monuments that can never have been obstacles: Thornborough, Rudston C, Potlock, Fornham All Saints, Welshpool and Holywood South. And it is the cursus-like appearance of the Shap avenue that catches our attention.

Lady Lowther's drawing (*51*) and antiquarian accounts leave little doubt that the southern section of the great monument was an avenue some 20m wide. It apparently terminated at a stone circle (Kemp Howe) wrecked when the railway line was built. But Colt Hoare is less clear about this: 'the avenue ... closes with a row of stones placed in a semi circular form.' He may have been recording the partially wrecked circle, as Aubrey Burl suggests, or was he describing the stone equivalent of a convex cursus terminal? Shap lies midway between Holywood North and Thornborough (100km in either direction) so would be well placed as an intervening type A cursus. The supposed circle's diameter was estimated by the Royal Commission in 1936 to have been 24.4m, remarkably close to the width of the avenue as the 1775 sketch shows. As an avenue this would be highly unusual – even the 'addition' at Callanish was only half as wide as the circle it approached.

North of the town of Shap, as the alignments curved away from their north–south alignment, there is less certainty about their form. Isolated stones – some of them massive – extend nearly another kilometre to the north-west to align on the Skellaw cairn: 'the place of skulls.' This section may represent the remains of separate single alignments, may never have been finished or may be a later addition. Pit avenues were found beyond the Milfield avenue and the Thornborough cursus.

PIT AVENUES

Pit alignments are ubiquitous. They occur on almost all river valley soils and overwhelmingly appear to have played a mundane, demarcating role in land division. There are, however, a few double pit alignments that are different – the pits are spaced rather than touching, and paired across the blank interior rather than randomly positioned. They are also self-contained, unattached to other pit alignments or ditches. Those that have been excavated have produced evidence of a Late Neolithic/Early Bronze Age date quite different from the almost invariable Iron Age date of the mass of sites.

A 50m-long, 2m-wide double alignment at Milfield appears to have held posts that were subsequently extracted. Cremated bone came from the pit fills and charcoal returned a date of 2400-2100 BC. It thus appears to be contemporary with the northernmost of the adjacent henges that stood just 200m away. This east–west pit avenue stopped in line with the sight line through the entrances of the henge – possibly symbolic or possibly abutting on to an undefined pathway akin to the defined avenue passing through the Coupland monument.[14] The same pattern is evident at Thornborough where a longer and wider free-standing avenue (350m x 10/12m) composed of irregular (perhaps sequentially added) sections ran north-north-east to stop in line with the common entrance axis of the three henges. Ring ditches stood beside each end (*49*). Jan Harding's excavation has demonstrated a similar date to the comparable Milfield pit avenue. Other pit avenues in the Vale of York have returned dates of 2600-2300 BC and been associated with Grooved Ware.

Whatever their precise role, these avenues were clearly of ritual purpose but can scarcely be regarded as cursus-like. They were narrower even than long enclosures, and at least half a millennium later in date it would seem. Comparison of the adjacent cursus and pit avenue at Thornborough underlines the contrast. It is possible that they were rooted in a common ideology but outwardly they could hardly be more different. Parallels for pit avenues lie not in cursuses but in stone sites such as Cerrig Duon in Powys (40m x 5m) that runs tangentially to a stone circle, and to the myriad Dartmoor rows of which at least 25 are double. The self-contained nature of sites like those at Merrivale and Watern Hill with their large terminal stones may echo aspects of cursus architecture but they are the exception. Overwhelmingly these very narrow (1.3m on average) double rows/avenues run from round cairns in the same manner as the post avenues attached to Early Bronze Age round barrows at Canford and Ogden Down in Dorset.[15] These rows – whether of wood or stone – were in essence embellishments for burial mounds, something cursuses decidedly were not.

HIGHLAND ZONE CURSUSES?

Only two sites measure up to, and have the characteristics expected of, highland zone cursuses. Unfortunately the Kennet Avenue is poorly dated by a few sherds of Grooved Ware in stone holes and by Beaker burials, while Shap is wholly undated. It can, however, be seen to fit quite comfortably into the Scottish tradition of post-defined cursuses. Elsewhere evidence for spaced posts at sites such as Scorton could result from contact with the early northern avenue tradition but, like the post settings within Holywood North, is as likely to reflect symbolic rendering in the Scottish 'hall' tradition.

Avenues are primarily a feature of entrance architecture that might easily have been independently re-invented from long barrows to round barrows. They are, after all, a widely recurring theme of world architecture in time and space; cursuses are not (see *1*). And where they achieve independent, or near independent

52 Dwarfed by the monument: a hunt unconsciously processes along the Dorset Cursus. Monument marked by hedge on right and light soil mark on left

status, they are characterised by regionally focused traditions (Dartmoor rows; Welsh tangential avenues; northern post avenues) that contrast with the broad unity of cursuses. There is every reason to feel that they are associated with quite separate manifestations of ritual action: avenues with contained movement and focal entrance; cursuses with defining a far larger precinct for action, whether human or divine (*52*).

We return then to the point from which we started – where are the highland zone cursuses? Perhaps an answer lies in the evidence we found for cursus definition in the lowland zone (chapter 4). The inexplicably long survival of several sites as landscape features suggested an archaeologically invisible component – perhaps stake fences on banks subsequently colonised as hedges. If lowland cursuses looked somewhat like fields, might that also have been true in the highland zone? If so, and the same pattern of incorporation occurred, highland zone cursuses could lie disguised and subdivided within later field systems. Recognition would be a major challenge. Even the clustering of round cairns would be no certain indicator since lowland cursuses are by no means invariably – or even commonly – associated with concentrations of ring ditches. They could, however, be predicted in regions such as the Peak District that witnessed monument building throughout the Neolithic and where early medieval infield walls mark out long linear divisions.

9
INSCRIBING THE LANDSCAPE – LAYOUT AND ITS IMPLICATIONS

Simply to state that cursuses are overwhelmingly straight monuments does them scant justice. Looking down on the Dorchester, Aston on Trent or Greater Stonehenge Cursus from the air it appears as if as vast ruler had been used to score parallel lines across the landscape. What is more, the terminals are often laid out with geometric precision. Given their huge size, this would have been difficult both to achieve and to appreciate on the ground as inaccurately laid out modern football fields illustrate (*53*). The fact that the slightest error in layout on sites of this size leads to exaggerated mis-alignment emphasises the achievement of the builders.

Prior to the appearance of cursuses there is little that immediately suggests that Neolithic builders were concerned with precise layout – causewayed enclosures have irregular ovate or circular plans, houses are irregular rectangles and those long barrows edged by post revetments rarely present a picture of geometric precision. Nevertheless it is amongst the latter that cursus layout is prefigured.

MECHANICS OF LAYOUT

We have already seen that two basic terminal forms exist (A – convex; B – squared) and that the latter, in Bi form, represents the most precise manifestation.

Seeking antecedents for the convex form in the long mound tradition presents some difficulty. Convex ends may have simply have arisen *de facto* due to dump construction or the collapse of mound revetment but rarely it seems were they planned in advance. Chalk buttressing the end of the rectangular stake-bayed South Street mound appears to have been deliberately curved outwards, but elsewhere any curvature that is evident is *inturned* – as a concave forecourt. By

INSCRIBING THE LANDSCAPE – LAYOUT AND ITS IMPLICATIONS

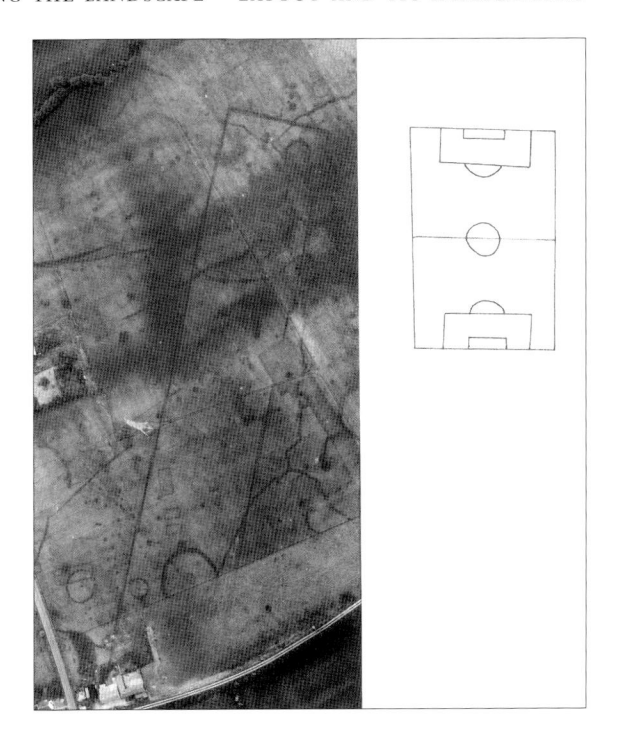

53 Contrasts in accuracy: Drayton South Cursus c.3200 BC. © Crown copyright. NMR; football field 1970. From Wilson 2000

contrast many long enclosures, particularly in East Anglia, have convex ends and, as we have seen, may represent ploughed-out long barrows. The surviving example at West Rudham in Norfolk suggests these were convex-ended mounds.[1] Early 'halls' like Claish in Scotland also furnish antecedents for convex terminal form (*36*).

There is some evidence from the regularity of post spacing in the Claish and Balbridie structures that units of measurement were being employed in the process of layout. Hogg suggests locally variable units such as a pace. Interestingly this may be repeated in the only comparable site in the south – an open structure in front of the mortuary area at the Nutbane long barrow in Hampshire. It was subsequently incorporated in the forecourt wings and only infilled and burned at the final stage of long barrow use. The posts of its straight, western side are separated fairly consistently by about 1.3m; not so dissimilar to 1.546m at Balbridie and close to double the 0.689m suggested at Claish.

Use of some unit of measurement is implied on other sites. The proximal (front) end of the trapezoidal enclosure revetting the Fussell's Lodge mound was twice as wide as the distal (rear) end, and the same pattern is repeated, although rather less precisely, elsewhere (e.g. Willerby Wold, East Yorkshire, and Wayland's Smithy, Berkshire). At each of these sites the burial structure exactly bisects the façades and in the first two cases, if projected, would also exactly bisect the distal

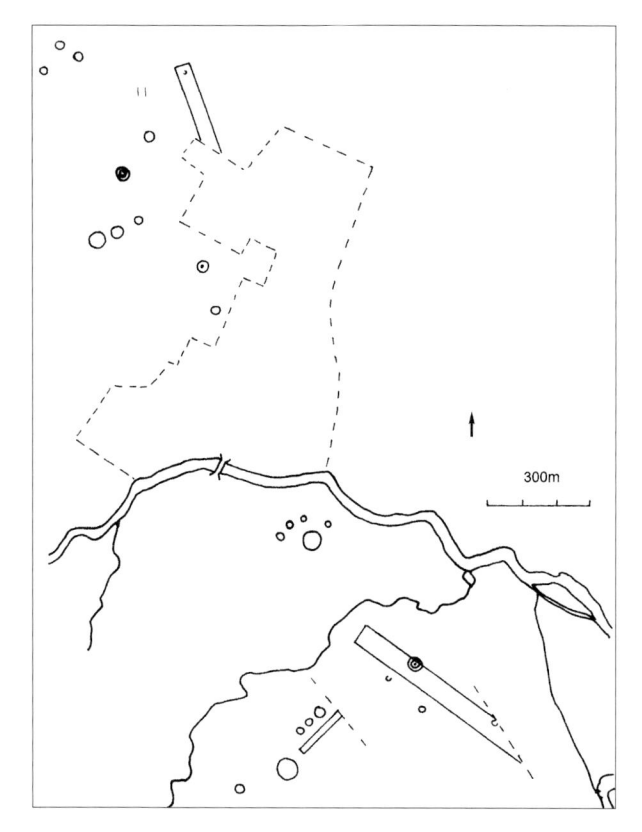

54 The Buscot–Lechlade complex

end. This is most unlikely to have been achieved by chance but close-set posts or stones prevent recovery of the possible unit employed.[2]

Just as trapezoidal layout appears to be linked to a basic geometric figure, so parallel-sided sites often approximate to true rectangular form. The sides of revetment 'enclosures' of wood at Wor Barrow, Dorset, and Kilham, East Yorkshire, and of turf at Holdenhurst, Dorset, hardly diverge except for bulges in the latter two cases (that at Kilham made explicable by the desire to incorporate an earlier mortuary house) (*26*). In almost every case ends were set at close approximations to a right angle. That seems equally true of a number of cursiform long enclosures that probably mark former bank barrows (*54* & *44*).

Interest in such right-angled layout may initially have arisen in the European background of long house construction where it would have been vital if transverse post lines were to provide the necessary combined vertical and lateral strength. If this was the case, we are left with the challenging question of how such procedures were transmitted, particularly as the Danubian long houses ceased to be constructed at least 500 years before British long barrows were first built. The possibility that the principles were independently worked out by British

Neolithic communities seems less likely in view of the relative irregularity of the (admittedly few) Neolithic houses so far discovered. On balance it might appear that transmission of the long house/long barrow concept was accompanied by procedural rules. The striking rectangularity of many Mecklenburg mounds supports the idea. Such rules might be comparatively simple in monuments of no great size, such as measuring the diagonals of the structure or even utilising a template. Applied to a cursus, however, these would be useless – it would be extremely taxing to measure the diagonals of even a limited length of such huge sites, while wooden templates would be of insufficient length to prevent drift and distortion across widths of 60-100m. If the geometry of the Bi cursus type had its origins in the long mound tradition evidence of rather different procedures must, it seems, be sought. We will return to this point later when examining the evidence from Bi terminals.

DITCH ALIGNMENT

Long barrow layout then may prefigure cursus plans but the procedures involved to maintain visibility over distances of a kilometre or more and to prevent the workforce from deviating, were clearly of a different order. Setting out posts are implied by the straight edges of barrows such as Kilham and Waylands Smithy II and the use of a plumb bob was suggested by Ashbee from the almost perfectly vertical post holes of the Fussell's Lodge palisade revetment. Such a system could be extended over a considerable distance on level ground by a simple leap-frog system of phased construction: sighting from a previously laid out segment, across the last segment to be dug, in order to layout the next one. This appears to have been the case at the Drayton North cursus where excavation revealed a series of ditch segments separated by causeways that marked slight drift in overall alignment. Deviations noted at regular *c.*11m intervals along each segment suggested gang labour. Despite this, an essentially straight alignment was maintained along the 450m of excavated cursus, a fact that suggests some consistent distant sighting element was employed – perhaps a large post. Evidence of such posts would inevitably be removed in the process of ditch digging, although a single post hole on a causeway across the northern ditch at Dorchester upon Thames may represent one that escaped destruction.[3] Elsewhere post holes within the ditch of the Stanwell cursus/bank barrow were too irregularly placed to have fulfilled this function and the large post hole on the alignment of the North Stoke bank barrow is more likely to have been a feature of the small long enclosure within which it stood. It is not inconceivable, however, that slight post/stake avenues – like the early examples recognised in Scotland – were set up in advance of cursus ditch digging. They would not only have eased the process of sighting but provided a model for alternative cursus definition by posts.

There is clear evidence for the use of earlier monuments for sighting purpose. The northern bank of the Pentridge arm of the Dorset Cursus runs for over 2km up to and over a long barrow (Pentridge IV), while from its southern extremity the Gussage arm runs straight for 2.5km across a valley to the long barrow on the top of Gussage Hill (see *17*). It has been claimed that the dog-leg correction of cursus alignment on the other side of that hill (to the north) reflects drift caused when work groups approaching from the other direction lost sight of the barrow in the lee of the hill. That is not the case. It is clear on the ground that long before the barrow disappears from sight the cursus had drifted away from it. An alternative explanation must be sought for this extremely unusual sinuous section of monument. We will return to the problem later. Other cursuses were aligned directly upon earlier monuments: the Greater Stonehenge site on the Amesbury 42 long barrow (although it stops short of it); one side of the Dorchester upon Thames cursus on, and across, the Site VIII long enclosure; and one side of the Stadhampton cursus apparently on a somewhat trapeziform-shaped enclosure.

Round mounds may also have been the focus of cursus ditch alignment. Aerial photographs of the Springfield cursus in Essex appeared to confirm this, its southern ditch being deflected from its near parallel alignment with the northern ditch to kink around a small, internally placed ring ditch (see *33h*). Excavation revealed a different story: the ring ditch was interrupted where it crossed the former cursus bank line and then clearly cut through the silted cursus ditch. It was of later date. The excavators suggested it had been dug to commemorate an earlier, now invisible feature.[4] A group of fine-quality flint blades found there (two with evidence of deliberately ground edges) could represent grave goods under an earlier, unditched turf round barrow that had been redefined by a ring ditch some time after the cursus had been built.

At Aston on Trent in Derbyshire the cursus ditch follows a remarkably straight alignment for 1500m until it meets a ring ditch. It curves around this before continuing on a similar, but displaced, alignment to the terminal (*55*). Excavation revealed that the wide cropmark where the cursus rounded the ring ditch was not the aggregate of two ditches but a much widened cursus ditch that had completely cut away the fully silted ring ditch. It can only be concluded that the cursus ditch diggers were respecting what then stood within it – an earlier round barrow. It appears to have been substantial enough not only to allow them to sight on the edge of it from 1.5km to the north-east, but also to block a clear view beyond – hence the misalignment to the south-west.[5]

Apart from this brief, hesitant misalignment the cursus ditch at Aston on Trent appears remarkably uniform. This is very much a feature of the Bi type

55 The Aston on Trent cursus showing alignment of the right-hand ditch on and around the ring ditch, and the accurately laid out terminal. *Copyright reserved Cambridge University Collection of Air Photographs*

but is also notable at sites such as Dorchester and Fornham All Saints. At Maxey a distinction is abundantly obvious, from aerial photographs alone, between the irregular, meandering ditches of the north-western arm and the straight, even, ditches of the south-eastern arm; numerous sections of the latter cut by Francis Pryor confirmed its consistent width and shallow, flat-bottomed profile. This is unlikely to have been achieved by chance and implies even closer control of the workforce than simply following sighting posts. It is difficult to know how common this pattern was, since a large number of ditch sections are needed to safely assess a degree of consistency. Only two other sites currently furnish such evidence: Springfield and Drayton North. The ditches of the first (a Bi site) are remarkable uniform given the gravel subsoil in which they were dug; those of the latter considerably more variable and markedly different along each side of the monument. The comparative uniformity at Springfield implies more than gangs following a single line. Definition of inner and outer ditch edges seems likely, perhaps by de-turfing or clearing in advance of the main workforce. Suggesting, as this must, the presence of what might be termed specialists, it has major implications to which we will return below.

Of course most of the foregoing is dependent upon the lack of natural obstacles to clear sighting and accurate layout. It is perhaps not inconceivable that the irregularity of the Thornborough ditch line owed something to its apparent woodland setting but the markedly irregular ditches of the North Stoke site were cut in open country. Ditch plan, it seems, cannot be explained away in environmental terms but is a direct reflection of the skill and control of those planning and executing the monuments.

Parallel ditches

Richard Atkinson first noted the pattern of regular, and opposing irregular, ditches when surveying the Dorset Cursus in the 1954. He concluded it arose from the method observed in long barrow timber revetments – laying out one side by offsets of variable accuracy from the 'master' edge. It is exemplified by cursus A at Rudston where the extreme irregularity of the eastern ditch near the Wold Top contrasts with the smooth line of the western ditch. Similarly the section of the Dorset Cursus examined by Richard Bradley revealed contrasting ditch sections. This pattern recurs in less pronounced form throughout the cursus series.

Amongst the Bi series the evidence is muted, obvious care being taken with this as with every other aspect of their layout. An irregularity near the midpoint of one side ditch at Benson probably points to an inaccurate junction of work by offsets proceeding concurrently from each terminal while, on the other hand, gentle curvature of one ditch as evident at Barford (*14c*) and Stratford St Mary suggests continuous, but adjusted, construction from one terminal to the other. Interestingly, when an earlier monument is incorporated, it often appears that the straighter ditch is on the *other* side of the cursus (e.g. Dorchester upon Thames, Springfield and possibly Pentridge). If that is regarded as a 'master' layout ditch, this has important implications. It suggests that cursus width was determined in advance and not arbitrarily established at the terminals. It also suggests that earlier monuments were not the primary aligning feature.

TERMINAL LAYOUT

The precision of terminal layout varies considerably. A few appear from their random angles to have resulted from a simple linking of side ditches but the majority approximate to geometric figures. The fact that they often represent the most regular feature of the entire monument confirms the importance attached to their layout.

Thornborough exemplifies the pattern: care was obviously taken with its evenly rounded terminal and the 75m or so of ditch running from it to a causeway. Thereafter alignment and ditch regularity degenerates. The terminal was constructed separately it seems by those with a knowledge of the procedures,

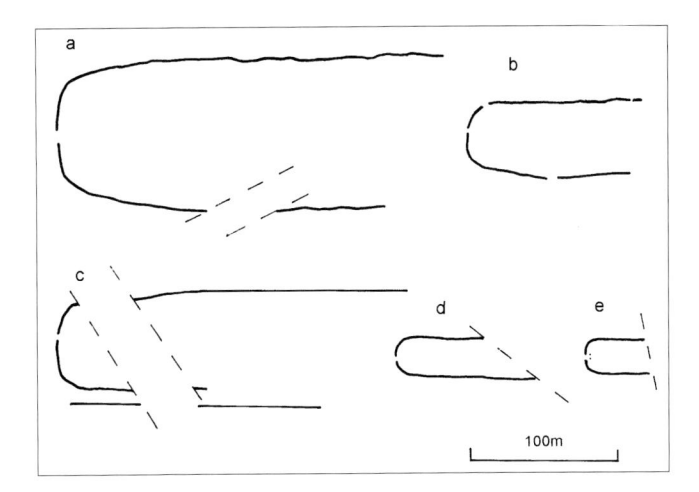

56 Type A terminal plans:
a) Curriestanes, Dumfries.;
b) Thornborough, N. Yorkshire; c) Dorchester, Oxfordshire; d) Feering, Essex; e) Lawford, Essex

presumably in advance – perhaps well in advance – of the main work party. It does not represent a full semi-circle or chord, however. At its centre there is an approximately 8m length of straight ditch. From this run curves on quite different arcs (56b). This could suggest the site was laid out by eye alone but the good general correspondence of each arc to circles of some 20m and 15m in diameter perhaps argues for layout either side of a now-vanished central obstacle corresponding to the straight central element. Interestingly the excavators recorded the discovery of an unaccompanied crouched burial in a stone cist set about 4.5m back along the centre line of the cursus from the terminal ditch. It is conceivable that this lay under the end of an axial mound, akin to that in the nearby Scorton cursus.[6]

A very similar pattern of contrasting layout is to be found at the Curriestanes cursus near Dumfries (56a & 59). There, the regular terminal ditch is less convex than that at Thornborough but it was marked by a central causeway in the same way. Curiously its closest parallel lies not at nearby Holywood North, where curvature of the terminal is pronounced, but at Dorchester upon Thames some 450km to the south (56c). In both these cases the terminals appear to have been created by initially slightly inturning the side ditches, then affecting a more acute curve towards the central causeway. This very specific approach is unlikely to have arisen by chance. It suggests there was a common principle. That may preserve evidence of two-phase construction: first the short incurved sections (akin to long enclosure sites such as Brampton), followed – perhaps after an interval – by the lightly curved main terminal ditch. The latter must have been set out by eye since the degrees of curvature at each site are so slight as to require a marking out circle of huge diameter. That is equally true of site 1 at Bannockburn where additionally, despite its very different pit construction, the same even terminal and irregular extending ditch plan is again in evidence. At Dorchester on Thames it takes a rather different form, not irregularity of ditchline but change of alignment – some 70m from the terminal the southern ditch curves, clearly but evenly, out to meet the main cursus ditch. This was not done on the northern side where cursus ditch and terminal side ditch run side by side (*56c*). It has been suggested that the terminal is in fact an earlier large enclosure 135m long closed at the other end by a causewayed ditch, but that ditch now seems likely to be related to an Iron Age field system.[7]

At these sites then it appears the terminals were laid out in advance, were open ended and, in the case of the three ditched sites, of strikingly similar length – some 70-80m. There is no way of knowing if they remained that way for long before a less-accomplished workforce extended them. One certain open-ended cursus has, however, been excavated – the Lesser Stonehenge Cursus. Although its terminals were very crudely laid out, there is clear evidence of planning behind its two-phase construction: the earlier western enclosure and the eastern – open-ended – extension ditches *both* comprise units measuring some 200m x 60m. The neat ends of the ditches of the eastern section leave no doubt that they had reached their planned extent, although their almost immediate backfilling with clean chalk rubble suggests work was stopped and the monument 'closed down' for some reason. This duplication recalls the four cell post-defined cursus at Milton of Guthrie on Tayside with two *c*.110m x 27m enclosures at one end and two *c*.180m x 27m enclosures at the other. Clearly some unit of measurement – or a length of rope equivalent to the primary enclosures – was employed.[8] Similarly the small Bi-type enclosures found at Fengate, Yarnton and Charlton scattered across the Midland/East Anglian region are notable for their almost identical internal widths (*c*.25m) and very similar lengths (50-60m); the Handley Hill site on Cranborne Chase is little larger (*c*.70m x 30m). Again a common numerical code of construction seems to be indicated, perhaps affected with somewhat variable units. Dimensional regularity can also be witnessed further up the Bi series: three Upper Thames cursuses (Lechlade, Buscot and Stadhampton) are all about 50m in width, double that of the small Bi enclosures. Nearby the Benson and Drayton South monuments are both 65-70m in width, perhaps replicating the width of the great Dorchester upon Thames monument (65m), but just conceivably recording approximate doubling across the wider region – the Longbridge and Charlecote cursuses in the Warwickshire Avon are both *c*.30m wide. Whatever the case, such close dimensional clustering could not have been achieved had the sites been set out by eye alone.

That is equally true of the laying out of rectangular terminals, particularly those of Bi type. Site after site in this series possess corners set at remarkably close approximations to right angles (*60*). It is so striking that when cursus of his type were first identified (chapter 2) they were immediately assumed to be of Roman

INSCRIBING THE LANDSCAPE – LAYOUT AND ITS IMPLICATIONS

date. This is not surprising: no rectangular structures of this size or regularity had existed before, nor were to be seen in Britain again for 3000 years. They were truly prodigious. The question of their method of layout is not so much begged as clamoured, yet oddly has scarcely received a mention. This is probably an understandable reaction to the extravagant claims of Alexander Thom that highly sophisticated geometric patterning, and micrometer-like accuracy, underlay the construction of British stone circles.

Humphrey Case has made reference to right-angled layout at cursus sites but what might the underlying principles have been? It is reasonable to assume that they arose through refinement of layout procedure, not as an independent intellectual construct or a mechanism derived from laying out quite different sorts of monument. Thus whilst it is possible to establish right angles by projecting lines from the the ends of a circle's diameter to a single point on the circumference, this is an improbable route given that precisely circular monuments were not a feature of the period. Added to this, it is impossible to straightforwardly project a right angle from a ditch line by this method. Bisection of a ditch line by a line drawn between intersecting arcs on either side can also be dismissed as implausibly sophisticated. This leaves checking the diagonals of a quadrilateral – incredibly difficult across even the *c.*70m lengths of accurately laid out terminal – or the 3:4:5 triangle. Despite the association of the latter with Pythagoras it need not imply advanced mathematical knowledge. David Hogg has noted regularity in the spacing of posts at Claish and Balbridie that points to the use of simple broad units, such as a pace or the arm, used in chosen multiples to achieve preconceived plans.[9] Use of a rope that had been knotted at these intervals to ease layout might lead to recognition of regularity in setting out corners and to rule of thumb application of the 3:4:5 triangle. Regular spacing of posts had also been a feature of Danubian long houses that were interestingly founded on transverse rows of three posts. It may not be coincidental that single, near accurate right-angle corners along the Yarnton and Handley Hill ditch lines comprise 3:4:5 triangles when measured from their entrance causeways (*57*). Setting out triangles of this size would easily permit accurate projection of a cursus terminal ditch line.

Sites such as Drayton South (*53*) reveal exceptionally precise layout that, as the football pitch analogy emphasises, would never have been obvious on the ground. Its purpose was undoubtedly to create a site worthy of the 'others', a universal theme of ritual architecture that is embodied in the Egyptian name for the great Karnak complex –'Most perfect of places.' Those responsible for such layout possessed esoteric knowledge, a major element in the establishment of social difference. Of course not all Bi sites achieved a level of perfection. Often only single right angles were laid out with real care. The plan of the western terminal at Springfield exemplifies the point (*58*). This suggests that the basic method of layout was to align one side ditch as the base line, to project terminal ditches from it and to lay out the opposing side ditch by measured offsets. The greater number of these used, the greater the level of accuracy. Poorly achieved this would result not only in an irregularly aligned offset ditch but also in final corrections to meet the terminal ditch. Thus it is not uncommon to find nominally square-ended cursus sites with one incurving side ditch. The fact that it is also possible to find examples of outcurving side ditches (see *11*) confirms that this is evidence of correction rather than a specific form of terminal architecture. And of course it is possible to find, as with the convex series, a number of roughly achieved terminals that clearly involved no specific expertise.

Most of the square-ended sites from Scotland are irregular in layout. This cannot be put down simply to the greater difficulty of achieving even lines with spaced pits or posts since it is also a feature of the few ditched sites north of the border. Only one corner at Blairhall approximates to a right angle, along with one at the small Douglasmuir enclosure and the central division at Milton of Guthrie; elsewhere random oblique angles characterise both structural traditions.

There seems little doubt then that the two distinct terminal forms, found on juxtaposed monuments at Bannockburn and Holywood, were often laid out in advance to clear patterns, and that the most precisely surveyed sites (Bi series) were largely restricted to the Midlands/East Anglia where they were often found in small Barford-like groupings of monuments. Major sites like Benson and Aston on Trent were the exception.

This begs numerous questions of which the most important – for the moment – is why were such forms considered important.

CURSUS: FORM AND PURPOSE

The often hugely extended forms of cursuses maximised the labour needed to enclose a given area of land and maximised the impact on movement through the landscape. The fact that the vast Avenue of the Dead linking the principal temples in the ceremonial centre at Teotihuacan in Mexico occupied less than a tenth of the area of the great Dorset Cursus complex furnishes a measure of their impact. Clearly there must have been a compelling reason to construct monuments in this form.

Cursuses have been variously interpreted as:

1. Processional ways, perhaps formalising earlier routes
2. Structures linking pre-existing or significant areas
3. Physical barriers between areas of differing significance

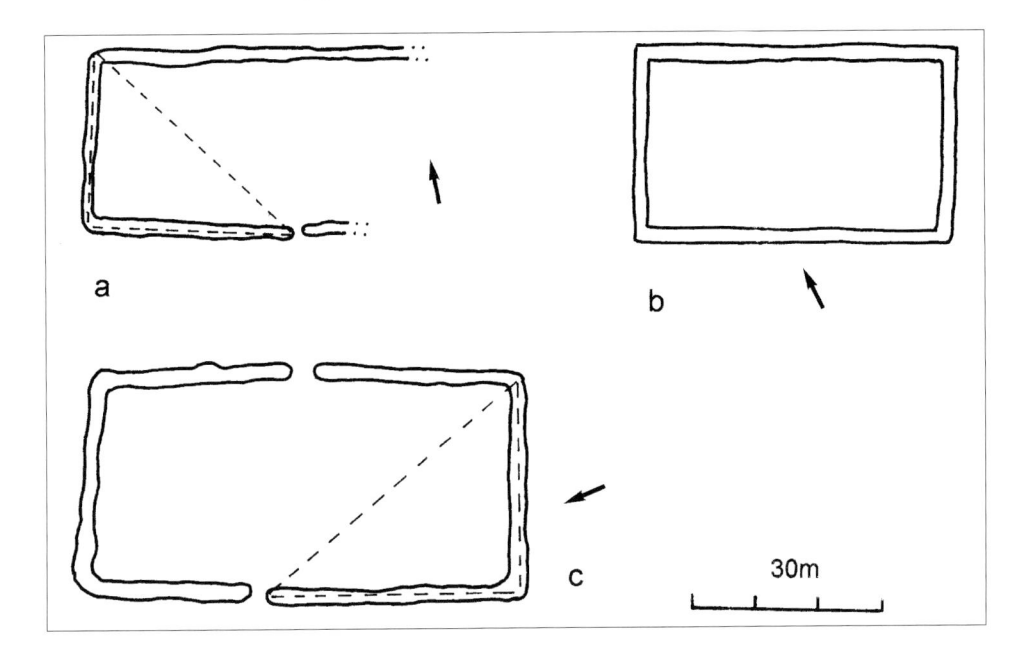

INSCRIBING THE LANDSCAPE – LAYOUT AND ITS IMPLICATIONS

57 Above: Right-angled layout in small Bi-type enclosures: a) Yarnton, Oxfordshire; b) Fengate, Cambridgeshire; c) Handley Hill, Dorset

58 Right: Springfield, Essex: western terminal. *From Buckley et al. 2001, courtesy of Essex County Council*

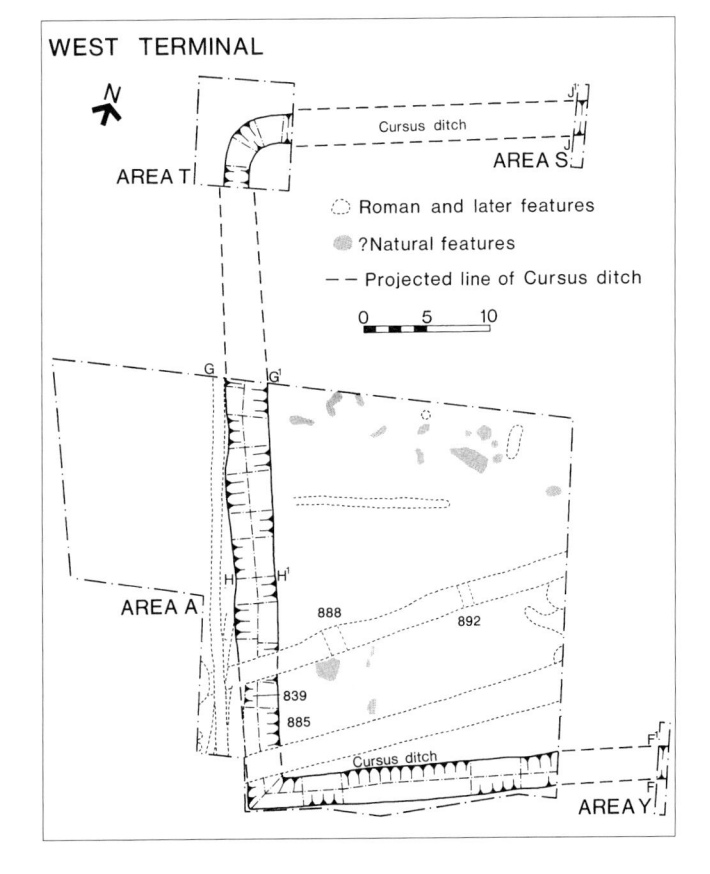

4. Alignments on a place or astronomical event
5. Symbolic rivers
6. A symbolic project – the physical expression of a social or ideological need
7. Arenas for celebrations and games
8. A temenos[10]

These are not necessarily mutually exclusive – processions (1) and games (7) might take place in a temenos (8) constructed as a symbolic project (6) to link pre-existing significant places (2) located on the boundary of cleared and wild land (3). Only when such interpretations are advanced in isolation as a primary *raison d'être* do problems arise. Most have arisen from fieldwork at a single monument where a combination of features and locally unique topography furnish a convincing case; transposing it to other sites clearly built in the same tradition is usually far less compelling. Thus we have seen that there are few points of contact between avenues and cursuses; that major cursuses seem too wide for processions (*59*) and minor ones too short (see *14*). Equally although a very few cursuses link existing monuments, most do not and hypothesising natural points of significance is fraught with danger. Explanatory value is also limited here to sites of sufficient length to have acted as links; most minor cursuses are excluded. Even more problematic is the notion of cursuses as alignment devices since they are too wide to have been useable with any approach to accuracy and landscape features are a rarity even on the chalkland landscapes where a small minority are sited. And only in the latter landscapes do cursuses achieve a level of monumentality that might have permitted them to have acted as physical barriers – for which purpose their wide, empty interiors seem wholly inappropriate.

The most important considerations, however, are their linearity and recurrent terminal forms. Clearly these had strong symbolic significance yet appear totally irrelevant to most of the above. Rivers do not exhibit these features, nor do boundaries, aligning devices or processional ways – but house plans do. And they furnish the *only* source for convex and square terminals closing straight parallel-sided structures. We have already seen that houses such as that at Claish appear to have generated the long enclosure concept (chapter 6) and that, in a more monumental form, bank barrows arose from the exaggeration and symbolic reduction of Danubian long houses (chapter 7). Cursuses appear to have arisen from the interaction of people constructing monuments in these two traditions. But to fully appreciate the significance of the symbolism, and to enable us to relate it to the vastly overblown monuments that resulted, it is worthwhile seeking ethnographic parallels.

The long house is a recurrent physical manifestation and symbol of group/lineage identity from Amazonia to Oceania. Very different from the medieval long

59 Curriestanes Cursus, Dumfries. Note the irregular ditch running from the well laid out terminal. Cars and the road furnish a dramatic sense of scale. Crown copyright © RCAHMS

house that was intended to house a simple extended family and its animals, these long houses were either communally occupied by a large number of families or set aside for particular use as a 'club house', 'mens' house' or cult house. In many cases these functions are combined as in the rectangular malocas of the Barasana of Columbia. At their centre, marked by eight major upright posts, is an open area used for communal meals but most importantly for ritual and initiation dances. The rear of the houses (that may be square or semi-circular) is screened off for everyday female activity; stalls along the sides are occupied by nuclear families and the front of the house is set aside for male activities.[11] With its rear and front doors, for exclusive female and male use, it recalls Claish where a central bay similarly appeared to be structurally emphasised and contained pits with burnt deposits. Symbolic expansion and representation of either a maloca or a house of Claish type as a sacred enclosure (temenos) would result in few internal features, and even less that might provide a suggestion of purpose. Such a site might also attract mass gatherings, elite officiation or be reserved for the otherworld of the ancestors and spirits without leaving a shred of discernible – or surviving – evidence.

Discovery of a pit with evidence of burning, fragments of Earlier Neolithic Grimston bowl and a remarkably high number of carbonised grains of emmer wheat (800+) on the old land surface at the centre of the Aston on Trent cursus indicates what may have been lost. These features had been fortuitously preserved because a round barrow had been raised for a Beaker burial placed over them and, by incredible good fortune, that barrow had not been ploughed out. Radiocarbon dates from the grain and from charcoal found in the cursus ditch close by are statistically indistinquishable and centre on the mid-fourth millennium BC. A deposit of carbonised material with cereal grains found at the base of the nearby Potlock cursus could have resulted from similar internal activity and at Maxey Francis Pryor remarked on the 'curious but consistently observed phenomenon common to both ditches, of a discontinuous layer of comminuted charcoal mixed with soil' close to the ditch bottom. At Aston on Trent it could be that the barrow was deliberately sited at an earlier significant point in the cursus confines: it and other ring ditches are almost uniquely aligned along the centre of the cursus (see *14e*).

This recalls the positioning of later hengiform, post circle and ring ditch along the axis of the Dorchester upon Thames cursus. None of these appears to have marked earlier cursus-related activity though, but a pit containing charcoal, wood ash and splinters of human bone dated to 3800-3400 BC lay on the axial line near the south-eastern terminal. Since this date is considerably earlier than that from the cursus at it north-western end, it may relate to an early stage when the U-plan terminal ditch stood alone. Elsewhere a substantial pit containing placed stones and charcoal lay by the northern terminal ditch of the Holywood North cursus where it had been later cut by the internal post setting, and at Springfield many features at the eastern end contained sooty soil with burnt flint and pebbles; one small feature also contained cremated cattle, sheep and possible pig bones that appear to have been burned *in situ*. These may equally relate to the post circle that was situated at this end of the cursus (*60*). Added to this an unaccompanied crouched inhumation in a cist was found just within the terminal ditch at Thornborough on the monument's axial line, and at Maxey a Group VI axe from an axial pit. This leaves little doubt that axial demarcation and spaced deposition was central to cursuses as well as the 'hall' sites of Lowland Scotland, whether before, during or after their construction.

The critical point remains however – why would symbolic house sites be so hugely magnified? Here it is instructive to turn to other longhouse-using groups. Amongst the Iban of Sarawak long houses represent a linear village under one roof. They can reach lengths up to 300m – equivalent to the Holywood South cursus – and house as many as 500 inhabitants in family apartments set along one wall. In North America the long house's central importance to the Iroquois was enshrined in their tribal name – 'The People of the Long House' or 'The Lodge Extended Lengthways'. With its partitions and separate fires it was a symbol of their identity and a metaphor for their remarkable Confederacy of Five Nations – apparently existing prior to European contact and extending over an area equivalent in size to England – some 500km x 300km. So totally did it symbolically structure their world that within this territory the Mohawks were

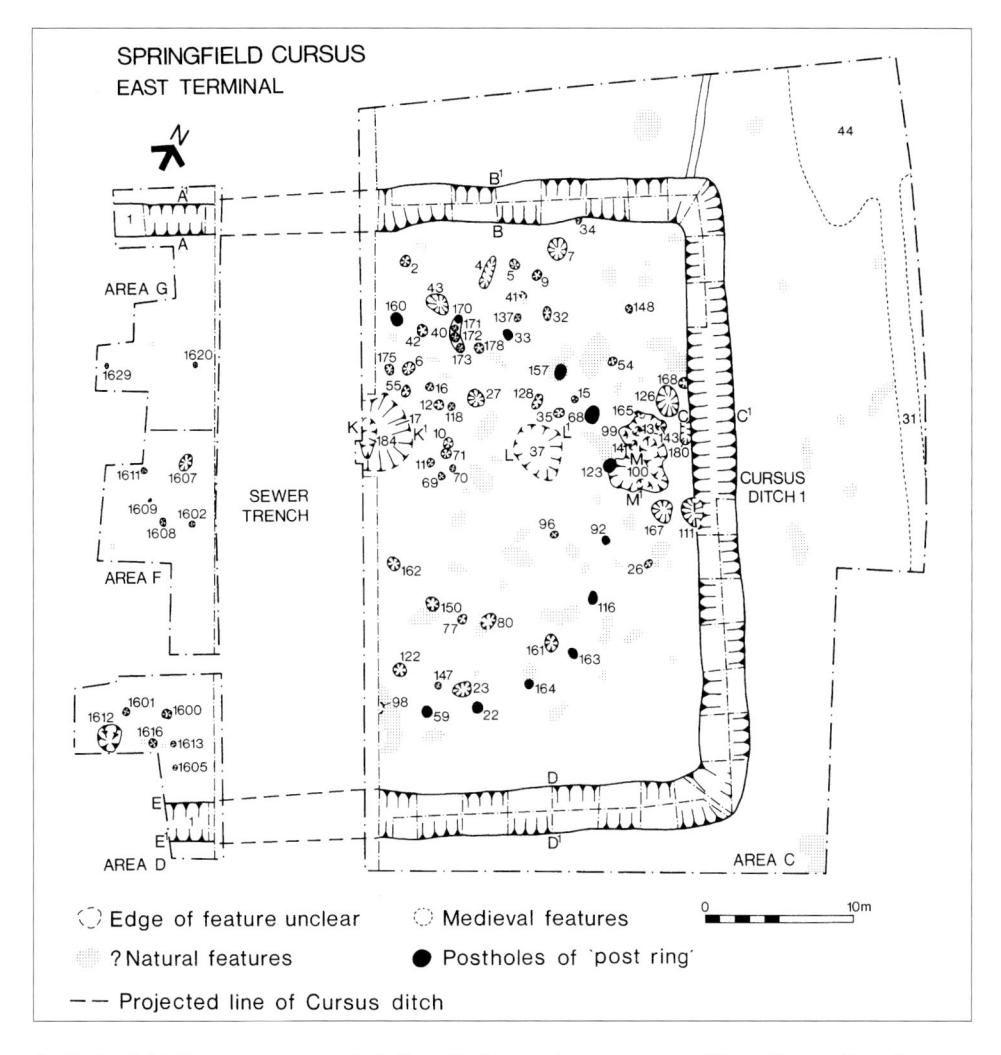

60 Springfield, Essex: eastern terminal. *From Buckley et al. 2001, courtesy of Essex County Council*

known as the 'Keepers of the East Door', the Senecas 'Keepers of the West Door' and the centrally located Onondagas, 'The Firekeepers', and hence hosts of the great councils.

Their houses were rectangular in plan with an end storage area. Individual family stalls lined the sides with spaced hearths shared between families in opposing units set along a central corridor. Such houses could be extended indefinitely to accommodate additions to the matrilinear clans that occupied them. By the fifteenth century AD they were on average 48m long with upper recorded limits of 122m and 124m (equivalent in length, but only a third the width, of the Barnack cursus).[12] Two structures were on occasion larger, particularly amongst the neighbouring Huron – those of the civil and war chiefs. This was not because they were wealthier – there is little evidence of differentiation in Iroquoian society – but because they served as the venue for village and other councils, and for some feasts and dances. Although no earthworks marked out the locations of the Great Councils that drew people from the farthest reaches of their vast territory it is easy to see that had they done so it is likely that they would have taken the form of a symbolic long house.

Clearly the cursus builders of Britain were neither Iroquois, Iban nor Barasana but these groups do furnish insights into the extent of cosmological structuring that may be generated by the long house. Ian Hodder has proposed this 'domus' concept as the basis for much of the development of the European Neolithic. More specifically Colin Richards has proposed it as a source for tomb and henge architecture in Orkney: the Stones of Stenness with their square central 'hearth' and spaced circle of uprights symbolically rendering the sub-circular house forms of nearby Barnhouse.[13] Such a leap – from 3m for normal houses to 20m for the outer walls at the monumental structure 8, to finally 44m at the Stones of Stenness – appears moderate, however, compared to that being proposed for cursuses. That is only true if we allow ourselves to be dominated by the dimensions of the major sites; akin to proposing a one-off leap from Barnhouse to Avebury. Small sites and minor cursuses furnish possible stepping stones, and incidences of possible dimensional doubling mentioned above may record the route to magnification.

Despite the fact that the great Danubian long houses of Europe had disappeared long before, they may have been an invisible but all-pervading symbolic influence. We have seen that the concept was clearly symbolically central to the emergence of bank barrows in Europe and that enclosure of houses like Claish by a fence points to a similar house-based origin for the long enclosure tradition. In much the same way the basilica remained central to the Christian tradition long after its civil basis in Roman administration had been lost in the mists of time. Likewise the extension of cathedrals to ever greater lengths was a product of monumentalisation within that tradition, not the desire for longer processional ways. Acceptance of such a symbolic core to the cursus tradition helps us to understand the many points of overlap with the bank barrow tradition. Rather than representing different stages of a common process with inexplicably contrasting outcomes (closed or open interiors), these two monument types can be seen to have shared sources in a common concept – the long house. We might reasonably conclude then that the cursus concept was largely symbolic from the outset. As symbolic 'houses' the monuments might physically define a social grouping in this world (a confederacy; or a dominant lineage) or the 'other' (the ancestors or deities). Importantly the latter would require no roof but the sky.

10

RIVERS, HILLS, SUN, MOON AND STARS – CURSUSES IN THE LANDSCAPE

There seems little doubt that cursus plan derives from the house, whether as a symbolic and ideological reference to the great Danubian long houses or as a home-grown expression of gigantism. The overwhelmingly straight nature of the monuments, their terminal plan repertoire and the selection of level ground for their siting, when away from the chalklands, all point in this direction. But the linear form chosen maximised the labour required to enclose a given area of land and also maximised the impact on movement through the landscape. Their extreme linearity must have made them uniquely demanding, not just to construct but to live or move around.

Cursus	Hectares enclosed
Barford	0.7
Longbridge	0.86
Cardington	1.02
Holywood South	1.05
Holywood North	1.4
Stadhampton	1.8
Balneaves	1.12+
Lesser Stonehenge	1.73
Stratford St Mary	1.94
Springfield	3.06
Drayton South	4.76

Thornborough	4.78+
Drayton North	5.52+
Fornham All Saints	5.81
Scorton	6.4+
Benson	7.3
Maxey (NW & SE)	7.68
Dorchester	9.92+
Aston	18.0+
Greater Stonehenge	28.76
Rudston A	18.9
B	11.16+
C	8.14
D	30.0+
Total Rudston	68.2+
Pentridge	43.0
Gussage	58.0
Total Dorset Cursus	101.0
Comparative sites	
Avebury	11.4
Karnak complex	40.0
Precinct of Amun-Re	27.0

Were the builders refining the techniques of alignment and geometric construction for purely esoteric/ritualised reasons or was it associated with a greater cosmological conception integrating the monument, the landscape and the heavens? All cursuses by virtue of their linearity possess an obvious capacity to align on distant features; the longer the site, the greater the precision. This route to explanation is seductive but peppered with pitfalls. First, unlike long barrows, we have no idea which was the 'business end' of the monument and hence which of the two opposing alignments was considered important. Added to that cursuses were overwhelmingly constructed on flat gravel terrace landscapes where skyline features were few and decidedly unimpressive. But all of course lay under the great vault of the heavens where it is certain some star will fall into the target line. To select individual sites with neatly satisfying alignments as a basis for explanation would be deceptive; the commonality of monument plans suggest a similar commonality of explanation, albeit tempered by local variation and change through time.

RIVERS

Having excavated at Maxey, Francis Pryor concluded that the cursus alignment there was 'manifestly illogical'. It cut diagonally across a gravel island that was later practically divided by field boundaries set at right angles to the water's edge. Adjacent ring ditches aligned with it preclude the idea that it was simply a short-lived feature. It does, however, run towards the Welland. That fact had led the Royal Commission in 1960 to postulate a processional connection between cursuses and rivers. The idea was encouraged by the mis-identification of Roman roads running to rivers at Ufton Nervet and Dorchester Overy. Realization that these sites were not cursuses, and that the open-ended nature of the Maxey cursus adjacent to the Welland merely reflects alluvial masking by a very mobile river, removed the main force of the argument.[1]

The juxtaposition of cursuses and rivers is nonetheless striking. Most run along gravel terraces parallel to rivers, terminate near stream ways and undoubtedly cluster close to major stream confluences (e.g. the Thames and Leach at Lechlade; the Thame and Thames at Dorchester). But does this reflect ideological intent? As flat land appears to have been a prerequisite for cursus construction away from the chalklands there would rarely have been much option but to lay them out parallel to the river. Their often massive dimensions precluded other orientations if terrace step edges were to be avoided. (What at first sight appears to be one continuous cursus running from upper to lower terrace at Drayton seems certain to have been two monuments; no sign of a link was found in excavations across its course at the terrace edge.)[2] Equally, small streams dissect terraces and would create natural boundaries, while the meandering of larger water courses could furnish a false impression of deliberate alignment. The only way to test the significance of the association is to observe the orientation of small sites unhindered by topographical constraints, and that off major sites on the extensive flat lands of river confluences.

Several small sites along the Warwickshire Avon and East Anglian Stour valleys do broadly follow the orientation of their meandering rivers but others, as at Barford, are set too far away from the river for it to be seriously considered an obvious – or even visible – influence. Closely similar orientation of the Warwickshire sites does, however, suggest a common source, a point to which we will return. Maxey and Dorchester upon Thames furnish closely comparable major monuments on wide floodplains and in neither case can the cursuses be said to run parallel to their adjacent rivers. This is almost equally true of the sites at Buscot Wick, Wilts, and Scorton, North Yorkshire, that lie on similar alignments to the former sites. They simply run beside an elbow of their adjacent river. Only at Fornham All Saints where the terrace gravel was restricted did a comparably sized cursus closely follow the course of a river (*41*). Sites such as Benson, on quite different alignments, show no sign of river-related orientation but are strikingly not far removed from the orientation trend revealed amongst minor sites in Warwickshire.

A deeper significance, unconstrained by notions of parallel or right-angled alignment may of course have linked rivers and cursuses. There is no doubt that the monuments are often sited at river confluences. Such locations are known cross-culturally as places of sacred significance but they also had potential as communication hubs. With this in mind it is perhaps significant that a number of cursuses also coincide with historically important river crossing zones: on the Thames at Dorchester and Lechlade; on the Great Ouse at Bedford (Kempston? and Cardington); on the Welland at Maxey – Barnack (bracketing the Roman King Street crossing); on the Avon near Warwick (Barford and Longbridge); on the Nith near Dumfries (Holywood and Curriestanes); on the Swale at Scorton (by the Dere Street crossing); on the Severn at Welshpool; and near the Icknield Way crossing of the Lark at Fornham All Saints. Despite the fact that river courses are likely to have been considerably different three to four millennia before these crossing points were first recorded, the coincidence remains. One locality – the Middle Trent – is strikingly highlighted by the distribution of stone axes made from Charnwood Forest stone (Group XX). Their source lies 14km south of the Trent but their densest distribution is some 40km north in the Peak District. Logic suggests they were taken across the Trent along the obvious route between these points – and the *only* cursuses in the valley lie there (*61*). This cannot be dismissed as a chance result of partial aerial reconnaissance. Cropmarks have been recorded in abundance along the entire length of the valley. The importance of the zone is additionally underlined by the presence within it of a double entrance henge monument with a large central round barrow (the Round Hill) and nearby a rare, nucleated round barrow cemetery at Swakestone. This prehistoric monument zone represents the principal historic crossing zone for nationally important north–south routes. If it performed a similar role in the Neolithic it does not of course follow this was mundane. The river formed a natural boundary for potentially hostile groups and may also have been a repository for the dead; at Langford Lowfields near Newark human and animal remains were discovered accumulated against a log jam in a former channel of the river.[3]

Rivers may then have been regarded as liminal zones where crossing could be fraught with danger, either from this or the 'other' world. It has been suggested

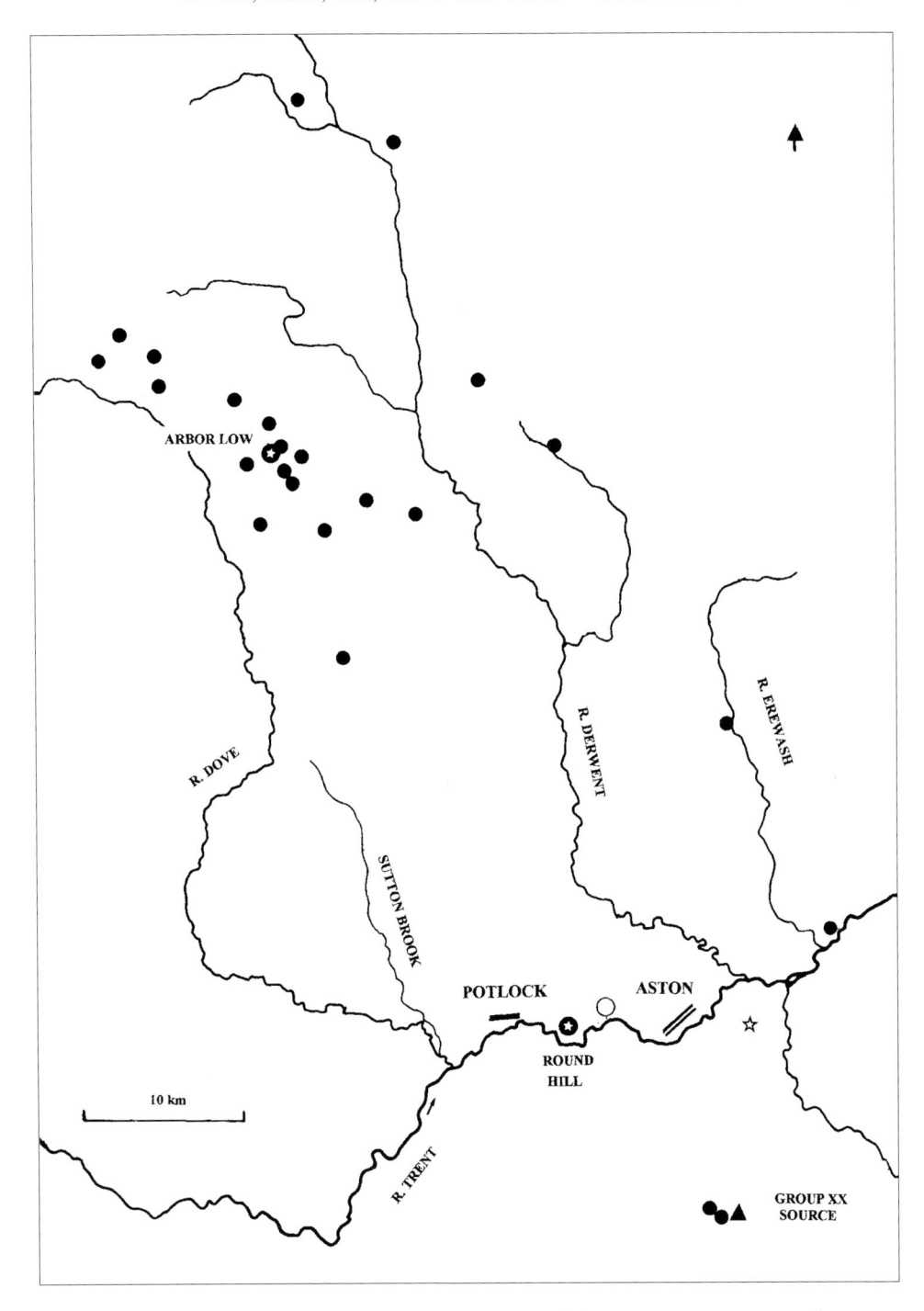

RIVERS, HILLS, SUN, MOON AND STARS — CURSUSES IN THE LANDSCAPE

61 Local Group XX (Charnwood Forest) axe distribution and the Trent monument zone (dot: axe find; dot with star: henge; open circle: Swarkestone barrow cemetery; open star: Lockington Early Bronze Age dagger and armlet deposit)

that cursuses were more – ritually designed as controlled, rationalised metaphors for rivers along which human populations could flow.[4] There are problems with this, not least because rivers, unlike cursuses, are never straight, and small cursuses would appear to 'flow' nowhere. Viewed instead as symbolic houses dedicated to dominant lineages, tribal confederacies, the ancestors or the gods, their positioning perhaps makes more sense – either to placate the otherworld at liminal locations or to furnish an integrative or neutral facility for disparate groups. The latter may have been of particular importance since the often expansive locales chosen for cursus construction are directly comparable to those chosen historically for the gathering of hosts (e.g. Athelstan and northern rulers at Eamont Bridge, Penrith in 927; the barons at Runnymede in 1215; Thomas of Lancaster and a claimed 18,000 retainers at Cotes Bridge, Loughborough in 1318).

This is not to deny the possibility of an active ritual element in the relationship between rivers and cursuses. It is rather to suggest that it may have been far more subtle than anything that can be read from monument plans or alignments, perhaps akin to the clear but loose Celtic association of Newgrange with the deified Boyne. The fact that the Dorset (Cranborne Chase), Greater Stonehenge and Rudston cursuses all lie on seasonal spring lines perhaps supports the idea.

Cursus alignment in relation to rivers, then, lacks the consistency that would allow us to see it as a ritual imperative akin to that prescribing monument plan, but there are other possible foci – the landscape and the heavens.

HILLS

It is rare indeed for cursuses to point to significant landscape features, largely perhaps because there are so few. The Greater Stonehenge Cursus does align on the lower, northernmost prominence of Beacon Hill 8km away, and looking north-east from its Thickthorn terminal the Dorset Cursus roughly aligns on Penbury Knoll, although this rapidly drifts and the monument skirts by it. No natural targets exist for the chalkland sites at Rudston nor for the vast majority of monuments that lie in river valleys with the exception of that at Welshpool that points at the Breiddin, 10km away. In flat localities like Maxey there can be no suggestion of landscape targets.

Regional patterns of orientation confirm a lack of landscape targets. Had they existed it could be predicted that where a number of monuments lie not far apart they would be seen to focus in to that one point. This is not the case. Instead they are often closely similar in alignment, a situation that forces us to delve deeper.

SUN AND MOON

The heavens are a bran tub from which orientations can always be plucked – if the rising and setting points of the sun and moon are too constrained there are myriad stars in the northern and southern vaults. Caution is therefore vital. This was missing from the famous article by Penny and Wood setting out the case for the Dorset Cursus as an astronomical observatory.[5] Of their six proposed alignments only two were broadly contained *within* the monument itself: that from the Bottlebush terminal to the skylined long barrow on Gussage Hill (midwinter sunset) and that from the long barrow to the south-western terminal on Thickthorn Down (minimum midwinter moonset). To achieve accuracy in the latter case however, the authors suggested a bonfire at the terminal – since it was not actually on the skyline – and movement of the observer on the hill toward the side of the cursus. Whilst both are possible, it hardly supports their case for the cursus as an astronomical observatory. The absence of a *single* significant alignment within the Pentridge arm of the site leaves little doubt that astronomy did not lay behind the planning of the complex.

Richard Bradley, excavating a large flint scatter overlying the cursus at the head of the Allen Valley, found the midwinter sunset alignment over the Gussage Hill long barrow a compelling symbolic feature. He concluded it was intended to impose a massive solar alignment on a series of separate monuments (long barrows) orientated towards the rising moon and thus place the cursus builders beyond challenge by relating their monument to the movement of the heavenly bodies.[6] The alignment is far from straightforward however (see *68*). From the Bottlebush terminal the monument runs straight as a die (see cover photograph viewed in the opposite direction) for over 1200m on an alignment to the *southern side* of the long barrow before short 'corrections' in the valley bottom realign it to the *northern side* of the barrow. It was brought back after a short distance but not fully; only the southern cursus ditch was aligned toward the long barrow. This line was followed for some 600m, even after sight of the long barrow was lost in the lee of the hill, before finally a major dog-leg correctly aligned it for the last 250m to the top of the hill. Observers at the Bottlebush terminal would not then have seen midwinter sunset over the long barrow along the course of the cursus but an oddly meandering track that was almost completely off target. That may have been symbolically important but it cautions against the assumption that the cursus functioned primarily as a track for the sun – only some 500m of a 10,000m-long monument were correctly aligned.

Claims of solar alignment have similarly been made for the Greater Stonehenge Cursus – in this case equinoctial. Here again real caution is needed since the monument is clearly not laid out on a true east–west course. Aubrey Burl, noting that its 263-283 degrees bearing was *not* astronomically significant, added that it may have casually marked the equinoctial sunrises.[7] This has since frequently been translated as a statement of fact. It was not. Burl's point about casual alignment is of real importance though since the equinox, being an abstract notion rather than an extremity, is difficult to observe. Equally the alignment could generally relate to those of earlier monuments nearby – the Lesser Cursus is not dissimilarly aligned nor are the Stonehenge car park post holes that can be securely dated to the Mesolithic. It is worth recalling the very early dates obtained from post avenues/cursuses in Scotland.

The alignment of the western section of the Dorchester upon Thames cursus appears more accurately related to a solar event – broadly midsummer sunset if viewed one way; midwinter sunrise if viewed the other. Bradley and Chambers have suggested its intention was to reorientate the earlier long enclosure (Site VIII) that was directed to the rising moon.[8] But had that been so surely the cursus would have been directed to the solar event along its entire length: instead more than half of its known track follows that of the long enclosure. Nor is there a distinct point at which both ditches realign as would be expected if precise orientation change was involved. Observers would be in some difficulty positioning themselves correctly between the staggered reorientated ditches to witness midsummer sunset. Such imprecision is inexplicable on the part of builders whose impressively straight cursus ditch lines confirm their ability to follow an alignment. Should we then conclude that the slight curvature of the site was deliberate but that the solar alignment was secondary and less precise?

We have already noted the general similarity of the Dorchester cursus to sites at Maxey and Fornham All Saints (*15*). They are similarly directed north-west/south-east, as are comparable sites at Buscot and Scorton, yet all wilfully miss significant alignments. Buscot is close but Maxey lies some seven degrees too far south for midwinter sunrise and the south-eastern arm is even further removed, lying beyond even the minimum lunar rising. Fornham All Saints, despite its multiple alignment changes, achieves a significant solar alignment only along its shortest, and most obviously linking, section. In northern England the Scorton site lies a few degrees from midwinter sunrise and at Thornborough the apparent orientation of the final section of the cursus to midwinter sunset is inaccurate by some seven degrees. Yet given that the alignment of these sites is often, as Francis Pryor said of Maxey, 'manifestly illogical' in terms of local topography and potential land use, there seems no doubt that there was a compelling motive behind it. Could the problem be ours rather than theirs?

Despite having moved beyond the extravagant claims of Alexander Thom, the astronomical debate is still largely conducted in terms of precision – necessary rigour if observational and calendrical claims are being made; much less so for

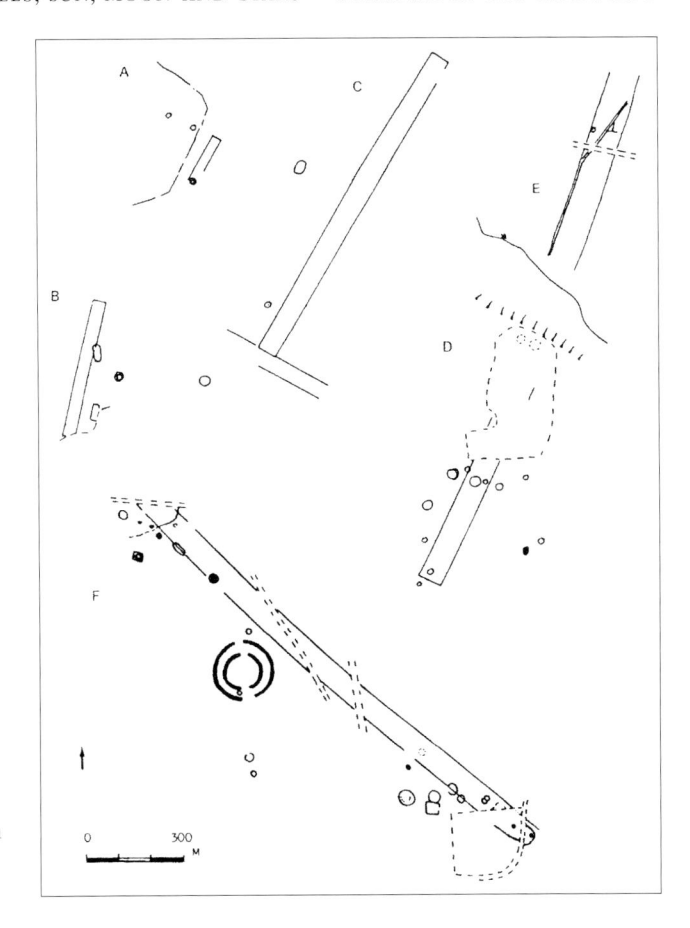

RIVERS, HILLS, SUN, MOON AND STARS — CURSUSES IN THE LANDSCAPE

62 Dorchester upon Thames and 'satellite' monuments: a) Drayton St Leonard; b) Stadhampton; c) Benson; d) Drayton (Sutton Courtenay) South; e) Drayton North; f) Dorchester upon Thames

purely symbolic ones. Cursus builders may well have aligned their monuments on the sun several days or even weeks before midwinter (or midsummer) because gatherings had been inadvertenly mis-timed. Such a resulting sweep would also include inexact alignment *within* the 18.6 year lunar maximum rising arc that extends either side of the solar extremities. We might then comfortably conclude that broad general solar and lunar risings explain cursus layout. We might, were it not for a very significant number of sites that are aligned to the northern and southern arc of the heavens where neither sun nor moon ever rise.

STARS

Again inexact orientation must be considered. These sites could be generally aimed at the moon when at the highest point of its journey across the night sky. That can be comparatively easily tested since judgments of height by the builders, unlike risings and settings, are subjective. Significant variation should therefore be evident within a region possessing a number of north–south aligned monuments. The Upper Thames is just such an area. There a series of Bi cursuses orbit the great monument at Dorchester upon Thames (Stadhampton and Drayton St Leonard some 5km to the north; Benson 6km to the east and Drayton 7km to the west). Their contrast with the central site could hardly be greater (*62*). It is round-ended, greatly elongated and the focus for a series of hengiform rings; they are precisely rectangular and largely uncluttered by later monuments. Most striking is the fact that their alignments cluster within about 16 degrees of each other (three within just six degrees), whereas they differ from Dorchester by as much as 100 degrees.[9] Such clustering is improbably close for judgements of the maximum height of the moon by the builders of the separate monuments. Yet no common horizon target is possible within 50 miles so slight is their convergence. And simple estimated replication can be dismissed – sites separated by 6km or more could not be laid out within six degrees of each other without some target. Since solar and lunar ones can be ruled out there seems no alternative but to see this as stellar. The 10-degree alignment range precludes the rising point of a star (notoriously difficult to observe anyway) but might be appropriate to a constellation. A clue that this was the case is furnished by the Lechlade cursus 40km upstream (*54*). It stands in the same relationship to the major cursus at Buscot as the Bi sites do to the Dorchester cursus and, most importantly, has almost exactly the same bearing *west* of north that they have *east* of north. This strongly suggests alignment on a constellation as it rotated through the night sky.

Constellations eternally circling the northern sky ('the imperishable stars' of the Egyptians) or on arcs across the southern sky, might equally result in this pattern of alignments. Given the neutral, non-directional form of cursuses it is unlikely that we will be able to establish the exact target. The northern sky, with its empty polar centre in the mid-fourth millennium BC, would have exhibited a tighter rotation for Ursa Major than is now the case. Its orbit would lie within the range we are considering but is improbably high in the sky to be the focus for a monument form with little apparent height. In the southern sky on the other hand there is one constellation (or at least part of it) that is almost universally recorded in ethnographic contexts – the Belt of Orion. This very obvious line of three stars demands attention and has generated a wide ranging mythology – from the barque of Sah/Osiris in Egypt to a plough in Java (the belt identified with its arm).[10] The striking linearity of the three stars might easily serve as metaphor for a cursus. Its track across the southern sky in the mid-fourth millennium BC was considerably lower than today and broadly in place to appear along the lines of the Upper Thames cursuses when climbing or dropping; risings lay 20 or more degrees beyond the range but are often

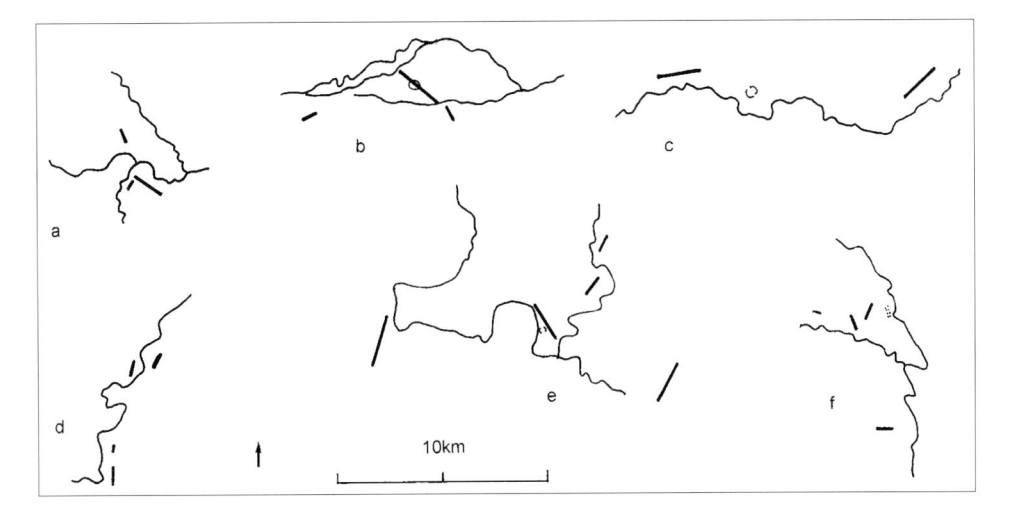

63 Examples of monument clusters: a) Buscot-Lechlade; b) Maxey-Barnack; c) Potlock-Aston; d) Charlecote-Barford; e) Dorchester upon Thames; f) Curriestanes-Holywood-Fourmerkland

feeble on the horizon and rendered invisible by the moon or the presence of trees.[11] A further possible focus is provided by Sirius, the brightest star in the sky. Following the Belt of Orion this describes a lower arc that might broadly coincide with the range of cursus orientations. Again the significance attached to the star is abundantly recorded.

There is little to choose between these possible targets in the Upper Thames. Seeking evidence from further afield we can turn to the Warwickshire Avon (63). There the monuments are small and consistently aligned north–south, or in the case of Barford, 20 degrees east of north. Amongst these sites is the Charlecote long enclosure that could have served as a model. The distance separating it from other sites excludes the possibility of simple visual copying of alignment. That is equally true of the river that is hardly an obvious visual feature nor consistently flowing north–south. In the absence of obvious landscape features, stellar targets must be presumed. These could be related to the Charlecote long enclosure if stellar alignment at the time of celebrations at that site attained significance. This might then be replicated at other sites *if* the celebrations enacted at the site occurred at a fixed seasonal point in time (e.g. after harvest in the early hours of darkness). Thus the north–south orientation of the Warwickshire cursuses could have arisen from fortuitous orientation of a paradigm site. Alternatively they might all have arisen from deliberate seeking of the centre point of that ever dark zone of the north marked by the rotation of the circumpolar stars. As in the Upper Thames these closely bunched alignments seem unlikely to result from chance. It is noteworthy that the four principal bank barrows outside Wessex similarly run north–south.

Moving to the borders of Scotland we find a complex at Dumfries that in many ways resembles the pattern found in the Upper Thames (*63f*). The large Curriestanes cursus on a potential equinoctial alignment similarly possesses 'orbiting' smaller monuments at Holywood. These have alignments of 152-6 degrees and 26 degrees, almost identical to those of the Lechlade and Dorchester Bi sites. Even if such distant parallels are dismissed, the fact that the two Holywood sites lie equidistant either side of north must surely point to deliberation. What is more the sites appear to have been aligned to furnish long skyline views to the south, not easy in such hilly terrain; to the north the monuments point into the Lowther Hills. The southern cursus follows the valley of the Nith to look out across the Solway Firth, while the northern cursus is aligned just off the edge of Long Fell to do the same. This would appear to suggest that the southern sky was the focus of interest. There the Belt of Orion would be an obvious target. Although rising and falling outside the cursus alignments, it would have stood some 10 degrees clear of the horizon when lined up with them, sufficient to clear middle-distance trees and for the stars to shine out brightly. What is more the highest altitude reached by the Belt at this latitude in the mid-fourth millennium would be some 15 degrees, just sufficient to take it over the considerable bulk of Criffel that lies 15km due south from the complex.[12] This 'event' that saw the Belt rise over the line of the southern cursus, follow the line of Criffel (already marked out as a point of interest by the presence on its upper slopes of the Slewcairn long mound) and fall along the line of the northern cursus, is most unlikely to have been fortuitous.

Interestingly the dates from the Holywood complex are somewhat later than most Scottish sites. It may then reflect development of a complex mythology, akin to that suggested by the Dorchester sites, that incorporated solar and stellar elements. What is certain is that cursus alignment – whether at the sites we have been examining or at more randomly disposed monuments elsewhere – was neither precise nor esoteric. But in the recurrent patterns across great distances we are witnessing dynamic change: from dispersed to clustered ritual foci; from moderately sized closed mortuary monuments to huge open, ancestor referencing ones; from regional monument traditions to inter-regional ones. It is to the changes that this wrought in Neolithic society that we now need to turn.

11

SACRED LANDSCAPES

Cursuses are intriguing monuments. Far bigger and, in many cases, better laid out than anything that had gone before; engaging far more people and taking far more land than was strictly necessary. Opulent if not monumental. Signalling devices probably to be read from above by the gods rather than on the ground by figures dwarfed by their dimensions. But to understand their importance we need to move beyond the particular: to see form as an encoding of ritual information rather than an end in itself; size as a measure of the dynamic social process of construction and use; and their relationships (local, regional and national) as a reflection of the wider forces moving society. The fact that cursuses really were the first monuments to override regional patterns of construction and adhere to a type recognizable from Dumfries to Devon is of hugely greater significance than ultimately unresolvable questions about how precisely they were used. Classical Greek temples furnish a useful analogy, albeit at a vastly more complex level of social development. Like cursuses, they are comparable from one end of the Greek world to the other but functioned at local, city state or pan-Hellenic level according to the site's significance. That is where their importance lies, not in a barren analysis of the patterns of use and movement that they imposed on worshippers. Cursuses were built at a crucial point in the development of society in prehistoric Britain. By reading them we may be able to read it.

Cursus monuments were massively larger than anything that had gone before (except perhaps the Stanwell bank barrow) and dominated whole landscapes. Nowhere is this more evident than in the Thames Valley. There the 1.6km-long, nearly 10ha site at Dorchester upon Thames was not only respected for over 1000 years (to judge from the later monuments positioned along its axis) but the whole landscape in its vicinity was peppered with other cursuses. In some areas this might simply be put down to the heightened awareness of flyers in the vicinity of a site

143

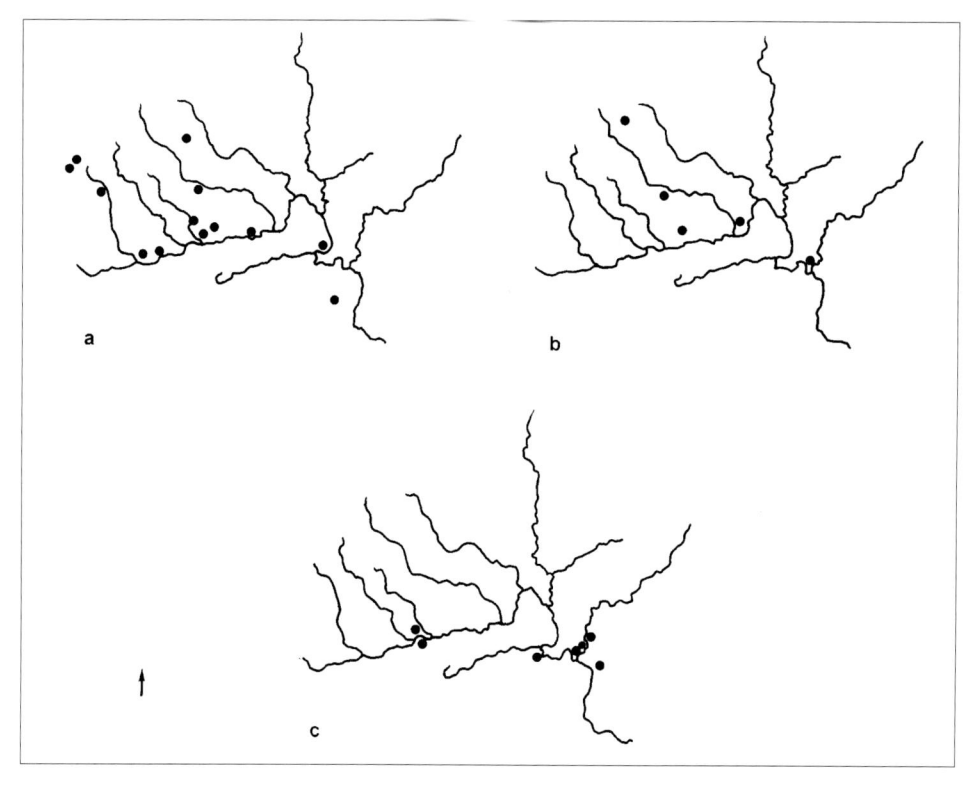

64 Monument patterning in the Upper Thames catchment: a) causewayed enclosures; b) henges; c) cursuses. *After Holgate 1988*

made famous by a pioneering excavation. Not here. The whole Thames Valley has been intensively overflown but the only new cursus discoveries in the last 20 years fell within its orbit – Drayton St Leonard and Stadhampton. They only served to intensify a pattern of regional clustering that contrasts markedly with what went before (Earlier Neolithic causewayed enclosures), and what followed (Late Neolithic henges) (64). With the probable exception of Drayton North, all the 'orbiting' sites around the focal sites at Dorchester and Buscot are of the precisely laid out Bi type and quite differently orientated. This could be explained in terms of their later date but not it seems in terms of their disassociation. They are far too close together to represent separate territorial foci, as the widely spaced causewayed enclosures and henges appear to have been. They seem instead to be part of whole landscapes associated with the central site.

Elsewhere the pattern is repeated: at Holywood – Curriestanes; Rudston – Burton Agnes; Maxey-Barnack; and perhaps Kempston – Cardington. Small sites of long enclosure or minor cursus type lie even closer to the Dorset Cursus, to the Greater Stonehenge Cursus (the Lesser Cursus) and possibly to

SACRED LANDSCAPES

the Thornborough cursus, but in no case are they physically incorporated in the manner of Site VIII at Dorchester. The implications are huge – not only the monuments but the areas *between* them were, it seems, set apart. That need not mean that they were empty of settlement but it does suggest a landscape where the assembling of large groups was common but the resident population low: agricultural practices would have been inhibited by the extended lengths of cursuses while their substantial acreages would have significantly reduced the carrying capacity of their areas.

We can gain some idea of the size of such assemblies by estimating the labour needed to construct each monument. This, in itself, is fraught with difficulty, since calculations based on the volume of spoil to be dug, assumes constant ditch size and profile. That is rarely the case. Figures in the work estimate table below provide an approximate indication based on Bill Startin's assumption of teams of two moving 0.5 cubic metres of chalk per hour or 0.68 cubic metres of gravel (estimates for three-man teams have been added for those sites of more significant earthwork size since a basketer would also have been needed).

Cursus	Dimensions (m)	Estimated ditch spoil (cu m)	Man hours 2 Man teams (3 Man teams)	Estimated days taken by 100 men working 10-hour days
Gussage	5640 x 100	356,400	141,600	142
			(212,400)	213
Pentridge	4290 x 100	26,400	105,600	106
			(158,400)	160
Rudston A	2700 x 58	14,683	58,733	59
			(88,098)	88
Grt Stonehenge	2730 x 100	5,750	23,000	24
			(34,500)	34
Aston	1700 x 100	11,529	33,908	34
Scorton	2000 x 32	5,400	15,882	16
			(23,823)	24
Dorchester	1600 x 60	5,983	17,597	18
Thornborough	1200 x 40	1,954	5,747	6
Springfield	680 x 40	1,552	4,564	5
Maxey (SE)	1710 x 55	972	2,858	3
Lechlade	300 x 50	696	2,047	2
Barford	185 x 40	220	647	0.5

Assuming these teams worked concurrent 10-hour days, it emerges that small sites like Barford and Lechlade – comparable to Stadhampton and Drayton St Leonard near Dorchester - could have been constructed by a workforce of 100 in a few days at most. Figures rise steadily for major sites but are heavily dependent on ditch size. Maxey is far larger than Springfield but using the slight ditch profiles of the excavated south-eastern arm as the sole basis for calculation indicates it could have been built in little over half the time. Even the Greater Stonehenge Cursus made quite moderate demands. Labour requirements only leap upwards for the great Rudston and Dorset monuments. We will return to them later. Focusing on the Dorchester area we can see that ditch digging at Drayton South may have taken about five days for a 100-strong workforce and, assuming similar ditch size, Benson may not have taken significantly longer – perhaps 7-8 days. To that figure would have to be added the uppermost layers of the ditch subsequently eroded away (perhaps as much as a third) and initial site clearance – so perhaps 15 days.

That may seem rather longer than the time span of a single festival event during which the workforce might be assembled, but of course doubling the workforce would halve the time. A workforce of 200-300 might then complete the Benson cursus during a week-long gathering, assuming there were no wooden structural components. Since the four Bi sites differ strikingly from the Dorchester cursus itself, we could presume that they were constructed and used by separate groups. Perhaps then the region witnessed gatherings of hundreds, if not thousands, of people at specific times. The probability of other major structures in the landscape increases the likelihood. Another cursus is probably represented by parallel ditches abutting the southern end of the Benson cursus at right angles (cf. Rudston) and they may extend on towards the great Dorchester cursus as the irregular parallel ditches recorded at Shillingford (see *14*).

It is not just the clustering of cursus sites in this region that sets it apart, however. The major focal site at Dorchester also has more hengiform sites around it than are currently known at any other place. Three multiple irregular ring ditch sites (I, II & XI) and as many as six small ring-ditch sites; the former probably enlarged and redefined turf-built barrows subsequently levelled, the latter low mounds or pit/post circles. Ordinary cropmark ring ditches could mask such sites elsewhere; at Wyke Down on the Dorset Cursus, for instance, Martin Green's excavation of a horseshoe-shaped ring ditch revealed instead a monument of conjoined pits. But both hengiform types are most commonly found close to cursuses so the number of such potential sites is limited. Many of the sites destroyed without excavation at Maxey could have been of this type as, to judge from Canon Greenwell's findings in the nineteenth century, might some

SACRED LANDSCAPES

of the round barrows on Rudston Wold, but there are few other potential localities.

Subsumed under the title 'hengiform' because they seemed originally to be mini henges, these sites furnish the little evidence we have for burial from the Middle Neolithic onwards. At Dorchester, Site I produced evidence of a surface laid inhumation (probably because it alone retained vestiges of a covering mound)[1] while two pits at the centre of Site II produced cremations, one accompanied by a stone macehead, a flint flake, a fabricator and a long bone pin. An adjacent pit had deposits of cattle bones. What really sets the sites at Dorchester apart, however, is not the rare evidence for Mid/Late Neolithic barrow burial but the overwhelming number of cremations found around the edges of Site II and the smaller sites. The little 10m-diameter Site VI produced as many cremation deposits as Stonehenge (97.5m diameter) and Duggleby Howe (a mound 36m in diameter and 6m high). What is more, the total number of cremations from Dorchester greatly exceeds the combined totals for these two sites (see table showing Middle/Late Neolithic cremation deposits below).

Duggleby Howe		53
Stonehenge		52
Dorchester upon Thames	I	4
	II	21
	IV	25
	V	21
	VI	49
	XI	3
	2	28
Total for Dorchester upon Thames		156
Cairnpapple		11
Llandegai		6 + small fragments
Sarn y bryn caled 2		4
Barford A		2
Wyke Down		2 + skull fragments

It does not, however, follow that these hengiform monuments were first and foremost cremation cemeteries. Cremations were only placed in their ditches in any numbers after a considerable amount of silt had formed; that need not necessarily have taken long given the rapidity of silting on the gravel subsoils of the site but it is sufficient to suggest a different primary purpose. Nor can the large numbers at Dorchester be taken to indicate survival of the prolonged, collective burial practices seen in chambered tombs. At Site VI for instance, only a couple of cremations were placed towards the base of the ditch, the rest, as Richard Atkinson noted, 'followed the profile of the ditch side' at a higher level. Notably there was no evidence of cremations at a range of different depths in the centre of the ditch as would be expected if they had been deposited over a considerable period of time. This leaves little doubt that the process was short lived, not ongoing.[2] Since it is unlikely that bodies would be stored for later cremation on the site (the rite depending in considerable measure on the presence of body fats) we are presented with two possibilities: that they had been cremated in their home territories and brought to Dorchester for interment in association with a particular assembly/festival or that they represent a specific population dying at the same time – the implications of the latter we will return to discussing Duggleby Howe.

The fact that elsewhere far smaller numbers of cremations were the norm leaves little doubt that Dorchester should be ranked as a sanctuary site of premier importance. Radiocarbon dates indicate that its importance may have grown over time: the hengiform sites regionally concentrated there are several centuries later in date than the cursus, although Site IV and the post circle clearly respect its axis, and the construction of a large monumental henge (190m in diameter) beside the cursus probably followed after another century or two. The importance of the sanctuary into the Late Neolithic is emphasised by the exotic nature of this henge monument. Unlike the comparatively common single ditched sites, this is defined by two concentric ditches 7 9m wide and finds its only clear parallel some 300kms north at Thornborough in North Yorkshire where one of three such henges overlies a cursus.[3]

SANCTUARIES AND PILGRIMAGE

Clearly the Dorchester on Thames monument complex – and we must assume the surrounding area – was hugely important over a considerable period of time. It can be clearly distinguished not only from small, 'local' monument groupings such as the Barford-like complexes, but also from major sites of apparent 'regional' importance such as Aston on Trent. It in fact possesses features that would declare it as an inter-regional sanctuary if encountered in an historical setting, namely intensity of monument construction, longevity of respect, addition of later exotic monuments with far flung parallels, large numbers of burials, and placement in a landscape structured, partly at least, by other monuments. These elements recur

65 The Sinodun Hills, capped by Wittenham Clumps

from Delphi to Uppsala, and from Pachacarmarca to Mecca at sites that Marcia Elaide has termed hierophanies – locations where the otherworld of gods and ancestors communicate with the living.

Mountains, hills, rocks, islands, springs, caves, groves and individual trees commonly form their core since there is a universal need to anchor mythology in geography. Such sites might also furnish an oracular conduit: at Delphi through the Pythia seated over the supposed chasm after drinking from the sacred spring; at Dodona through the rustling leaves of the venerable oak; and at Olympia through inspection of the entrails of sacrificed animals. Pausanius tells us that these pan-Hellenic sanctuaries to Apollo and Zeus were originally sacred to Gaia, the earth goddess. Then they probably comprised little more than a defined temenos (to contain the otherworld forces and protect the unwary), an altar (probably little more than a huge ash heap, as it remained throughout Olympia's history) and a cult structure (that at Dodona remained small and awkwardly fitted into the large precinct). A similar picture is presented by Adam of Bremen's description in AD 1070 of Old Uppsala in Sweden. He mentions a temple with cult figures, a spring used for divination (unfortunately only activated by plunging a living man into it), a huge tree and a sacred grove hung with the bodies of sacrificed people and animals.

Patterns of propitiation and sacrifice will inevitably vary according to cultural context but there are a number of features here that could be accommodated within the findings at Dorchester. Equally the location of the later henge beside the cursus recalls a common process of realignment at such sites. Thus the temple of Pythian Apollo at Delphi was located beside what appears to have been the earlier sanctuary to Gaia where a temple dedicated to Athena Pronaia overlies deposits of Mycenean female figurines. Similarly, the Incas were so in awe of the great shrine of Pachacamaca when they conquered the region that they dare not disturb it. Instead they built their site beside it and sanctioned them conjointly.

Finally the cleanliness of such sites is often accorded priority. This is aided by the commonly cyclical nature of activities associated with them (e.g. originally only annual consultations at Delphi, festivals every four years at Olympia and nine years at Uppsala).

There is little at Dorchester upon Thames to mark the location out as unusual but it does lie just across the river from two singular hills, today capped by the distinctive Wittenham Clumps (65). These Sinodun Hills have long attracted the attention of visitors: 'From the great sea like plain … rise two curious, isolated, round hills. Although the highest of them is under 300ft (92m), so flat is the surrounding country that they dominate it completely and form a landmark on the countryside for many miles in every direction.'[4] They are perfectly visible from the Ridgeway 18km away, both to the east and to the west. Chris Tilley has emphasised the crucial part part played by such landscape features in ritual practices. He points to the Avatip people of Papua New Guinea seeing deities and ancestors reflected in the topography around them, and the Irish Dindshenchas record a similar world view in early medieval Ireland: 'Behold the paps of the king's consort here beyond the mound west of the fairy mansion' (cairns K & L at Newgrange). Twin hills are not infrequently termed paps in Ireland and the Western Isles of Scotland, most significantly perhaps the Paps of Anu in Kerry since Anu can be convincingly demonstrated to refer here to be a Celtic mother goddess. It is not entirely inconceivable then that the Sinodun Hills, visible from so far, were thought of in similar terms. Certainly they were perceived in anatomical terms far more recently: Camden in the sixteenth century AD stated that locals, referring to the Lady of the Manor of Wittenham, called them 'Mother Dunche's Buttocks!'[5]

If these distinctive landscape features were the focus of interest it is easy to see how the whole Dorchester region might be invested with great significance. The cursuses that ring the area give substance to the idea and recall sacralised topography at sites such as Mecca and Vaygash Island. In the former case the Haram or sanctuary area extends for 30km x 9km around the Ka'ba and includes various hills, springs and standing stones; in the latter case, the island represented the premier sanctuary of the nomadic Nenet people in the Siberian tundra and was held to be the 'first earth' that grew out of the sea in the shape of a man. Like Mecca it drew an entire people to it. Pilgrims returned with holy relics (fragments from the body of the 'first man' – an anthropomorphic stone) and constructed a hierarchy of sanctuaries branching out from this ancestral centre

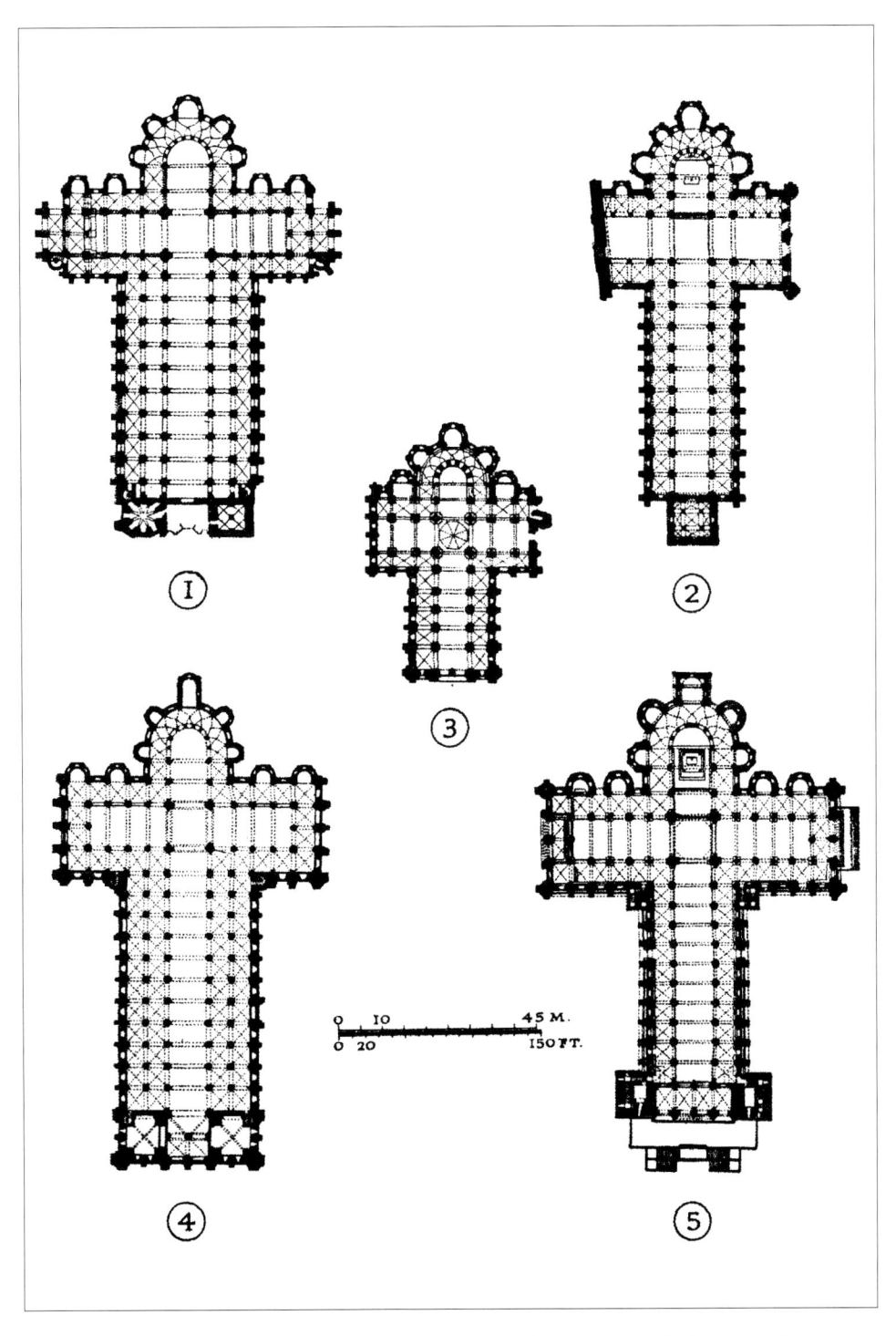

66 Pilgrimage and replication: 1-4 churches on separate roads to Compostella (1 Tours; 2 Limoges; 3 Conques; 4 Toulouse), 5 Santiago de Compostella. *From Conant 1993, courtesy of Yale University Press*

that resembled each other in character and their main components, ' ... the holy places of the Nenet varied only with regard to detail.'[6]

This reminds us of a further characteristic of inter-regional sanctuaries: their capacity to inspire replication. This is a universal phenomenon unaffected by either the complexity of the structure or of the society constructing it. A classic example is to be found in the great shrines built along each of the medieval pilgrimage roads leading through France to Santiago de Compostella in north-west Spain (*66*). Transcending the localism of the period each was built in the peculiar style of the great church that was the pilgrims' goal.[7] This pattern of replication of a cult site paradigm is perhaps the clearest evidence we have for the pilgrimage process.

Dorchester, Maxey and Fornham

Architecture, like all aspects of ritual, is based upon repeated formulae that are regarded as essential to the maintenance of cosmological order. Its forms may be rationalised to accord with the beliefs of those using the site but is not a functional response to ritual procedures nor is it often the subject of dogmatic formulation – there are no prescriptions for laying out Greek temples or medieval churches. Rather, early sites are adapted as paradigms. At a local level this results in regional patterns familiar from chambered tombs to medieval churches; at long distance it points either to itinerant architects (cf. Durham and Kirkwall cathedrals) or to pilgrimage. If peculiar features of one of the sites are slavishly replicated, the latter seems certain.

The Dorchester upon Thames cursus, as we saw in chapter 6, lacks antecedents in its area; there is nothing to suggest it arose from the progressive magnification of local long enclosures. It is of simple form, with the exception of an unusual side ditch arrangement at the south-eastern terminal, but it does change direction towards its centre by several degrees. The fact that this reorientation is not synchronous on opposing sides suggests it is a deliberately engineered feature rather than misdirection following interrupted construction. As we have seen, the closest parallel for the Dorchester cursus lies 120km away at Maxey, a site that potentially possessed even more hengiform ring ditches around it (see *15*). The course of the two main arms at Maxey similarly diverge but cropmark evidence there leaves no doubt that here two separate monuments were involved – one with shallow, regular ditches, the other with deeper, irregular ditches. These would be unlikely outcomes of a pilgrim's 'mental map' of Dorchester, but Dorchester could well record experiential 'mapping' of Maxey.

Even more important to this argument is the highly atypical site at Fornham All Saints that apparently uniquely possesses a series of sharp angled bends along its length. Again, as at Dorchester, the ditch cropmarks suggest a unified plan with the possible exception of the narrower northern arm. We could seek to explain its plan in terms of the vagaries of adjacent river meandering or of attempts to redirect the monument across the centre of the causewayed enclosure but neither very convincingly. It is difficult to see why the established form, rigidly followed elsewhere, was subverted for such minor objectives. The cult-paradigm site replication approach, however, furnishes a mechanism and a compelling imperative. A mental, experiental 'map' of the Maxey cursus, *with its Etton extension*, would closely resemble the Fornham monument constructed some 90km away (see *15*). As with Dorchester, it seems more likely that the unified structure copied the multi-phased one, than vice versa. Assuming the Etton arm to be a later addition, we could envisage Dorchester replicating Maxey when only its north-east and south-east arms were present, and Fornham doing so when the paradigm site had reached a more developed stage.

It would follow from this that the monuments on the Maxey island were the most venerable. It might also follow, if all aspects of the cult site were being replicated, that Dorchester, like Maxey-Etton and Fornham, should possess a causewayed enclosure. That could prove to lie in the pastureland obscuring the north-western end of the cursus, or even beneath the adjacent oppidum earthworks at Dyke Hills. Causewayed enclosures furnish a precedent for the assemblies needed to undertake major cursus building programmes.

Unfortunately it may never be possible to test this hypothesised relationship between the three major complexes of the Midlands and East Anglia. It is one thing to point to their regional distinctiveness and distant similarities; quite another to find organic material that will deliver dates fine enough to establish a sequence that may be measured in decades rather than centuries. Material culture could assist. Melanie Silverman has suggested from a study of a Peruvian pilgrimage centre that if ritual and iconography are representative of the areas from which pilgrims are drawn, it should be possible to identify the catchment area of the sanctuary.[8] Sadly cursuses are noted for their barrenness. Francis Healey's work on a large flint scatter near the Thornborough cursus hints at future possibilities though, since the flint can be seen to have come from a range of non-local sources. Pottery – the classic indicator of regional affiliation – is conspicuous by it absence; none at all came from Maxey and only a scrap of Beaker from the top fill of the Dorchester ditch. Peterborough Ware in simple Ebbsfleet form did nonetheless come from the near contemporary secondary silts of the long enclosure (Site VIII) cut by the cursus.

Peterborough Ware is associated with a number of other cursuses in this Midland/East Anglian region. At Drayton North a few sherds in the Ebbsfleet style came from near the base of the ditch but far more from tree throw holes close by, perhaps placed there during the process of clearance for cursus construction. At Springfield, in Essex, pottery in the more elaborate Mortlake style came from the lower secondary silts of the eastern terminal ditch and from pits and post circle holes just inside (67) and at Potlock in Derbyshire similar pottery came from low in the ditch fill. Farther afield, along the line of the great Dorset Cursus, Peterborough Ware followed Earlier Neolithic plain bowl pottery in the ditch after a comparatively short period and dominated the 'occupation site' set across the monument. It is not the exclusive pottery type from these monuments – carinated bowl pottery came from Holywood North near Dumfries and from Bannockburn – but there is a notable association. That is all the more striking since the dates for southern cursuses (3600-3000 BC; the questionably early optically stimulated luminescence dates from Eynesbury excepted) overlap with those for Peterborough Ware (3400-2500 BC).[9]

Peterborough Ware

This pottery tradition marks a major break from earlier patterns. Unlike previous regionally distinct patterns of decorated bowls (e.g. Abingdon Ware in the Upper Thames; Mildenhall Ware in East Anglia), Peterborough Ware exhibited a 'dynamic expansion and development' that Isobel Smith noted in 1974 ' … contrasted strangely with a gradual loss of cultural status.' By this she meant its virtual absence from the primary levels of structures and lack of securely associated diagnostic artefacts. Although still true in part, subsequent research has associated Peterborough Ware with the chisel form of transverse arrowhead and with elaborate edge-polished flint knives and axes, as well as with some cursuses, post circles and individual burials under round barrows. This gives context to what was a uniquely expansionist ceramic tradition; its spread across almost all areas of southern Britain was unprecedented and only later superseded by Grooved Ware. Its origins, and the dynamic behind its expansion, remain obscure. Smith's recognition of a developmental pottery sequence from Ebbsfleet to Mortlake and then to flat-based Fengate styles has been called into question by recent radiocarbon dating, while almost exclusive use of quartz as a filler in Welsh Mortlake-style pottery has no apparent practical explanation and has led Gibson to suggest a ritual component to manufacture.[10]

Iconography might better explain the obsessive use of bird bone to impress decoration (even extending to cut and sliced quills e.g. Barford[11]) than an increased dependence on hunting. Shared cosmology appears more credible than expansion of regional identity or the 'export' of a distinctive potting style. But how could this have been achieved across such an unprecedented area? Aggression and dominance are the obvious mechanisms but there is little to support this; chisel arrowheads so closely associated with the Peterborough Ware phenomenon were not a feature of the clusters that testify to violent

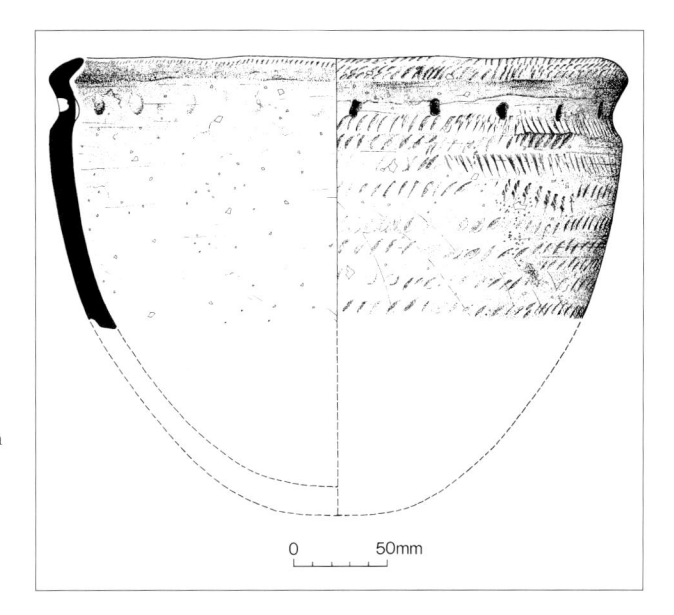

67 Mortlake-style Peterborough Ware bowl from a grey lens in the lower ditch silts of the east terminal at Springfield. *From Buckley et al. 2001, courtesy of Essex County Council*

attack on the causewayed enclosure at Crickley. Emergence of confederacies like that of the Iroquois, discussed earlier in relation to the long house (chapter 9), may produce 'remarkable concordances' of culture across very considerable territories[12] but, if voluntarily entered into, are invariably ideologically triggered. The role of ideology is not restricted to the formation of such rare social groupings, however. Convergence of large numbers of people at sites deemed to be sacred could play a more passive but no less effective role. From the Andes to the Peloponnese it is recognised that gatherings at neutral, pan-regional cult centres enabled heterogeneous groups to exchange goods, compete and debate, and so establish a sense of common – even national – identity. The key articulating roles of Delphi and Olympia in this process are well known. Less well known is the role of Chavin de Huantar in the coalescence of Early Horizon communities in Peru. From a purely regional cult centre with a local deity, Chavin developed to monumental proportions and elements of its temple architecture and iconography were copied at far flung centres. Regional spheres of interaction became interlocked to form a pan-regional network extending up to a staggering 950km. In the absence of defensive architecture it seems probable that this was articulated by an expansive cult. As Berger puts it: 'In societies based on ideologies of kinship and reciprocal exchange … new religious beliefs can provide the energy and direction to overcome the fears and antagonisms produced by long standing provincialism.'[13] Participation in rituals, dancing, feasting and competition during pilgrimage events, without conflict that would have angered the deity, would serve to bridge inter-group hostilities and encourage the broadening of identity beyond the local. This is nowhere better illustrated than by the conscious decisions of groups to alter local shrines so they shared features in common with those of different cultural backgrounds. This returns us to the possibilities of recognising signs of replication between major cursus centres in the Midlands and East Anglia.

The Midlands and East Anglia in the Middle Neolithic

The distribution of Peterborough Ware extends well beyond this region to Wessex, Wales and Yorkshire but it does have some claim to be considered its heartland. The simple Ebbsfleet style is particularly well represented here. Importantly the remarkably well laid out Bi cursus type appears almost exclusive to this region and so does another type of monument tightly linked to ceremonial centres – the multiple ring hengiform. We have already seen that these are unusually clustered around the Dorchester upon Thames cursus (see *22*) and probably existed in equal, if not greater, numbers around Maxey SE. They have also been noted around the southern terminal at Fornham All Saints (see *15*) and, since they appear to have originally been barrows, it was suggested that surviving mounds beside the chalkland cursuses could hide further examples. These hardly represent a major surviving resource, however. Paul Ashbee excavated one beside the Greater Stonehenge Cursus (Amesbury 51) and reviewed the evidence from similar excavated sites.[14] He concluded that most causewayed ditch round barrows have only one causeway and that only half a dozen had ditches with more than 5; notably one of these was Rudston LXIII adjacent to cursus A. *None* had multiple ditch circuits. Nor has such evidence emerged as chalkland sites are ploughed out. They have proved to mask single-circuit mini henges like Dorchester IV, V and VI (e.g. Wyke Down) but rarely it seems multi-ditched sites; the Neolithic sites excavated by Terry Manby at Grindale 5km from the Rudston cursuses are rare exceptions. Harding and Lee's survey of henges show that single segmented rings occur from the north of England (e.g. Marley Knowe beside the Milfield 'avenue') to the south (e.g. Handley barrow 27), and that single causewayed rings occur across an even greater distance – from the Moray Firth to Dorset – but that multi-ditched sites of Dorchester type are regionally restricted. Even at the great Forteviot post ring enclosure, with its numerous attendant hengiform sites, none occur. They are, it seems, almost entirely restricted to the vicinity of Midland/East Anglian cursus sites.[15]

It would be foolish to suggest that they are a particular monument type: the ditches record no more than successive redefinition. Nor are they all of Mid/Late Neolithic date. They can define barrows of the Early Neolithic (e.g. Aldwincle, Orton Longueville and Grendon, Northamptonshire) or the Early Bronze Age (e.g. Barnack, Cambridgeshire; West Cotton, Northamptonshire;

Aston on Trent, Derbyshire). Yet the fact that the latter two sites, although significantly later in date, are situated beside cursus or cursus-like monuments emphasises the enduring nature of the regional connection between redefined round barrows and cursuses. Peterborough Ware sherds came from all three of the multi-ditched sites excavated at Dorchester. Radiocarbon determinations confirm that Dorchester XI is as much as three centuries later in date than the cursus, and a similar date returned by the multi-ditched site at Barford (still often described as a henge) suggests a similar separation there, although the adjacent cursus is undated.

Garwood and Barclay have noted a burst of monument refurbishment and building at Dorchester from 3000-2600 BC that contrasts with marked lulls at the nearby complexes of Drayton and Radley that would later witness major barrow building programmes in the Earlier Bronze Age. This was not a response to population shrinkage: recovery of Peterborough Ware in surface scatters from the great expanse of the second terrace gravels and the enlargements of flint scatters dateable to this period both point to expanded settlement.[16] Monument concentration at Dorchester appears to have been deliberate at this period, as we could equally assume it was at Maxey. The widespread Peterborough Ware phenomenon can then be linked to cursuses: from the outset at some sites or in association with refurbishment of round barrows and the construction of pit/pots circles placed at others. Its dynamic expansion far beyond the limits of previous regional pottery traditions may well be linked to the development of pan-regional sanctuaries. Pilgrimage to sites such as Maxey could have acted as a powerful integrative agent amongst heterogeneous groups, aiding the convergence of material culture that we witness. Equally by generating the drive to replication the potential existed for premier sites such as Maxey, set apart in its island fastness, to be eclipsed by more extensive sanctuaries like Dorchester that encompassed whole landscapes, within the duration of a single pottery tradition. As noted with regard to the Nenets' great sanctuary on Vaygash Island, minor sites and complexes of Barford type may represent local foci imitating the major examples to be found at, or around, the premier sanctuaries.

THE GREAT SITES

The picture of cult-paradigm site development, coupled with pilgrimage, as the main motors behind the cursus and Peterborough Ware phenomena in the heartland of their distribution, offers some useful insights. There is no doubt that this was a period of major change – ideological as well as social. But whatever its validity for the Midland and East Anglian region, it completely excludes the mega sites in Dorset, Wiltshire and Eastern Yorkshire. Their difference must be addressed.

A glance at the work estimates for the two greatest complexes – Rudston and Cranborne Chase – flawed as they inevitably are, suggests a huge inflation of the labour force. This is not just a consequence of their vastly greater dimensions; they were also it seems far more monumentally constructed. But it is not just size and monumentality that sets them apart. The landscape of 'orbiting' lesser monuments examined at Dorchester upon Thames and noted elsewhere (e.g. Buscot; Dumfries; Thornborough) seems to be missing. Except for the Lesser Cursus at Stonehenge, 'orbiting' minor sites are of little more than long enclosure size. On Cranborne Case and the Yorkshire Wolds it seems the focal monuments dominated their regions mentally and physically.

The principles on which these two complexes were laid out appear to have been significantly different: in Dorset the cursuses were abutted so as to produce a single monument of great length that was aligned on, and incorporated, two long barrows; at Rudston the cursuses were laid out across each other and nearby long barrows were totally ignored. The Dorset complex lacked any clear focus; that at Rudston is focused onto a narrow zone of the valley floor around the great monolith. Seemingly the builders had different objectives. Yet in both places the monuments are equally recognizable as cursuses, dip into and out of valleys when adjacent ground was far more level, and have monumentalised terminal banks. There was clearly an underlying common ritual 'grammar' that was adjusted to local circumstances. Other shared patterns may clarify their relationship.

As with Fornham All Saints, it is most productive to focus on anomalies. The most obvious is the pronounced curvature of Rudston A just below the crest of Rudston Wold. There is no visible junction to suggest phased construction. In fact quite the opposite – the cursus curves evenly around to the terminal. There is only one obvious parallel for such a pronounced dog-leg – on the Gussage arm of the Dorset Cursus at least 400 weary kilometres away (*68*). This seems an absurd distance across which to seek parallels but it is worth recalling that Rudston lies just within the outer limits of the Ebbsfleet Peterborough Ware distribution that also covers Dorset. If pots – or the ideas governing them – travelled as far why should not the ideas underlying cursus form? First we must assess the importance of these dog-leg features. Unusual they may be, but are they any more than surveying mishaps?

We have already seen, when discussing potential solar alignment, that the dog-leg on the Gussage arm of the Dorset Cursus can not be explained in terms of loss of alignment on the long barrow as the builders came into the lee of the hill. Quite the opposite: the builders had been off target for some considerable distance. The curvature was, it seems, deliberately contrived. Examination of the

SACRED LANDSCAPES

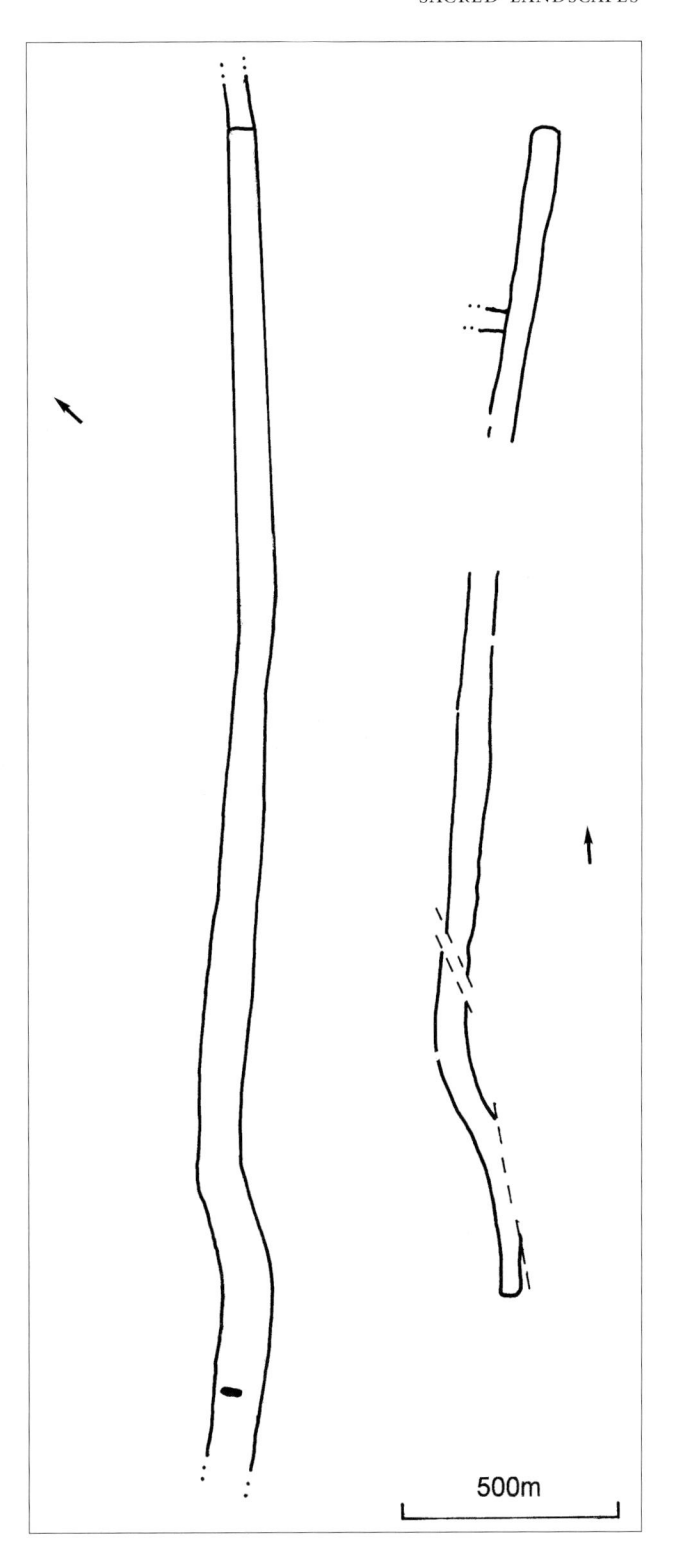

68 Rudston A (right) and the northern half of the Gussage cursus (left): coincidence or replication?

500m

ground along the line of cursus A at Rudston delivers a quite different answer, as Chapman's GIS progressions along the site clearly demonstrate. There, as the cursus climbs from the valley bottom, the terminal on the Wold Top is invisible. It only comes into view near the dog-leg. An error could well then have been corrected here, assuming either that the terminal had already been laid out or that the location was already a site of some significance. It was certainly significant later. Of the seven burials found by Canon Greenwell when he trenched the terminal bank, two of four in a vertical grave stack under the south-western corner mound were accompanied by Beakers. This remains unprecedented: single Beaker burials have been found along former side bank lines at Drayton South and Curriestanes, but no more.[17]

If the idea of cult-paradigm site replication applied to the anomalous features of Fornham, Maxey and Dorchester has any relevance here it would seem to indicate that Rudston A was the model. There is a major objection, however: whereas Rudston A terminates on the hilltop immediately after the dog-leg, the Gussage monument does not. It runs on for a further 2.8km crossing another valley. The hilltop is nevertheless covered in a tangle of ditches of Iron Age date, one of which beside the long barrow suspiciously alters direction slightly to cross the cursus at a near right angle. It is not inconceivable that this obscures an earlier terminal – one, like the Bottlebush terminal, that was superseded as the cursus was extended. Only excavation will tell but there is a striking similarity between cursus A at Rudston and the truncated Gussage site.

Clearly there were no Neolithic plans but the topography of the Allen Valley crossed by this section of the Gussage arm of the Dorset Cursus is not dissimilar to the valley at Rudston. They also share one potentially very similar feature: headwater springs for their river systems. Today in wet weather the headwater spring of the Allen migrates up the valley and appears between the banks of the cursus where it forms a lake overlooked by the occupation spread at the top of the Pleistocene river cliff excavated by Richard Bradley. We do not know if the Allen rose at that point in the Middle Neolithic, or where the main springs were located for the even more variable Gypsey Race, the only running water source in the central wolds of Eastern Yorkshire. Terry Manby considers them to have lain adjacent to the valley crossing of Rudston A. Certainly the acute right-angled turn of the valley at that point is likely to have generated the appropriate hydrological force, and increased flow is indicated by the capacity of the stream to support dual channels just 150m downstream. If this were the case, the great monolith on the spur at Rudston would have occupied a position comparable to that of the occupation scatter across the Gussage cursus. It is also interesting that Ros Cleal, reporting on pottery from the Gussage scatter and the adjacent area, noted that the only material in the Early Neolithic Eastern (Grimston) Style came from a deep pit excavated by Pitt-Rivers on Handley Hill overlooking this part of the cursus. The pit was stepped as if to hold a post and also contained dismembered human and ox bones. Such pottery, prevalent around Rudston, is here considerably further west and south than expected. Clearly there are too many unknowns here and the distance separating the sites is huge but we should not forget the partial nature of our distribution maps. Intervening sites in locations such as the Gogmagog Hills of Cambridgeshire where evidence of ritual activity has emerged, may yet furnish stepping stones.[18]

There are also tantalising hints of more local replication. As noted earlier when discussing avenues (chapter 8), the Kennet Avenue at Avebury possesses puzzling dog-legs at each end. It also has an occupation site set across its course that can currently only be paralleled by that across the Gussage cursus. Both look out to adjacent circles: Faulkener's circle at the former; the Wyke Down henge at the latter. Both were also areas of headwater springs. Might the Kennet Avenue (or avenues, since there is a possibility of a gap along its length in the valley) have represented an attempt to copy the more obvious features of the earlier Dorset site? The great Obelisk within Avebury's southern circle lacks local parallels but, had it pre-dated the great henge and stood independently in conjunction with the avenue, would have challenged the Rudston monolith.

Whether or not we are witnessing replication of architectural elements – however blunderingly initiated – that were sanctified by their presence at major sanctuary sites, the fact remains that these mega sites each represent a quantum leap in manpower terms. Either vastly greater numbers of people were assembled than appears to have been necessary to construct say the Dorchester upon Thames cursus, or the workforce was engaged for far longer. Both scenarios have major implications. Put simply, is this conceivable for the probable size and duration of Neolithic gatherings? Phased construction, suggested in Dorset by the awkward linking of straight sections of monument, renders this more manageable but the manpower requirements remain huge. We often rather uncritically assume monument construction was undertaken spontaneously (even enthusiastically!) by Neolithic populations driven by corporate religious zeal. This owes more than a little to erroneous notions of how medieval cathedrals were built and has been encouraged by the association of monument building with Late Neolithic Grooved Ware-using groups whose ideology precluded the marking of individual status at death. Thus it has been possible to talk of complexes such as Stenness/Brodar in Orkney as sacred centres fulfilling integrative functions for acephalous societies.[19] Cursus layout, as we have seen, often suggests something quite different – careful planning and close supervision of the work teams. This has more in common with the engagement of tribute labour by specialists. It could point to the use of ritual to bolster individual power.

12

SACRED SITES AND POWER – TRANSFORMATION IN THE NORTH

'There's such divinity doth hedge a king'
Hamlet 4.5.123

Religious monuments are vital theatres. Without them an individual claiming divine/ancestral sanction for the exercise of power appears vulnerably mortal. By contrast the Pharaoh entering the vast temple complex at Karnak to escort Amun to the Luxor temple at the great Opet festival, or the Byzantine emperor officiating alone, save for the patriarch, in the great soaring nave of the Hagia Sophia, was set apart; reinvested with divine authority as much by the setting as by the rituals. And that need not have taxed the ingenuity of the ruler. Charlemagne legitimised his theatrical elevation as the new 'Emperor of the Romans' by constructing the palatine Chapel at Aachen as a close copy of St Vitale at Ravenna while Prince Vladimir followed the Byzantine route in Kiev. In both cases exotic architecture in general (from palace baths to golden gates), and religious architecture in particular, signified affiliation and distinctiveness.

These examples clearly greatly exceed the level of social development reached in Middle Neolithic Britain, and in the latter cases reflect the role of peripheries drawing on more advanced core areas. Nevertheless the principles are probably constant: core areas need not have been hugely distant nor the architecture hugely sophisticated, simply highly charged spiritually. In order to assess the potential of cursus complexes, not merely to reflect but to aid, the emergence of individual power we need to ask what social conditions are needed to permit this development and how such 'partisan' centres can be distinguished from neutral sanctuaries?

THE EMERGENCE OF INDIVIDUAL POWER

Autonomy is not lightly surrendered. Village, region or country will resist amalgamation, even in twenty-first-century Europe when there are perceived advantages to the course. Intangible identity is invoked as justification centred on local practices and the status of local structures — witness local government reorganization and the European Union. There is every reason to suppose that such attitudes would be far stronger in the Early Neolithic when group identity centred on a local landscape of clearings, burial monuments and causewayed assembly points. This identity is only likely to have been abandoned in conditions of stress, of which warfare is the most familiar. This was, for instance, claimed by the Iroquois as the *raison d'être* for their remarkable league: to make their lands '… invulnerable to attack from without and to division from within'. Excavations at the causewayed enclosures at Hambledon Hill and Crickley Hill have recovered clear evidence of attack and at Abingdon near Dorchester upon Thames a new defensive ditch circuit appears to have been added. Coupled with the recently recognised evidence for cranial injuries in long barrow skeletal remains,[1] this leaves little doubt that the Early Neolithic was far from a peaceful idyll. Francis Healey has noted a broad correlation between the abrupt abandonment of the great Hambledon Hill enclosure, where extensive excavation revealed only one semi-complete Peterborough vessel and a few scattered sherds, and the construction of the Dorset Cursus 12km away, where it was the sole ceramic from the extensive occupation scatter across the monument's interior. Both are the greatest monuments of their time, and destruction dates for the former (skeletons with leaf-shaped arrowheads in their ribs 3500-3100 and 3600-3300 BC) are not significantly different from a date of 3360-3000 BC from the early secondary silts of the cursus ditch. Similarly Peterborough Ware is rare at Radley (only three sherds came from the Abingdon causewayed enclosure) but the dominant ceramic 10km away at the Dorchester cursus complex.[2]

The emergence of individuals as war chiefs in such circumstances is not unusual but this rarely results in the establishment of hereditary power. Earle, reviewing the global evidence for the evolution of chiefdoms, concluded that the potential for control based purely on military force was quite limited. More was required to ensure stability and that, almost invariably, lay in the claims of individuals to mediate with the ancestors/gods.[3] Thus in the context of African kingdoms we hear: 'Every (Ashanti) lineage is believed to be protected by its own ancestors but it is the dead rulers, the ancestors of the royal lineage, that guard and protect the whole tribe of the chiefdom.'[4] And 'Kingship seems to be inseparable from the belief that the potential for rule is the possession of a particular lineage, and this appears to be much more fundamental than the idea of the kingdom as a

INSCRIBED ACROSS THE LANDSCAPE: THE CURSUS ENIGMA

material possession.'[5] For such claims to possess any credibility certain conditions would need to apply, principally those demonstrating the 'otherness' of the chief/king. At its most extreme this might involve the elevation of outsiders. The foundation myth of Benin, for instance, suggests its royal dynasty was founded by a prince given to its elders at their request from Oyo, a kingdom exercising ritual supremacy over all the Yoruba states. More commonly it is likely to have involved a chief emerging from a lineage set apart in some way: perhaps by good fortune (larger herds; greater capacity for feast giving), but more frequently through its ritual role. Belief that ritual powers are hereditary, and so the monopoly of particular lineages, appears common and much older than kingship.[6] Examples of such lineages include the Iamids, a family of seers who served the cult of Zeus at Olympia, and individual clans of the Quorash who administered particular elements of the sanctuary area at Mecca.

Emerging from such a group, or in alliance with them, an individual 'Big Man' who had gained renown might consolidate his power. Such support would be vital to any claim of ritual mediation. This need not imply the existence of an organised priesthood, merely groups applying esoteric knowledge such as that apparently involved in the laying out of certain cursuses (chapter 9). Nor, unfortunately, need they be archaeologically visible. 'Keepers of the Faith' arranged and conducted ceremonies at the great festivals across the Iroquoian confederacy but possessed no special privileges and wore no special emblem.

The Rudston sanctuary

As the scene for the elevation of a local chief or 'Big Man' as a paramount, an earlier sanctuary with its supra local and integrative role would clearly be advantageous; significantly in early medieval Ireland such complexes appear as inauguration sites for kings. Once accorded this role, subsequent monumentalisation would be expected.

We have seen that, of the two great monument complexes that we have been considering, Rudston has the best claim to be considered as the paradigm. It is there then that we should look for the first signs of the emergence of individual power. They are abundant. Within a radius of 5km of the cursus complex the fields have produced an unparalleled range and quantity of elaborate flint and stone artefacts. Many are truly exquisite items: waisted axes with carefully fashioned concave sides and blades polished to a glass-like smoothness, along with broad, thin, rectangular flint knives so totally polished that all trace of the flake scars have been removed (69). These items also appear as the first significant grave goods with intact burials. Added to them there is, in the same region, a greater concentration of fine polished-stone axes from the Langdale Pikes (Group VI) than anywhere else in the country, despite the fact that the source in

69 Rectangular polished flint knives: larger knife 115mm x 80mm; smaller knife 80mm x 54mm. Martin Green collection

the Lake District lies some 200km away on the other side of the country.[7]

We must of course be careful not to telescope the evidence. This material need not necessarily have all been in use at the same time, nor have been contemporary with the cursuses. In fact the cursus complex has often been wholly disassociated from it on the assumption that the monuments were by that date archaic, redundant features of the landscape. Instead it has been proposed that individual power in the society that developed here was based on secular control of access to 'prestige goods' in contrast to the corporate, ritual-orientated society of contemporary Late Neolithic Wessex.[8] This picture has been very enduring despite the fact that dates are slowly but steadily demonstrating a Middle, not Late, Neolithic date for the appearance of individual burial with prestige artefacts (3500-2900 BC Whitegrounds burial), for the intensification of working on the Langdale axe quarry sites (3500-3100 and 3700-3400 BC) and for most cursuses (3600-3300 BC). Admittedly, the cursus dates apply almost exclusively to southern England; many of those from Scotland, as we have seen, are several centuries earlier.

Sadly the date of the Rudston cursuses remains uncertain. Probably the best indication comes from a pit that cut the primary silts of the eastern ditch of cursus A. It contained a very fine ogival flint arrowhead of the type found with articulated burials under round barrows accompanied by Towthorpe pottery. This was a long-lived tradition that existed alongside classic Earlier Neolithic long barrow burial and continued through the Middle Neolithic. The pit in question may have been dug through a recut in the ditch but that recut may itself represent opportunistic use of an old ditch for Iron Age/Romano-British trackway construction. In any event, it seems certain that the pit forms an element in the remodelling of the cursus; interestingly Peter Mackey noted that an arrowhead, so similar that it could have been produced by the same person, came from one of the pits of the independent double alignment near the Thornborough cursus (chapter 8). He also noted flintwork of typical Early to Middle Neolithic date from the cursus ditches at the two points where they had been sectioned and from an adjacent Earlier Neolithic pit containing Grimston ware. This could all derive from earlier occupation of the site (as at Llandegai) but the absence of such material in fieldwalking away from the cursus gives it an appearance of deliberation. By contrast Grooved Ware is rare near the cursus but clusters some 1-3km distant along the Wold Top. Peter Mackey has also noted a marked reduction in Late Neolithic/Early Bronze Age flintwork in the fields as the cursus is approached. It seems reasonable then to assume that cursus A at least is of Early/Middle Neolithic date, was possibly remodelled by Towthorpe Ware using groups and exercised an increasing 'presence' in the landscape over time that prohibited adjacent mundane activity. The other cursuses may be later in date: cursus C appears to butt onto A, and the ditches of cursus D are interrupted to pass across C.[9]

One element of the great sanctuary site, however, bids to be considered much earlier – the great monolith. At 7.7m tall this is a stone without peer. The Devil's Arrows in the Vale of York (5.5m, 6.7m, 6.9.m), the Watch Stone in Orkney (5.6m) and the destroyed Obelisk at Avebury (6.4.m) are perhaps the nearest parallels. These have little in common with moderately sized outliers to stone circles. In fact the Devil's Arrows more closely resemble the posts set up in the Mesolithic on the Wiltshire downland where Stonehenge would much later rise. Strikingly the great monolith at Rudston appears to lie in a landscape set apart: the Rudston and possible Denby long barrows lie on the edge of visibility 2.5km from cursus A and are largely invisible from the other cursuses (GIS viewshed transects in Chapman 2005). And they, and the Kilham long barrow (a further 2km west), are the only Earlier Neolithic monuments within the vicinity of Rudston. The numerous other long barrows for which the Wolds are famous lie well away (70). This seems strange if the monolith is indeed an Earlier Neolithic element. But the fact that the cursuses effectively box it in makes it improbable that it was a later addition, particularly as that would seem to have necessitated dragging the stone across at least one of their ditch lines.

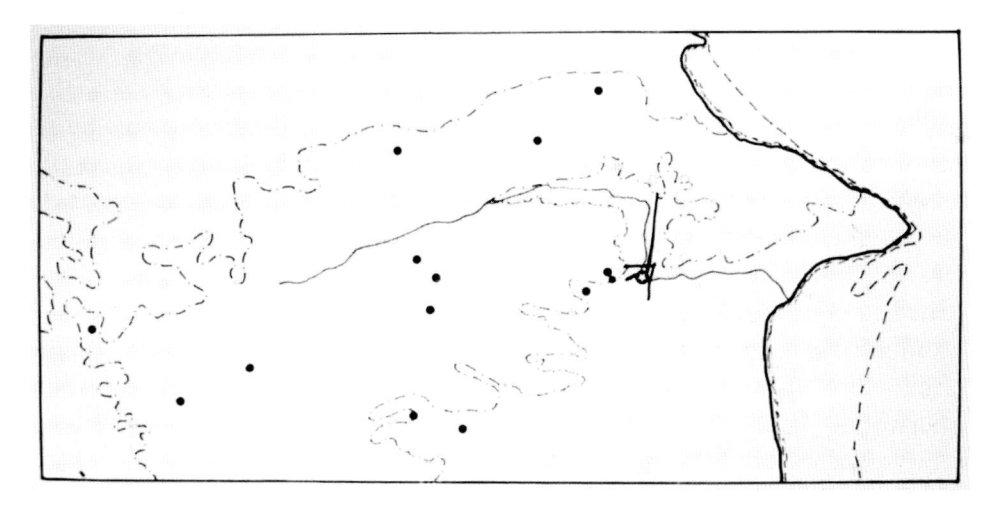

70 Long barrow distribution and the Rudston complex. Theoretical Neolithic coastline shown by dashed line. After Manby 1988

Might it instead have been a pre-existing feature respected by Earlier Neolithic groups who built their long barrows away from its confines? Along the Gypsey Race stream between Rudston and Bridlington there is clear evidence for Mesolithic occupation and the former existence of a substantial bay where it met the sea would have made it highly attractive to hunter-gather groups; no other such inlet existed for 60km north or south.[10] A post set up overlooking the capricious seasonal springs of the Gypsey Race could have generated a powerful and inviolate inter-regional hierophany, and been subsequently replaced in stone. If seasonal springs – albeit of the sole water source for the entire central Wolds – seem unlikely sources for awe, it is worth recalling the name of the river – Gypsey. This has a specific local meaning that Daniel Defoe encountered on his tour through England:

> The country people told us a long story here of gipsies which visit them in a surprising mannere … at certain seasons, for *none knows when it will happen*, several streams of water gush out of the earth with great violence, spouting up a huge heighth, being really natural … fountains; that they make a great noise, and, joining together, form little rivers, and so hasten to the sea. … the country people have a notion that whenever those gipsies, or, as some would call 'em, vipseys, break out, there will *certainly ensue* either famine or plague.[11] (author's italics)

Superstitious awe in the eighteenth century AD may have had a long ancestry; placing the church at Rudston beside the monolith suggests it, at least, still had strong pagan associations in Saxon times. We have, of course, no way of knowing whether the Gypsey Race ever behaved in this way at Rudston in the Neolithic. Indications that it may have done comes from a combination of features: restriction of the valley and its right angles turn at that point, multiple springs feeding the drained wetland just to the east of cursus A and the geomorphological evidence for increased flows downstream.[12]

Axes

Mark Edmonds has draw attention to the axe-like shape of the monolith (*71*). Whether deliberately selected or fortuitous, it is unlikely to have escaped attention during the Neolithic when, unencumbered by the eclipsing church, it imperiously towered over the valley. Powerful male and female elements may have been perceived in the conjunction of monolith and springs at Rudston, conceivably elevated to that union of sky and earth so familiar from creation myths. In such circumstances axes could be predicted to have attained major symbolic significance at the site. It is unlikely to be coincidental then that the eastern wolds area centred on Rudston has produced probably the greatest density of axes recorded in this country. Lake District axes (Group VI) are overwhelmingly concentrated in an area of some 20km radius from the monolith, while Cornish axes (Group I), Graig Lwyd axes (Group VII) and edge-polished flint axes are even more tightly clustered around it and to the east. The latter is explicable given local preferences: good-quality flint is abundantly available from the Flamborough Head cliff exposures. Stone axe concentrations are not.[13]

Even more striking than the huge numbers of Lake District axes (VI) that had to be brought the 200km and more across the Pennines, are the salients that the Rudston/Bridlington concentrations represent in the contained southern and Midland distribution patterns of Cornish (I) and North Wales (VII) axes. They point to strong distant attraction extending into the hinterland of these distantly sourced axes. It cannot be explained simply in terms of ease of coastal communication: Group I axes are found in considerable numbers in East Anglia but Group VII implements must have been brought overland to Rudston. Such distant attraction goes well beyond what might be expected of a simple chiefdom where territories were probably in the range of 10-40km diameter to judge from North European bronze stylistic zones and anthropological review.[14] If the ideology centred on the Rudston monolith was linked in some way to the axe this might be explicable. Certainly a symbolic role appears more credible than a practical/economic one generated by a dense population centre, given the distances involved and the lack of visible reciprocal commodities. Nor need it have excluded the Gypsey Race. The fact that the spring of the temperamental stream migrated westwards up the Great Wold Valley during wet seasons may have

71 Rudston – the monolith in the churchyard

mythically linked it to the long journey west across the Howardian Hills, past the Devil's Arrows or Thornborough cursus, up Wensleydale and on to Windermere and Langdale. It is not uncommon for the ultimate source of mythologised rivers to be sought in distant, sacred mountains, however geographically implausible.

Speculative though this is, it does help us to appreciate the possible 'sense of place' that generated the cursus complex. Yet it still need point to little more than a neutral pan-regional sanctuary. Offerings were, for instance, abundant at Delphi within a restricted artefact range (e.g. tripods, armour). If we are correct to conclude from the size, isolation and labour demands of the monuments that Rudston is qualitatively different from sites such as Dorchester upon Thames, we need to seek other archaeologically detectable ways of confirming this. To do so we must turn to sites where the evidence is either historically supported or less ambiguous.

SACRED SITES AS CENTRES OF POWER

Adam of Bremen in AD 1070 described the great pagan sanctuary at Gamla Uppsala in Sweden where a festival was held 'every nine years common to all the lands of Sweden.' Yet in addition to the temple, spring and grove that he describes in horrified detail, there were also halls and huge royal burial mounds constructed during the sixth century AD that his informants either failed to mention or he chose to ignore. They were not an aberration of the Migration Period; halls and burial mounds continued to be built into the Viking period. Historical sources, from the Ynglinga Saga to Beowulf, confirm that this was the royal seat of the house of Svea. It may have originated as a neutral sanctuary site but its subsequent pan-regional importance undoubtedly favoured its adoption as centre of power. Halls and burial mounds proclaim this.[15]

Chavin de Huantar in the northern highlands of Peru, as we have seen, emerged as a pre-eminent inter-regional cult centre in the Early Horizon (850-200 BC). Burger and others have proposed that pilgrimage led to the adoption of Chavin structural and iconographic patterns at local centres and that this initiated a huge multi-focal interaction field, extending at its zenith a linear distance of 950km. This was not an egalitarian phenomenon however. Unlike most earlier ritual architecture that had emphasised communal rituals, the cult focus at Chavin — a decorated menhir — was hidden within a labyrinth of passages under the temple. This strongly suggests restricted elite access. Pilgrim involvement was confined to the open plazas and terraces fronting the temple. The presence of a few rich graves containing exotic materials, obtained through the pan-regional network and inscribed with Chavin iconographic devices, clearly indicated that operation of the temple went hand in hand with elite dominance. Since the pattern is repeated at local centres, Burger has suggested: ' … regional leaders appreciating that egalitarian norms were embedded in the fabric of localised ideologies, intentionally encouraged the adoption of the Chavin cult in order to justify circumventing the long standing conventions prohibiting the unequal appropriation of goods for personal gain.'[16]

Chavin then furnishes a picture of elite emergence through dominance of a pan-regional cult site, and Uppsala probably likewise. Archaeological evidence for this lies in ritual restriction, elite residence, rich burials and the presence of exotic items from a wide interaction field. Burial and settlement are usually proscribed at neutral inter-regional sanctuaries.

There is much here that chimes with the situation at Rudston. The area around the monolith appears cut off by the cursuses, great burial mounds akin to those at Uppsala follow the course of the Gypsey Race to its rare, seasonal uppermost source, and a range of fine artefacts manufactured from distinctive local flint are concentrated in the vicinity. Elite residences and aggregations of population are difficult to record on the ploughed lands of the Yorkshire chalk. Nevertheless, settlement features (occasional or permanent) have been extensively recorded along the Wold Top immediately downstream from the sanctuary, and the massive flint scatter at Grindale provides even clearer evidence. There Tess Durden's careful fieldwork has revealed workshop areas indicated by concentrations of partially finished or broken high-status artefacts within the scatter.[17] The principal types – rectangular polished flint knives and ripple-flaked oblique arrowheads – may belong to the succeeding Late Neolithic when Grooved Ware was the predominant ceramic but that would not prevent association with the cursus complex, quite the opposite. Uppsala and Chavin demonstrate that an ideology focused upon a pan-regional sanctuary may form the bedrock for prolonged elite dominance.

A further example helps us to see the process by which neutral sanctuaries might become partisan centres. Amongst the pre-Christian Slavs, cult centres were simultaneously tribal centres or places very close to them. Radogosc in the lands of the Redars was one such: 'a temple standing alone within a triangular stronghold, adjacent to a lake and surrounded by a forest untrodden by the natives.' Adam of Bremen adds that this was the most powerful of the Slavic centres from which the Redars controlled the territories not only of the four tribes of the Lutizen Union (for which the temple appears to have been the seat of the assembly) but the whole area stretching from the Oder to the Elbe and the Havel to the Baltic – an area some 150km in diameter. The Redars considered themselves to be the most powerful of people occupying the centre of the world. Control of the sanctuary of a widely recognised deity undoubtedly helped in acquiring political leadership, although that dominance may have arisen in part from success in warfare, as the magnification of Amun by the New Kingdom dynasty of Theban nome governors in Egypt testifies. In the vastly less centralised contexts of Slavonic Radogosc – or Neolithic Rudston – however, such dominance could cause tension. In AD 1057 two of the four tribes of the Lutizen Union seceded for this reason. To the obvious sources of resentment that may have underlain this, we might add the often enormous tribute payable to such sanctuaries – in the case of the shrine of Sventovit in Arcona this was apparently paid annually from all Slavic territories since the god had attained primacy over all other deities.[18]

It is interesting that the area controlled from Radogosc corresponded roughly in size to northern England from the Peak District to Cumbria – an area across which Terry Manby has detailed remarkable similarlities of prestige artefacts and across which Lake District axes were moved in huge numbers. The four cursuses boxing in the Rudston monolith might similarly point to joint control of the sanctuary; unlike the Dorset and Maxey cursuses there is no question of any of these being additions aimed at extending and magnifying an earlier site. The splendid isolation of the site is also telling: other possible cursuses – but lacking the all important identifying terminals – lie 20-30km west at Fimber and at Kirby Underdale but the nearest certain sites are 80km away in the Vale of York.[19]

The Wolds area is also distinctive in possessing evidence of separate Early Neolithic populations from at least the mid-fourth millennium BC: one utilising

Grimston pottery and burying their dead in corporate-disarticulated fashion under long barrows; the other using Towthorpe pottery and buying their dead in corporate-articulated fashion, increasingly with grave goods, under round barrows. Causewayed enclosures, that in the south acted as integrative communal facilities for scattered communities, are missing. Here we can perhaps witness the seeds of stress that we earlier suggested might most readily explain the willingness of autonomous groups to accept the power of a paramount chief. Adoption and magnification of a venerable, neutral sanctuary site to sanction such elevation would have distinct advantage: both nullifying apparent sectional interest and, by seizing control of the past, the supernatural and (if the springs were pivotal) the natural, creating new principles of legitimacy. A period of confederate control of the sanctuary and attendant assemblies, akin to that of the Lutizen Union or the Amphictyonic Council of Delphi, could have eased the passage to individual power. Councils in confederate situations have the capacity to attract assembly from a vast area as we know from the Iroquois. Religious sanction would increase the motivation and is likely to have been associated with offerings (e.g. from all commoners at ceremonial and ritual occasions in Tahiti, from all Athenian territories to Eleusis, and from all Slavonic territories to Arcona). Movement from a dominant lineage to a dominant individual in such a context – eased perhaps if that individual arose from the lineage controlling the sanctuary – would open up access to considerable resources.

The site might witness further embellishment following the adoption of individual power. The island of Kana'i in Hawaii furnishes a clear example of such magnification. Timothy Earle records 122 heiau (elaborate stone platforms with enclosing walls) on the island, of which 28, fairly regularly spaced along the coast, are considered large enough to have hosted the ceremonies of the ruling chiefs. The residence of the ruling paramount chief had five large heiau. By contrast two other communities had two, and all others just one. Historically their use is well documented: as theatres for ceremonies of war when the paramount chief prepared for conquest, and for the annual ceremonies when the paramount acted the part of the fertility god. The latter facilitated the collection of tribute to support the chief, since a figure of the god was taken from the heiau to each local community shrine to collect annual contributions.[20]

ELABORATE ARTEFACTS

The size of the Rudston sanctuary and the abundance of high-quality flint 'prestige' aretefacts locally leaves little doubt that the two are linked – the monuments being used in some way to justify overt displays of status. But the choice of materials and forms for these items remain confusing. Prestige goods are noted as items fashioned from exotic materials and finished to the highest standards of craftsmanship. Yet the artefacts in question here are almost exclusively of local material (Flamborough Head flint, Whitby jet and antler) and, in the case of the axes, polished only across the blade area. Suggestions that partial finish resulted from rapid production of new forms to ensure the exclusivity of the new elite in the face of lower lineage emulation meets the difficulty that scarcely any variation is evident in the basic axe/adze forms over perhaps as much as half a millennium. Even more puzzling is the fact that Cumbrian axes (VI), that are known to have been circulating at the same time, were *fully* polished but are *never* found as grave goods in the new individual burials. An answer may lie with prototypes and antecedents.

Cumbrian axes had been circulating for a considerable period and, had they become tightly associated with a cosmology centred on the Rudston complex, it may have been unacceptable to include them as grave goods. Their role in other words remained restricted to the mythologies of the sanctuary. There is nothing to suggest a long ancestry for the waisted flint axe types (Seamer axes and Duggleby adzes), however (*72*). Simple inventiveness in the search novelty is possible but their concentration in Eastern Yorkshire, particularly in the Rudston region, suggest something deeper – that they are linked to the same ideology that drew so many stone axes there. Production of a waisted axe form in flint is extremely difficult and asymmetric adze blades amongst earlier flint and stone axes are rare. There is little to draw on here. A compelling novel prototype seems to be indicated. Earlier investigators had little hesitation in holding this to be the copper axe. Essentially the Yorkshire burials were seen as poor copies of richer Early Bronze Age ones in Wessex. Piggott's demonstration in 1954 that the burials were Neolithic undermined the idea and dating of the Whitegrounds burial finally scotched it – the axes were circulating at least 700 years before the earliest-known copper items were placed in Beaker burials in Britain *c.*2200 BC.[21]

In Europe, however, copper artefacts were passing along an exchange chain extending from Alpine production centres to the Baltic between about 3400 and 2900 BC, contemporary with the Whitegrounds burial. Might a few have been taken further? Flint axes of distinctive Scandinavian form have been found in Britain and Alan Saville has recently drawn attention to axes of a distinctive marbled flint that are almost certainly of Danish origin. Significantly these have been found almost exclusively along the North Sea coast. Had a very few copper axes also been conveyed to Britain they could be expected to have had a dramatic impact: nothing prior to metallurgy shone like the sun. Regarded perhaps as gifts from the gods they might have been placed in a suitable location – such as the sanctuary at Rudston – where they would occasion veneration rather than

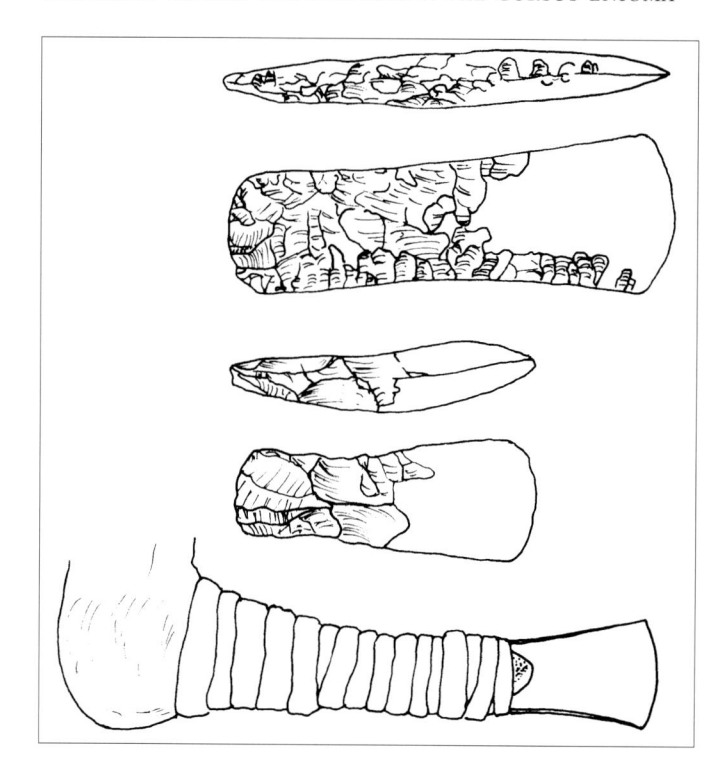

72 Waisted flint axes from York (top) and Willerby Carr (centre) (after Manby 1988). Reconstructed hafting of the Iceman's trapezoidal copper flat axe (bottom) (not to scale)

investigation. Thus, if hafted like the Iceman's axe, only the blade area would show. Is it purely coincidence then that it is this area alone that is polished – and often to a glass-like smoothness – on Seamer and Duggleby implements and that they were made from distinctive red, yellow, pink, orange and mottled flints – the colours of copper? Forms and profiles represent close matches to copper specimens; even the adze profile finds a ready parallel amongst copper axes cast in flat single piece moulds (*73*). Failure to replicate the flat sides of copper axes in flint could be related to their invisibility beneath the hafting of venerated specimens.[22]

We may never find these hypothesised prototypes: they would have been too valuable to be deposited, and later when metallurgy became commonplace and ideologies collapsed, too readily recycled. The lesson of the Iceman, though, is that copper items may have been in circulation long before they were sufficiently common to be placed with the dead and thus turn up in an archaeologically dateable context. We might nonetheless wish for some supporting evidence here.

It is furnished by another artefact type that appears at this time – the polished rectangular flint knife. These are remarkable. Manufactured from very broad flakes, often worked down to an incredible thinness, they have had all the flake scars polished away. Small, remarkably thin specimens were included as grave

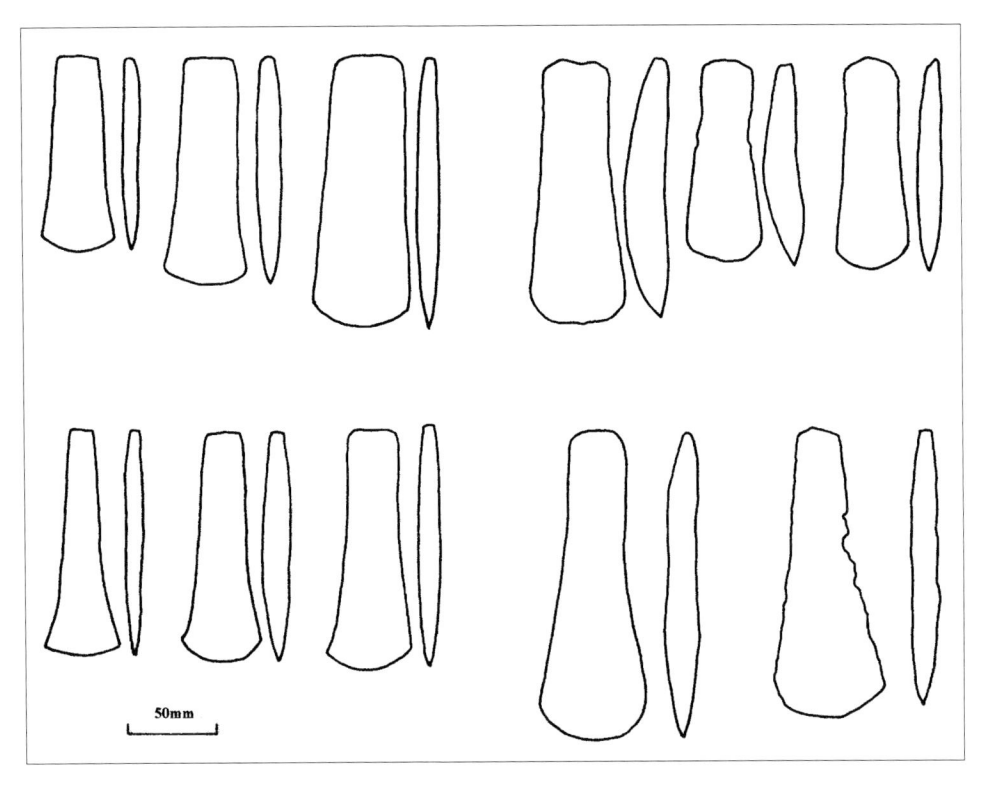

73 Copper trapezoidal axes from Poland and Moravia (left) and waisted flint axes (right)

goods with the new individual burials at Duggleby Howe and Aldro C75 (*c*.3300BC) and larger ones occur as stray finds, overwhelmingly in the great flint scatter at Grindale just to the east of Rudston. Although Tess Durden's careful fieldwork has demonstrated that they were being produced there, their precise dating remains uncertain. They were clearly highly prized items and closely associated with events at Rudston; unlike the round discoidal knife form to which they are technologically related, their distribution is closely contained – none have been definitely found in Yorkshire more than 15km from Rudston. Again the huge care taken in their production tells us they were greatly valued and, in the absence of any very convincing developmental sequence, we must presume a compelling prototype. The closest is the copper rectangular axe (*74*). These strange, often very thin, axes circulated alongside copper trapezoidal axes in eastern and northern Europe but unlike them may have been only lightly hafted for fine, plane-like, woodworking.

Just as the rarity of copper in Europe ' … is indicated not just by the small number of metal objects in archaeological contexts but by the imitations of copper objects which are widespread'[23] so polished rectangular flint knives and waisted

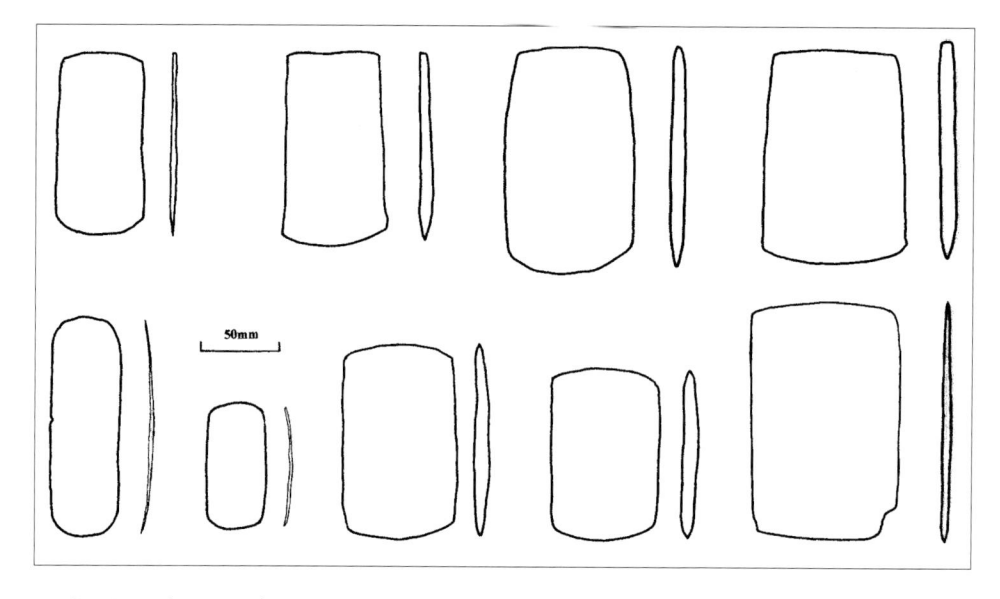

74 Continental rectangular copper axes (top) and rectangular polished flint knives (bottom)

flint axes furnish valuable evidence for the presence of copper axes in Eastern Yorkshire. The fact that great care was lavished on fabricating these copies, and that they represent the two dominant prestige items in the new 'package' that emerged there in the Middle Neolithic, suggests they were instrumental to the change that followed. As Mary Helms has pointed out an imitation speaks more strongly than an import about the local significance accorded to 'foreign' prestige goods.[24] It does not follow that this was a secular 'prestige good' economy unassociated with the earlier monolith/cursus sanctuary since the distribution of prestige artefacts is closely concentrated around it. Rather, as in Meso-American and Mississippian chiefdoms, it seems likely that 'special wealth objects were ... associated with powers that both symbolised and encapsulated the elite's divinity, or at least non local legitimacy.'[25] Possession of exotic and apparently magical copper axes might most readily mark individuals out as close to the gods and qualitatively different if their lineage were custodians of an inter-regional sanctuary rooted in an axe-related mythology. Control of both ceremonial and prestige items was vital to a perception of 'otherness' and membership of such an elite could be signalled by possession of a flint copy of one of the copper axes.

Burial

The nature of the power that emerged in Eastern Yorkshire is demonstrated most clearly not by the enormous size of the Rudston cursus complex, nor by the

75 Duggleby Howe

exceptional craftsmanship lavished on the production of flint prestige artefacts, but by the great barrow of Duggleby Howe (75). Significantly this stands close to the highest wet-weather spring of the Gypsey Race, some 23km upstream from the Rudston where it was suggested the main springs were located. Its great mound, 6m high and 38m in diameter, stands at the centre of a great enclosure 370m in diameter. The latter is unexcavated but the barrow was dug into by Mortimer in 1890. Over a period of six weeks he found a central grave shaft nearly 3m deep with a vertical sequence of bodies extending up from it to the top of the inner mound. A similar vertical sequence ran up from an adjacent shallow grave. In addition a body lay on the old land surface and 53 cremations had been placed around, but mostly above, these inhumations. This complex mesh of burials has been used to support a stratified sequence of burial development through the Middle and Late Neolithic.[26]

There are problems with this however.[27] The cremations, held to be the final burials on the site were not confined to the upper layer (some were as much as 2m down from the top of it) while the four burials held to have been secondaries dug through the mound above 'prestige burials' G and C very unusually did not disturb them or each other (76). Even more striking is the fact that both these 'secondary' burial stacks comprised a child (lower) and an infant (upper). It seems most unlikely that mortality patterns would coincide so closely. Coupled with the evidence for the depths of some of the cremations this suggests the burials in the mound cannot be separated; only the burials in the deep shaft seem to

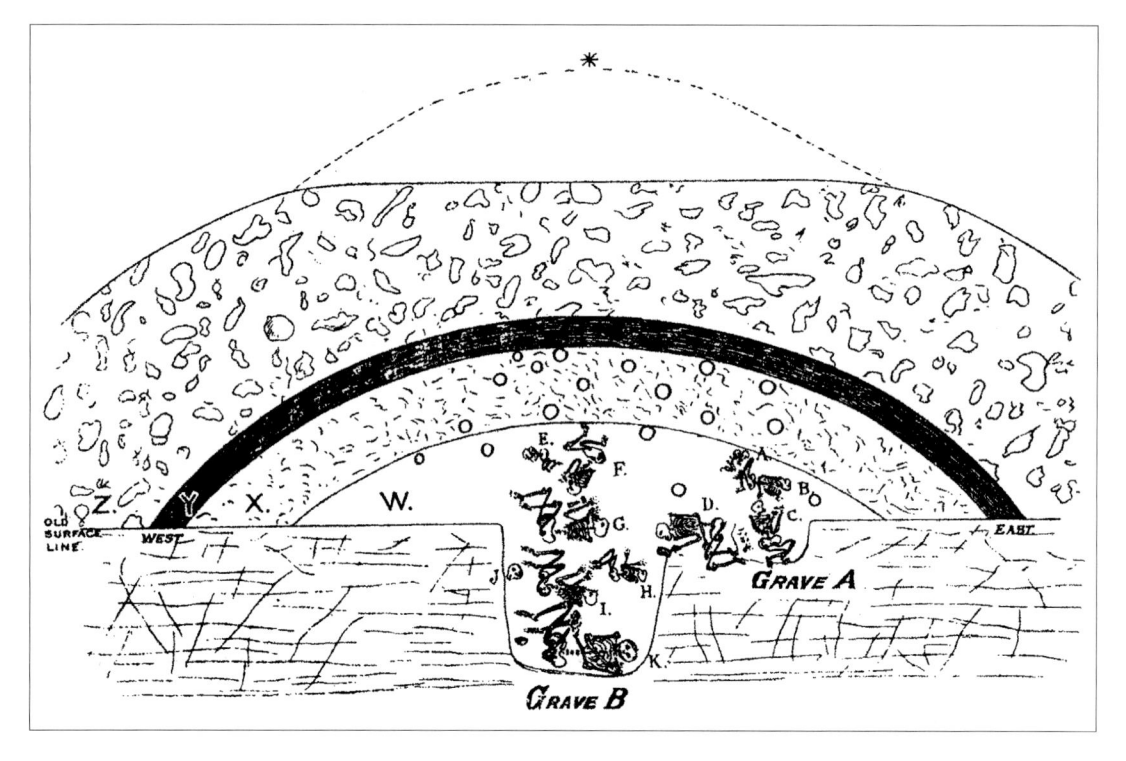

76 Mortimer's section drawing of the burials at Duggleby Howe; circles represent cremations

belong to an earlier phase. But why might so many burials have been made at the same time? One explanation could relate to the extravagance of the prestige goods: burial G – a waisted and highly polished flint adze, an antler macehead and a kite-shaped arrowhead; burial D – a fine highly polished flint knife; burial C – 6 transverse arrowheads, 12 boar's tusk blades, 2 beaver's teeth and a massive bone skewer pin. These are exceptional, as are the numbers of cremation burials. Together they hint at a global form of ostentation not uncommon at the outset of paramount kingship – retainer sacrifice. It occurs in circumstances not wholly dissimilar to those of Middle Neolithic Eastern Yorkshire from Cahokia to the Steppes.[28] Herodotus described such a funeral for a Scythian ruler in the fifth century AD:

> In the open space around the king they bury one of his concubines, first killing her by strangulation, and also his cupbearer, his cook, his groom, his lackey, his messenger, his horses, firstlings of all his possessions.... After this they set to work to raise a vast mound above the grave.... When a year has gone by, further ceremonies take place. Fifty of the best of the late king's attendants are taken and are strangled along with fifty of the most beautiful horses. (IV, 71-2)

There is much here that recalls Duggleby Howe: comparable infant and child burials over adult burials G and C seem more likely to result from a common rite than coincidental family/kin group mortality patterns; the grave goods of C are worn unlike those of G which were centrally placed and possessed a macehead; and the number of cremations can only be paralleled at the ceremonial sites of Stonehenge and Dorchester upon Thames.

Duggleby Howe is not, of course, the only such large round barrow on the Yorkshire Wolds. Willie Howe and Wold Newton 284 closely resemble it in size and lie close together on the floor of the Great Wold Valley, adjacent to another seasonal spring location just 4km from cursus D at Rudston. The only comparably sized mound within sight of Rudston (South Side Mount) was set beyond its confines and near the Wold Top.

POWER IN THE NORTH

However concentrated their distribution is in Eastern Yorkshire, waisted flint axes and rectangular polished flint axes are not confined to that region. In northern Britain scattered examples can be found from Lincolnshire to Aberdeenshire in a distribution pattern that emphasises the eastern seaboard. Waisted flint axes can often be identified as imports from Eastern Yorkshire by virtue of the distinctive flint used in their production. Discovery of a very distant outlier of an Aberdeenshire speciality – a carved stone ball – near Bridlington, points to a process of coastal exchange. But is that sufficient explanation? Unfortunately, except for Terry Manby's invaluable work on the northern English material we lack the detailed distribution maps that would enable us to better understand the patterning of stray finds. It does seem, however, that the Borders of Scotland may have been of particular significance. There in 1990 at Biggar Common in Lanarkshire, a waisted flint axe of Yorkshire derivation along with an atypical laurel-leaf point was found in an apparent burial pit dug into the end of an earthen long barrow. This very closely resembles burials in Eastern Yorkshire; that at Whitegrounds near Malton (dated *c.*3500-2900 BC) was similarly placed over an earlier long barrow and was accompanied by a waisted axe. Discovery of a further waisted flint axe at Biggar suggests the area may have been of some importance.[29]

South of Yorkshire in the Peak District there is a far more marked concentration of prestige artefacts, although interestingly no waisted axes appear to have been found here. Polished rectangular flint knives are tightly concentrated near Arbor Low whilst, as in Yorkshire, the round form are more widely scattered. At Biggin, not far from Arbor Low, lies the important round barrow Liff's Low. Beneath the mound lay a crouched burial of a male accompanied by two boar's tusk blades, two fine edge polished axes, an antler macehead, two lozenge arrowheads, a polished-edge knife, a serrated blade, two 'spearhead'/laurel-leaf blanks, three pieces of red ochre and a unique miniature vessel, decorated in Peterborough style but in form suggesting an ill-achieved copy of a European *Trichterbecherkultur* flask. The first three groups of items immediately recall those placed with burials at Duggleby Howe. Like the burial at Biggar Common then this appears to have been an outlier of the Yorkshire pattern. But that does it scant justice. Despite extensive barrow digging by Thomas Bateman and others no comparable burial has ever been found. In its area this burial must have been revolutionary. The multitude of possessions were clearly signalling status (and presumably power) in an unprecedented way to the living and to the gods. It must mark something more dramatic than simple emulation yet it is inconceivable that here, and perhaps at Biggar, we have evidence of direct political control from Eastern Yorkshire. Local chiefdom levels of political alliance may extend military power some 20-40km through raiding but nothing approaching 200-300km. Ritual or sacred power had the capacity to generate alliances beyond the local, however. And individuals at a distance using an ideology developed around the Rudston sanctuary to legitimise their assumption of individual power (as has been suggested for Chavin) would require access to the exotic wealth items that delineated their affiliation and 'otherness'.

It is equally, of course, not beyond the bounds of possibility that warfare was used on occasions to extend such influence. We too easily regard distant ventures as the preserve of state societies on the verge of empire. Long-distance raiding aimed at establishing hegemony and eliciting tribute may be practised by societies at quite simple levels of development. Fortification – the standard archaeological test – is an excellent indicator of endemic, local warfare but a very blunt instrument in this context. It is unlikely to record sudden irregular raids like those that drew armies from Bamburgh to Chester and from Anglesey to Northumbria during the formative years of the northern Anglo Saxon kingdom. In each case tribute was exacted, and at such a distance it must have taken the form of walking tribute – cattle.[30] There is little here inappropriate to the Middle/Late Neolithic when walking tribute might have taken the form of cattle or labour. Cumbrian axes and the Rudston cursuses may represent the material outcomes. Certainly refinement of a range of arrowheads at this time does little to suggest pacifism. Nor need Cumbrian axes have fulfilled a purely symbolic role.

Interestingly at neither Biggar nor Biggin is there evidence of a nearby cursus, although it is just possible that medieval field walls in the latter case obscure the evidence. Equally, as both are upland locations, it is possible that they occupied niches equivalent to Duggleby Howe with ceremonial monuments placed much further downstream. The Meldon Bridge post enclosure lies some 15km east of Biggar, and it is not inconceivable that Liff's Low lay at the farther end of a transhumance territory that extended from the cursuses on the Trent, a little over 10km further than the distance from Rudston to Duggleby.

13

SACRED SITES AND POWER – EMULATION IN THE SOUTH?

On the face of it the situation south of the Trent appears very different. The cursus complexes – whether of Dorchester or Bi type – resemble each other but not Rudston, and extravagant male burials with Yorkshire prestige goods are absent. Importantly single, all-encompassing pottery styles (Ebbsfleet, Mortlake and Fengate Peterborough Ware) cover the region in contrast to the regionally limited Rudston Peterborough style that appears to have co-existed with an older Towthorpe tradition in Eastern Yorkshire. There are nevertheless background similarities. As we have seen, both long and round burial sites were built particularly along the valley of the Nene. Concentrations of prestige artefacts recalling the clusters near Arbor Low and Rudston also exist along the eastern Fen edge (e.g. waisted flint axes, an antler macehead and a rectangular polished flint knife amongst other items from Burwell). Some individual burials also appear.

A ring ditch 1.5km away from the Dorchester upon Thames cursus at Mount Farm covered an adult male accompanied by an unpolished flint knife, struck flints and sherds of possible Peterborough Ware. Like the Whitegrounds burial in Eastern Yorkshire, it has been dated to 3500–2900 BC and recalls similarly dated burials in the long enclosure at Radley and in a ring ditch at Stanton Harcourt, both of which possessed jet sliders and edge-polished flint knives – classic Yorkshire items.[1] Coupled with primary burials assumed to have been plough-eroded from under the multi-ditched hengiform barrows that were added to the Dorchester upon Thames and other cursus complexes in the Midland/East Anglian region, this suggests significant development. It also suggests, as in the north, that the cursus monument may have been instrumental in the spread of an ideology that justified the magnification of the individual. Evidence of paradigm site replication, probably centred on Maxey/Etton, makes it additionally plausible that these ideas were seeded from the north. Maxey is ideally sited to have received them, whether transmitted by people moving along the eastern seaboard or the Jurassic spine of Lincolnshire.

It may be significant that a Cumbrian axe (Group VI) was found in a pit close to the axial line of the Maxey cursus, but this also lay within the henge circuit and the axe may even have become incorporated in a watering pit of yet later date. Nevertheless, Group VI axes do appear to have been deliberately deposited in the nearby Etton causewayed enclosure. The distribution pattern of these axes appears to record movement along the Trent Valley, the Jurassic ridge and East Anglian 'Icknield' line; virtually none occur around the East Anglian coast. They could well, then, have been exchanged during gatherings at the major cursuses.

Richard Bradley and Mark Edmonds have suggested that they were closely associated with ideas that facilitated the emergence of the individual from the anonymous, collective world of the Earlier Neolithic. The massive expansion in their distributional range was generated they suggest from Eastern Yorkshire during the period 3600-3200 BC when production was being intensively undertaken on the near vertical face of Top Buttress, Pike o' Stickle. Interestingly the waves of their dominating distribution appear to have reached little further than the Thames Valley. Beyond that point it is axes of Group I from Mount's Bay, Cornwall, that dominate.[2] Although predominantly associated with Late Neolithic Grooved Ware-using groups and the great Wessex henges, they are not exclusive to that period. One or two axes of this type were contained in a deposit dated *c*.3600-3400 BC in the great causewayed enclosure at Hambledon Hill on the edge of Cranborne Chase, and Cornish axes dominated at the Maiden Castle causewayed enclosure, although from various other sources.[3] The possibility presents itself then that Group I Cornish axes, with their iconic source area focus in St Michael's Mount, were increasingly produced and deployed in the Wessex area to counter the impact of Cumbrian (Group VI) axes. If so, and the latter did enshrine ideological messages, development of a comparable centre to Rudston might also be predicted. Significantly the first suggestions of clustering amongst Group I axes away from the Land's End peninsula source area occurs in Dorset, particularly around Cranborne Chase where the greatest cursus complex in Britain is situated.

THE DORSET CURSUS — POWER IN THE SOUTH?

We have already seen that the northern section of the Gussage arm of the Dorset Cursus strangely replicates certain features of cursus A at Rudston. There is, however, one very major difference — whereas the Rudston cursuses were laid out with total disregard to nearby long barrows, the Dorset complex was laid to incorporate them. This in fact appears to be a governing feature of cursus sites from the Thames Valley southwards: Dorchester upon Thames and Stadhampton incorporate long enclosures in their side ditches; the Greater Stonehenge Cursus and a long enclosure at Pentridge spatially respects long barrows lying parallel to their eastern terminals; and the Buscot, Long Bredy, Nether Exe and Dorset monuments all terminate beside long enclosures/bank barrows. By contrast, north of the Thames Valley these sorts of configuration are rare. The small long enclosure set across the end of the Barford cursus in Warwickshire is the only clear example; aslant positioning of the long barrow within the northern cursus at Eynesbury in Cambridgeshire is unusual in all areas. As the southern sites were the first to be discovered this relationship has long been central to discussions of cursus use. It indicated that cursuses were later in date than long barrow/long enclosures but linked to them structurally and functionally. Therefore they were places of death along which bones were paraded prior to internment in the long barrow, avenues linking the living and the ancestors, places for mortuary rituals or for the exposure of corpses.

This has all been called into question by radiocarbon dates that indicate that probable prototypes and the earliest cursuses are to found in Scotland where there is no hint of this relationship. And, as we have seen, this northern focus is supported by the paradigm site replication approach that elevates Rudston rather than Dorset as the premier of the two mega complexes. This potential later dating of the southern sites forces us to look at the long mound relationship again. Reminding ourselves that no cursus runs up to a mortuary structure at the end of a long barrow, in the manner of the Kilham and Kemp Howe post avenues, we must ask ourselves why instead several long mound sites were incorporated in the sides of cursuses. Access or continued use would have been impossible. The monuments appear to have been slighted and buried rather than respected and magnified. Is it possible then that these southern cursuses were intended to cut across and through long barrow alignments, and to imprison or obscure their structures? The same process was enacted at Rudston more than 4000 years later when the parish church was built beside the monolith; without our historical knowledge of the process of Christianisation we might easily conclude, as has so often been done with long barrows, that this was an act of respect. The fact that Peterborough Ware is associated with many southern cursuses may be significant since it appears on many long barrow sites in contexts that suggest they were being closed down.

Alignment of the terminals of the Dorset site with neighbouring long barrows on the other hand appears to register respect, particularly as monumental construction of the terminal banks has been likened to replication of these earlier mounds.[4] This may be true – certainly the last 600m of the Pentridge cursus appears to have been deflected to line up with the Pentridge 2a/b long barrow (*17*). But the same monumentalisation occurs at the earlier Bottlebush Down terminal where there are no adjacent long barrows; its corner mounds are still visible after decades of ploughing. Seeking an answer it is instructive to enlarge our view. Following the spring line that is so obviously the focus of the cursus into the next two valley systems – is revealing. Another alignment of long barrows like that on Thickthorn Down occurs on the next ridge to the south (Pimperne, Tarrant Hinton and Tarrant Launceston) and another clustering like that at Pentridge is found to the north (Knap Barrow, Grans Barrow and Rockbourne). Had the cursus reached these, or indeed stopped on Gussage Hill, similar patterns to those currently observed at the ends would be evident. It may be then that both long barrow and cursus builders were aligning on now invisible elements of the landscape – trackways that followed the ridge lines. Interestingly the monumental southern terminal of cursus A at Rudston (the only one at the complex known to have been exaggerated in this way) lines up with the Wold Gate – a ridge route that may stretch back deep into prehistory to judge from the extensive evidence of occupation along its length. This terminal bank had the same corner mound form as those in Dorset yet nearby long barrows were ignored by the builders and there is no indication from aerial photographs that the terminal masked a long barrow. What appears as monumental long barrow replication might as easily be explained as house façade replication. It is worth recalling the large size of the terminal posts at the earlier sites of Claish, Douglasmuir and Dunragit.

Rather than respect, then, we could be witnessing the imposition of a northern cursus-related ideology on a still resistant southern Earlier Neolithic society. That change was already afoot is indicated by the trend towards articulated burial of reduced numbers of people, mostly males, under long barrows. Rather than the 'tangled masses of humanity' under earlier long barrows such as that at Fussell's Lodge (14 males, 15 females, 22 children – all disarticulated), smaller, later barrows covered far fewer burials: Wor Barrow (6 males, 3 of them articulated) and Radley (1 male and 1 female, both articulated). These later barrows are often marked by U-plan ditches akin to small long enclosures in the Thames valley and are strikingly clustered around the great Dorset Cursus. Very significantly these barrows are *not* those imprisoned in the monument. It is possible, as Richard Bradley has suggested, that some were built after the cursus was constructed.[5] Their clustering is in some respects akin to that of Late Neolithic ring ditch sites at Dorchester and Maxey but, since they adhere to the common Cranborne Chase pattern of alignment along ridge tops at the spring line, this may be illusory.[6] It is probably the spring line that was of overwhelming importance to the builders of classic long barrows, small long barrows, the cursus and even Early Bronze Age round barrow cemeteries like Oakley Down.

Nevertheless, it is probably significant that the only burial like those in the Upper Thames Valley came from a round barrow (Handley 26) placed only some 10m from the front of Wor Barrow. Here, although the central inhumation had no grave goods, a second burial just to the west was accompanied by a jet belt slider. Mortlake Peterborough Ware sherds were found at the base of the ditch. Fifty or so metres from the other end of Wor Barrow lay another round barrow. Pitt-Rivers' excavation showed that it had an irregular ditch akin to the 'hengi-form rings' later identified at Dorchester upon Thames. It also produced a sherd of Peterborough Ware from its lower fill.[7] These are in no way comparable to the fine – sometimes extravagant – individual male burials under round barrows in Eastern Yorkshire but they confirm the suspicion that the emergence of this burial tradition was tied to Peterborough Ware and that the receptors on Cranborne Chase were the decendants of those who had introduced short barrows like that at Radley. Less clearly than in Eastern Yorkshire these subtly different long mounds may record divided populations and political manoeuvring. Other, finer, round barrow burials may of course have existed beneath the many barrows ploughed out around the cursus. Perhaps the greatest potential lies in the Wyke Down cemetery and by great good fortune that falls in the land of the indefatigable fieldworker Martin Green who has preserved it from further erosion.[8]

THEATRE OF POWER

Adjacent to the Wyke Down cemetery, at a point overlooking the seasonal spring of the River Allen, a 200m-diameter flint scatter crossed the cursus. Here Peterborough Ware was found. It accompanied a small quantity of animal bone composed chiefly of skull fragments and mandibles in the western ditch. Six of the 27 or so cattle represented by this material were wild species, an unusually high proportion. The presence of two human long bones, perhaps from different individuals, further sets this material apart. Whatever the cultural affiliations of the groups first depositing the bone in the ditch, Peterborough Ware-using groups certainly continued the practice; their pottery appears after 0.5m or so of silt had formed. Activity was not restricted to the ditches. A spread of flintwork covering the interior of the cursus at this point is dominated by scrapers, borers and fabricators suggesting domestic activity. This picture is backed up by evidence of heavy wear on some items and *in situ* flint knapping. On the other hand a polished-edge knife and part of a macehead suggest a high-status element since both are also found with individual burials. Analysis of the results of Richard Bradley's sample excavation across this scatter suggested a fairly clear,

77 The seasonal lake within the Gussage cursus: flint scatter to the left above the Pleistocene river cliff; cursus running through the corner of Firtree Field ahead to the long barrow above. Photograph: Martin Green

possibly cleaned, central area with domestic activity near the eastern ditch. The highest density of burnt flint and tool types occurred there along with three pits of a possible pit circle.[9]

Although strictly secondary to the cursus, this activity was structured by the monument and seems unlikely to have been domestic in any normal sense. Flake densities, as well as magnetic susceptibility and phosphate readings were a fraction of those returned from similar transect sampling at Wilsford Down and King's Barrow Ridge in the environs of Stonehenge.[10] Intermittent small-scale activity seems to better explain the pattern, with a strong ritual element to judge from the bone selection in the western ditch. It is unlikely to be coincidental that on that side the scatter overlooked the sudden drop of a Pleistocene river cliff below which the wet weather spring sporadically produces a lake filling the cursus earthworks.[11] This would have been invisible on the eastern side of the monument along the transect line, and there the flintwork had a more domestic quality (*77*).

If the cursus was built as a huge symbolic house set apart for the 'others' (ancestors or deities) whose roof was the sky itself, what was this 'occupation' debris doing inside it? Nothing like it has been discovered elsewhere. Features within the eastern end of the Springfield cursus produced little flintwork, while the only concentration revealed during stripping for road construction along the line of the Dorchester upon Thames cursus lay outside the monument, between the south-eastern terminal and the river. The probable answer returns us to those questions of power generated earlier by the labour figures for this and the Rudston complex. Taking – and being considered justified in taking – individual power almost certainly required evidence of divine sanction. That is unlikely to have been a once for all event. That legitimation would need to be demonstrated at cyclical events of the types recorded ethnographically and historically as first fruits, sacrifice and sacred marriage. It may even have required regular confirmation. The best known example of the latter is the Heb Sed. In this ceremony, that probably stretched back to the origins of kingship in Egypt, the Pharaoh was required to demonstrate his vigour by running around a large court built to symbolise his realm. Similar cyclical assembly, within a monumental structure with comparable symbolic overtones, might explain the relatively low level of activity recorded by the Dorset Cursus flint scatter. The events witnessed by this material were perhaps triggered by appearance of the seasonal lake or by midwinter sunset but the chosen location may have had a deeper significance – its near central position within the suggested initial section of the Gussage cursus recalls the central 'activity' space within earlier, prototypical 'halls' such as Claish and Balbridie.

SACRED SITES AND POWER — EMULATION IN THE SOUTH?

78 Above, below and opposite: The Thickthorn terminal – the human dimension: Inside looking north-west (opposite); inside looking south-east (above); outside looking at the terminal bank (below)

It has been suggested that the Dorset Cursus possessed high banks that restricted visual access to the esoteric knowledge encoded in its relationship to surrounding burial monuments and the heavens.[12] With a monument overlooked from every ridge, and with so short an astronomically significant alignment, this presents problems. Rather, like others of its type, it may have represented a visually permeable precinct within which those of 'other' status could be observed enacting the ceremonies that ensured cosmological equilibrium. Whether ceremonies of war or ceremonies of fertility – sacrifices or sacred weddings – took place within its confines; whether great assemblies or individual inauguration and re-dedication – All Things or Heb Seds – the symbolic house form of the cursus roofed only by the sky may have seemed certain to ensure the presence of the gods. And, as with a house, greatest importance seems to have attached to the façade. The surviving terminal on Thickthorn Down is impressively monumental when viewed from outside but much less so from inside where the bank is scarcely obvious. On such a well-preserved site it seems most unlikely that this reflects erosion. Was it contrived, in conjunction with the large ditch and falling topography, to allow those inside to be seen by those outside against the back drop of the sky (*78*)? A concentration of flintwork beyond the terminal at Dorchester upon Thames could record just such a location from which 'outsiders' observed those within. On a much larger scale that is also true of material scattered along the King Barrows Ridge overlooking the eastern end of the Greater Stonehenge Cursus. That terminals were the focus of attention at cursus sites is clear from a range of evidence: care taken with their layout; their frequently larger size (whether embanked as at Rudston and Greater Stonehenge or defined by posts as at Douglasmuir and Dunragit); and the presence of a post circle at Springfield, a burial at Thornborough, and ring ditches/round barrows at several sites.

Support for the idea that the Dorset cursus was tied to a pervading ideology of elite distinctiveness is provided by the notable increase in the percentage of polished flint tools found during fieldwalking as the cursus is approached. These include polished-edge knives, chisels and macehead fragments.[13] Additionally Yorkshire influence is indicated by a belt slider from Handley Barrow 26 (whether of jet or a copy in local shale) and, in the wider region, by waisted flint axes from Bournemouth and Bere Regis, the last of full Duggleby adze form. Cornish axes, including Group I, have also been found near the cursus. This may be significant if they do indeed represent a challenge to a northern ideology attached to Group VI axes. In such circumstances a nascent Wessex elite is likely to have sought comparable signals – axes of a distinctive stone with mythological associations, and a competitively constructed sanctuary site. We have already noted the points of similarity of the Allen Valley arm of the Gussage cursus and Rudston A. The distance separating the two – over 400km – seems excessive but it is worth recalling that it is not greatly farther than that between the Vale of York henges and Dorchester upon Thames and could have been aided by intervening sites signalled by concentrations of elaborate flint artefact in the Cambridge/Burwell area and in the Peak District. The huge distributional range of Peterborough Ware certainly points to a widespread transmission of ideas across the region while the long-distance exchange of exotic items, marriage partners and esoteric knowledge that marks out elites in all cultures would have aided the process.

Incredibly at Monkton Up Wimborne, some 800m from the cursus, Martin Green has found evidence for the movement of people involved in the construction of the great Dorset Cursus. There a 34m-diameter circle of open pits with Peterborough Ware in their upper fills surrounded a large central pit with a deep shaft. A multiple burial of a woman aged about 30, two girls aged about 5 and 10 and boy aged about 9 had been made in the side of the pit and carefully covered by chalk rubble. A radiocarbon date for the burial is indistinguishable from that for cursus construction. Isotope analysis of trace metals absorbed through the food chain from underlying geology takes us further. It suggests the woman had originally lived in a high lead-level area – probably the Mendips 60km away – and had travelled to Cranborne Chase where she stayed for some time before returning. She appears to have 'acquired' the two older children in the process; DNA analysis showed they were not related to her. She gave birth to the youngest girl in the Mendips and then all three returned to Cranborne Chase where, as Martin Green puts it, 'they ended their lives.'[14] It is difficult to feel that that end was natural and that movement across those distances was anything but compelled. Evidence that they suffered from iron deficiency but had a high protein diet points to one low in meat but possibly high in dairy produce – consistent with the herding of cattle, the 'walking tribute' of early historic times.

Despite the huge length and monumentality of the Dorset Cursus, the society that developed around it appears never to have advanced as far along the road to elite demarcation as that on the Yorkshire Wolds. The number and quality of the elaborate artefacts provide the palest reflection of the material around Rudston/Bridlington. Equally the jet belt slider burial (Handley 26) cannot hold a candle to those from Eastern Yorkshire, although admittedly Cranbourne Chase lacked Victorian barrow diggers with the appetite of Greenwell and Mortimer to amass the data. An answer may lie in the proposed later date of the great Dorset monument since, in Wessex at least, the ideological changes ushered in with Grooved Ware cut short the development of an individualising society.

14

CURSUS AFTERGLOW

Wessex, having been notable during the Middle Neolithic principally on account of the great Dorset Cursus, became indelibly imprinted in the Late Neolithic with massive henge complexes. These were almost exclusively associated with the new, flat-based ceramic. From extensive excavation of the Mount Pleasant henge enclosure 30km from the Dorset Cursus only 6 sherds of Peterborough Ware were recovered as opposed to 657 of Grooved Ware while only one sherd of Peterborough Ware came from the even more prolific Durrington Walls enclosure near Stonehenge.[1] That is equally true of the small henge-like enclosures on Wyke Down adjacent to the Cursus. Although this bespeaks exclusivity and possibly even wholesale replacement of the older pottery tradition – akin to the earlier virtual absence of Peterborough Ware from the great Hambledon Hill causewayed enclosure complex – it need not imply disdain for the earlier monument. The causeways of the small Wyke Down henges look out to the adjacent Peterborough Ware flint scatter within the cursus, and the presence of house structures (however ceremonial) beside these new monuments implies regular use of this cursus-focused group. The pit circle henge very closely resembles single ring examples at Dorchester upon Thames, one of which (Site IV) is aligned along the cursus there. In both cases they have been dated several centuries later then the multi-ringed type.

Martin Green has made the important suggestion that a 500–700m clear zone separated the Dorset Cursus from other early monuments (long enclosures and the Monkton Up Wimborne pit circle) and that the process of encroachment, that was to see round barrows cluster closely, was begun with Grooved Ware.[2] In addition to the Wyke Down structures a number of pits have been located at Down Farm with domestic and ritual deposits. These include a pit with a dog's skull and a polished flint ball; one with a banded pebble, a boar's tusk and a Cornish axe; and another with a cow's skull placed on top of an antler pick. A Cornish axe fragment and a bone from a brown bear were found higher up the latter pit. It is difficult to dismiss this as the result of simple opportunistic occupation of cleared land.

Farther afield Grooved Ware came from pits apparently aligned directly alongside the Drayton South (Sutton Courtenay) cursus and deposits were also made in the upper ditch fills of the Lechlade and Springfield cursuses. They are unlikely to represent rubbish disposal.[3]

Perhaps the clearest indication of continued interest comes from the placing of large ceremonial henges across or beside the cursuses at Thornborough, Maxey and Dorchester upon Thames (see *15* and *49*), a pattern repeated by a comparable post enclosure at Dunragit in Galloway. The cursuses were venerable by that date; ditches were silted up and Dunragit had been built and burned down as much as 1000 years earlier to judge from radiocarbon dates. Yet, as we have seen, hengiform and ring ditch alignment at Dorchester and Maxey confirms that their confines were still respected. Overlay cannot then have been fortuitous. Power was still perceived to be centred in these much older monuments. So much so perhaps that the Big Rings henge at Dorchester was placed to the side – a pattern that recalls respectful placement of new shrines beside, rather than over, the old at the great sanctuaries of Pachacamarca and Delphi. Subversion and redirection rather than aggressive iconoclastic slighting seems to be indicated (*81*).

These complexes, then, follow the pattern of succession expected of sanctuaries of any period. Those at Rudston and on Cranborne Chase do not. No large ceremonial monument lies across or beside these mega complexes. The Maiden's Grave henge beside cursus D at Rudston is moderately sized but hardly bears comparison with the great Thornborough and Dorchester henges (*17*), while beside the Dorset Cursus there is nothing larger than the 20m-diameter Wyke Down 1 henge. Nothing that is until 5km downstream at Knowlton (*79*). There a 230m-diameter henge is accompanied by a series of smaller henge sites and a huge barrow 6.5m high that resembles Duggleby Howe or, on a smaller scale, the huge mass of Silbury Hill. Martin Green has suggests that this site was chosen for the henge complex because of the presence of natural shafts, akin to those further up the River Allen near its source within the cursus. A further factor could have been the continued 'presence' of the cursus in the landscape – an unchallengeable cosmological force deflecting overt expression of the new power well away from its confines. A similar explanation could be advanced for the Rudston sanctuary – if a henge complex (conceivably constructed as a palisaded rather than ditched enclosure) had been similarly deflected it could lie eroded and obscured on the valley floor downstream. Perhaps significantly, Grooved Ware has been recovered from the valley side to the crest of the wold

79 Knowlton: the 'church henge' and the great barrow beyond

between Low Caythorpe and Boynton, and Harding has recently noted that the Durrington Walls style of the pottery (associated in Wessex with the great henge enclosures) is exclusive to pit deposits at this eastern end of the Rudston Wold distribution. The fact that they alone appear to hold the debris of communal events such as feasting makes this doubly significant.[4]

LATE CURSUSES

The clearest picture of continued respect is to be found in the Stonehenge landscape. In contrast to the confused, often invisible, nature of round barrow positioning in relation to the great stone circle,[5] the picture around the Greater Cursus could not be clearer. Round barrows are emphatically aligned alongside it (see *16*). Why should this have been? None of the barrow grouping around the far more monumental Dorset and Rudston cursuses demonstrate anything like the same spatial respect. An answer may have been revealed by the radiocarbon date for the monument – 2900-2500 BC. This is several centuries later than other cursuses and later even than phase I of Stonehenge. Doubts have been expressed regarding its integrity. Nevertheless, taken at face value, it does broadly correlate with the destruction of the nearby Lesser Cursus – an apparently unfinished monument. It may also explain the massive long barrow set back from its eastern terminal. Stukeley had falsified his findings by turning this into the end of the cursus and the seat for his judges but there is no denying its unusual size, orientation and apparent lack of primary burials. Aubrey Burl has suggested it was a dummy long barrow constructed by remodelling the terminal.[6] Aerial photographs and geophysical survey cast doubt on this but might it have been constructed as a theatrical backdrop copying the pattern observed on Gussage Hill? The remarkably straight alignment of the cursus and its cross valley layout closely resembles the southern section of the Gussage cursus dominated by the hilltop long barrow as it runs from Thickthorn Down.

It is not inconceivable that the Greater Stonehenge Cursus is a late example of the type constructed by groups wishing to magnify the importance of the henge monuments at Coneybury and Stonehenge I, both with unusually early in dates – 2900-2600 BC and 3000-2900 BC respectively. Addition of a cursus after the examples at Dorchester upon Thames and Maxey may have been perceived as vital to ancestral legitimization – albeit back-constructed. This could equally apply to the presence of a monolith resembling that at Rudston; the Heel Stone is ill dated and, strangely for a claimed late element, is virtually alone in being neither shaped nor smoothed.

A further possible example of back-constructing the history of a sanctuary complex is to be found at Llandegai near Bangor in Gwynedd. The cursiform long enclosure size of the monument there encouraged the idea that it was the earliest ceremonial structure on the site but a recent radiocarbon date has thrown this into doubt. A single date from oak charcoal found just above the bottom of the ditch suggested it was constructed between 2700 and 2550 BC, later than the large single entrance henge (site A) and contemporary with the double entrance monument (site B).[7] Further determinations are needed to confirm this but it is a valuable warning against too readily using size to predict date, particularly on a long-lived sanctuary site.

Intriguingly a very similar monument to the Llandegai 'cursus' (round ended and 100m x 20m) is to be found on the opposite side of the Irish Sea beside the great passage tomb at Newgrange. As at Llandegai, a very large ceremonial circle stands beside it (here a pit circle rather than a henge) and the cursus alignment, if projected, meets a large ditched circle. These 'echoes' strongly suggest this is another example of the replication of selected elements of one sanctuary by the builders of another. Less certain is the Banqueting Hall at Tara. This 225m x 25m sunken linear monument, hollowed out to provide spoil for its banks is aligned on the Mound of the Hostages passage tomb (dated 2600-2200 BC). It seems likely therefore to be later but just how much is unclear: the site has been closely identified in early medieval legend with the great banqueting hall of Irish kings and this was the most important of royal sites.[8]

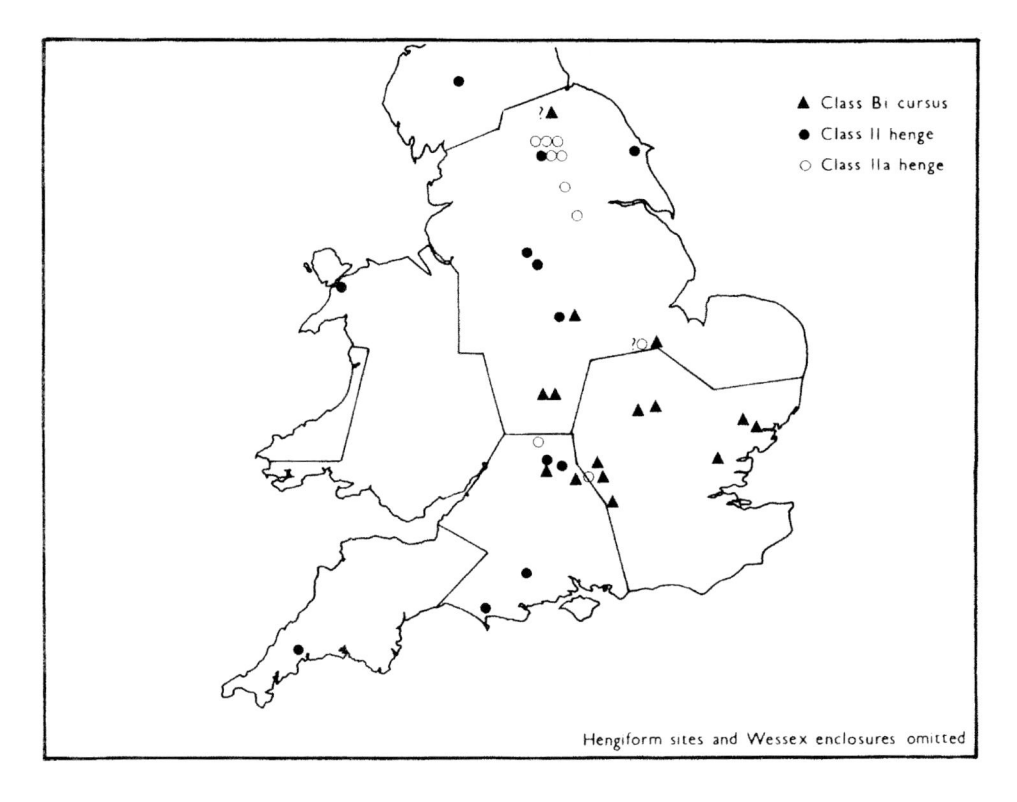

80 Bi cursus and henge distribution superimposed on Burl's henge zones (1969). Note broad correlation of Bi sites with Burl's empty SE zone

THE CURSUS LEGACY

Whatever the case with smaller, cursiform long enclosure sites, it is clear that nothing approaching cursus proportions was constructed after the mid-third millennium BC at the latest. Labour was now lavished on new theatres that ensured cosmomological harmony through their circularity. Yet it is strange that the principal of these – the henge – is all but absent from the Midlands/East Anglia. This was the southern heartland of the cursus tradition. It may all have begun here centuries earlier when long enclosures were extended not only in length (as in Scotland) but in width as well. And certainly it was here that the finest examples of the type – the Bi sites – were almost exclusively constructed (*80*).

Cursus ideology clearly had a strong hold in the region. It is tempting to imagine therefore that this led to finely planned rectangular monuments being built instead of henges. Ideological adjustment on the part of Grooved Ware users seems most unlikely though, as henge plans and pottery exhibit a remarkable nationwide orthodoxy. The evidence also contradicts it: Grooved Ware appears only at the top of substantially filled ditches at Springfield and Lechlade. Nevertheless the fact that it *is* found there, and often in pits nearby, probably points to the continued 'presence' of these sites. And the fact that multi-ditched hengiform rings occur beside Bi sites like Barford *and* at the major sanctuaries, but rarely away from cursus complexes, confirms that both types of ritual centre were in use when Grooved Ware made its appearance. Conceivably the earliest Grooved Ware-using communities met resistance in the region and were forced to construct their ritual sites away from these centres, perhaps in the less easily detectable form of post circles, a number of which have been recognised.[9] Only with increased dominance – either of the ideology, the group, or of both – might the confidence have arisen to construct major ceremonial henges at the great cursus sanctuaries. The fact that with a very few exceptions (e.g. Arminghall, Norfolk, and Stanton Harcourt, Oxfordshire) these were the *only* classic henges built in the region has major implications. It suggests not only that the Middle Neolithic Peterborough Ware hierarchy of cursus centres was maintained, but the social organisation that must have underpinned them. The great sanctuaries were, and remained it seems, exceptional (*81*).

Their distant similarity has already been explained in terms of replication through the pilgrimage phenomenon but their fairly regular, regional spacing hints at another factor. It suggests that while inspiration was drawn from paradigm ritual sites, they may have been constructed as much as a political act (to furnish a monumental tribal focus) as a religious one. Such ceremonial centres are exemplified by the great Late Neolithic henge enclosures of Wessex but their spacing across the landscape is far closer: 20-30km as against 90-120km. They accord with our evidence for the normal territorial extent of chiefdoms; Dorchester upon Thames-like centres do not. Elements of the Wessex henge complexes spread over limited areas (1km Dorchester, Dorset; 2km Durrington Walls, Stonehenge; 3km Avebury) whereas the Dorchester upon Thames sanctuary appears to encompass a landscape nearly 10km in radius. Clearly this reflects very differently organised societies.

Alistair Barclay has pointed out that satellites of minor cursus size in the Upper Thames Valley are sited close to tributary rivers.[10] This might suggest they were constructed on the edge of the central ceremonial territory by distant communities – explicable if cursuses functioned as symbolic houses for the ancestors of particular lineages or social groups. Their home-based counterparts are perhaps to be found in the minor cursuses at Barford-like centres whose distribution corresponds far more closely with the predicted spacing of chiefdom territories (e.g. Cardington, Eynesbury and Brampton on the Great Ouse; Grendon, Raunds (West Cotton) and Aldwincle on the Nene). Like Greek city-state treasuries at the venerable sanctuary at Delphi, the Bi

81 Dorchester upon Thames; Big Rings henge with cursus beyond. Allen 462 1938: Ashmolean Museum, Oxford

satellites at Dorchester upon Thames may be later additions that served different communities; their contrasting stellar orientation points to a cosmological, and probably hierarchical, distinction from the focal site. Unlike Delphi, the extent of this territory and its apparent survival into the mid-second millennium BC, with periods of monument building alternating across it from hengiform concentration at Dorchester to the Early Bronze Age round barrow cemetery at Radley, points to a political dimension. The nearest analogy would appear to be *not* the aggrandised Rudston and Dorset complexes but the Stonehenge landscape. There round barrow cemeteries spreading both west and east of the Avon demarcated a similarly extensive territory and permit us to appreciate the intricacies of its organisation.

Early Bronze Age 'Wessex' barrows in particular fail to ring – or even in many cases even to be visible from – Stonehenge as might be predicted. They cluster instead around the Wilsford dry valley to the south, where occupation material has been recorded and from which large numbers of the barrows are skylined.[11] The pattern is repeated by other barrow groups set around dry coombes. It suggests that this landscape is a product of a series of separate, probably seasonal, occupation niches in an area of exceptional sacred significance. Hierachical power, as witnessed by 'Wessex' prestige items and the monumental sarsen structure, is not in doubt but its display in such a landscape may have been deliberately oblique to avoid venerated ground. Likewise around Dorchester upon Thames while Late Neolithic cremation burials are concentrated around the central site, the early individual burial at Mount Farm is set about 1.5km away and the important Early Bronze Age barrow cemetery at Radley lies yet further out.

Dorchester then, and to a lesser extent the other major cursus complexes of the Midlands and East Anglia, may have functioned at an early stage as Stonehenge did at a later one – as the focus of a territory far larger than those of Late Neolithic Wessex. There the far more closely spaced henge enclosures could record subdivision of the undoubtedly huge territory called upon by the builders of the great Dorset Cursus, or might conceivably represent succession masked by the broad, predictive nature of radiocarbon dating. Tantalisingly the distinctive stepped back or minimal forms of 'Wessex fancy barrows' (bell, disc, saucer) appear alien to the chalklands where the structural stability of a barrow mound was not in doubt, but appropriate to the river gravels where it would have been. Could the Stonehenge landscape, then, record the imposition onto Early Bronze Age Wessex of a Midland/East Anglian cursus-based social structure that had survived – as henge patterning there implies – the transition to Grooved Ware?

A CHANGED WORLD

Parallel or axial alignments of Early Bronze Age round barrows/ring ditches at some major sites certainly tell of continued respect into the middle of the second millennium but this did not last. By the opening of the first millennium BC ceremonial monuments had been rendered obsolete. Claims of divinely invested authority that they bolstered had collapsed, a process perhaps taking no more than one or two generations: 'My grandfather used to think the king was a god. My parents used to think he stands between God and the devil. Me, I think he is the devil.' (International Herald Tribune 16 April, 2006 quoting a Nepalese protestor).

The Banqueting hall at Tara opens up the possibility of a late survival – or even re-invention – of the smaller forms of cursuses. If, as has been suggested, the monuments did represent magnified, symbolic houses this is not implausible. Several sites confirm this and suggest that we must be wary of automatically assuming that long enclosure cropmarks always represent Neolithic monuments.

On the continent two sites stand out (*82*). Aulnay aux Palnches in the Champagne closely resembles a Bi-type long enclosure, even down to its offset entrance. Pottery from the ditch dates it to the opening of the first millennium BC. Two inhumations and three cremations were scattered about the interior, stones had been set up inside each terminal and a pit containing an ox skull was

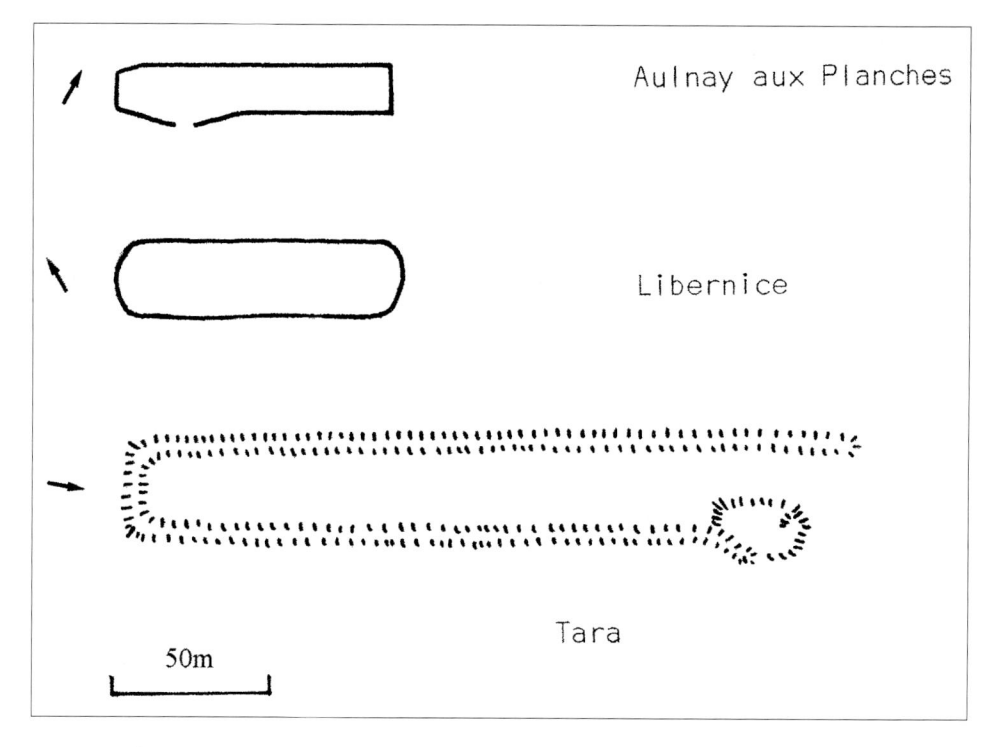

82 First millennium BC long enclosures

sited across the enclosure from the entrance. It was clearly related to an adjacent cemetery but not as an aggrandised burial enclosure or cremation site. Rather it seems to have been an attendant ritual structure perhaps additionally marked by posts set in the ditch. There is much here that recalls the Yarnton long enclosure where the ditch appears to have been recut in the Bronze Age. Aerial photographs make it clear that Aulnay is not alone, nor is it far removed from Britain.

Farther afield the site at Libernice in Czechoslovakia even more closely resembles a British long enclosure with its gently convex ends. Excavation dated it to the late fourth century BC. Inside there was a single, central burial of a richly adorned aged female and, at the eastern end, a large sunken area. This had been created by repeated pit digging and contained deposits of animal and human bone along with pottery. A 2m-high standing stone stood within it. Paired posts were set up in front of the stone and others flanked the sunken 'sanctuary' area.[12]

Until recently these two sites appeared to have little relevance to the British scene. Excavation of a long enclosure thought to be Neolithic at Bow Brickhill, Milton Keynes, changed this. The continuous ditch, very similar in plan to Libernice, produced pottery of mid-first century AD date and a radiocarbon date backed this up. The non-domestic nature of the site, hinted at by its shape

CURSUS AFTERGLOW

and lack of an entrance causeway, seems confirmed by a burial apparently cut through a former bank on the outer ditch edge. How many other such sites exist can only be guessed at but there is a marked concentration of cropmark long enclosures in the Trinovantian territory of southern East Anglia.[13]

Whatever the case with small sites that presumably reflected continental influence, there is no doubting the demise of the major sites. Now cursuses were slighted by field systems as the landscape was organised into blocks that often ran at total variance to their alignment. Elsewhere, as at the Lesser Stonehenge Cursus and on Gussage Hill, small group of fields were laid out from these monuments but this represents no more than opportunistic adoption of their bank lines. The same may be said of the great Late Bronze Age pit enclosure at Eynesbury (426m x 180m) that followed the slight curve of the side ditch of the northern cursus but cut straight through the southern one.[14] Adoption by lengths of much later field and trackway confirm the survival of sections of these monuments as relics in the landscape but no more than that.

Like aristocratic London residences subdivided and dilapidated as the centuries turned and society changed, so these sacred enclosures were reduced. Once vital engines for the maintenance of cosmological harmony and the legitimization of individual power, they were now, at best, no more than field boundaries. At worst, as at Maxey, they were totally forgotten. The most monumental were incorporated in linear boundary dyke systems – the Argam Dyke at Rudston and a triple dyke at Gussage, with other dykes focusing in on their opposing ends.[15] It is possible that in these cases they retained a little of the mystique that had led people to labour so long in their construction and to sacrifice so much precious land to their leviathan demands. A hint that this was so comes from a strange quarter: the only two certain cases of churches built on earlier pagan sites are amidst the cursuses at Rudston (71) and at Knowlton, the henge complex that drew on and superceded the great Dorset Cursus (79). And we might wonder was it purely the uncertainties of Middle Saxon politics that led Birinus to choose the completely peripheral site of Dorchester upon Thames as the seat for the bishopric of Wessex? At each of these places the symbolic, demarcating role of cursuses in the changed geography and emergent power play of the Middle Neolithic may have long passed but a broader sense of place perhaps persisted. Later practices could have focused on small elements of once huge complexes such as the square ditch enclosure around Site I Dorchester that closely resembles the Saxon shrine around the western ring ditch at Yeavering.[16] Alternatively they may have been enacted within unrecognised structures such as the complex at Warborough situated on the opposite bank of the River Thame to the Dorchester cursus and unparalleled in any period. Or wider *genius loci* may have endured loosely connected to the Rud Stone, 'gipsies' or 'Mother Dunche's Buttocks.' Whatever the case, the sites

INSCRIBED ACROSS THE LANDSCAPE: THE CURSUS ENIGMA

83 Reconstruction of the Springfield cursus. © Essex County Council. Original watercolour by Frank Gardiner

seem to have retained sufficient potency to activate Pope Gregory's instruction to Augustine to reconsecrate rather than remove pagan sanctuaries.

Elsewhere the monuments vanished until the keen eyes of Major Allen resurrected them from the air. Thanks to him and the aerial photographers who followed the trail he blazed, cursuses can now be recognised for what they were: not arbitary responses to the need to link or process but ideological signals to this world and to the 'others' founded on the long house. Their monstrous growth is the story of a society in flux: small enclosures delimiting 'halls' in Scotland; magnified through contact with the bank barrow tradition and adopted further south at major sanctuary sites; monumentalised at Rudston as the springboard for wresting individual power; and perhaps challenged from Dorset through the construction of the most extravagant of all their manifestations – as important to the emerging paramount rulers of Middle Neolithic Britain as Woden was at the head of an Anglo Saxon king's pedigree. For the inhabitants of prehistoric Britain these monuments were instrumental in changing the world (*83*).

APPENDICES

GAZETTEER OF WELL-ATTESTED SITES
(Scottish sites after Brophy 1999; Welsh sites after Gibson 1999.)

SITE	FORM	SIZE (metres) + : incomplete	ALIGNMENT (approx. azimuth)
Mega sites			
Gussage, Dorset	B	5640 x 106	51-59
Pentridge, Dorset	B	4290 x 102	31-43
Greater Stonehenge, Wiltshire	B	2730 x 100-150	83-85
Stanwell, Middlesex	?	3600+ x 22	165
Rudston A, East Yorkshire	B	2700 x 58	0-12
Rudston D, East Yorkshire	B	4000+ x 50-90	7
Major sites			
Scorton, North Yorkshire	B	2000+ x 32	132
Thornborough, North Yorkshire	A	1200+ x 42	53-63
Rudston C, East Yorkshire	?	1480 x 50-60	96-8
Rudston B, East Yorkshire	B	1550+ x 65-80	61-65
Aston on Trent, Derbyshire	Bi	1700+ x 96-100	33
Potlock (Findern), Derbyshire	?	1560+ x 72	74
Maxey, Cambridgeshire	?	1710+ x 35-65	126 & 116
Fornham All Saints, Suffolk	A	1900 x 25-32	166/146/132/137
Benson, Oxfordshire	Bi	1090 x 65	32
Drayton N., Oxfordshire	?	650+ x 75	18
Drayton S., Oxfordshire	Bi	750 x 70	26
Dorchester, Oxfordshire	A	1600+ x 60	128-130
Buscot, Wiltshire	Bi	750+ x 50	131
Old Montrose, Angus	B	600 x 60-81	93
Curriestanes, Dumfries	A	300+ x 95	90
Drylawhill, Lothian	?	300+ x 60	
Minor sites			
Nether Exe, Devon	Bi	210+ x 30	45
Lesser Stonehenge, Wiltshire	B	400 x 60	75
Sonning, Berkshire	Bi	250+ x 35	86
Stadhampton, Oxfordshire	Bi	400 x 45	13

Drayton St Leonard, Oxfordshire	Bi	390+ x 40	27
Lechlade, Gloucestershire	Bi	300+ x 50	154
Eynesbury N., Cambridgeshire	Bi	101+ x 65	10
Eynesbury S., Cambridgeshire	Bi	316 x 77	15
Godmanchester, Cambridgeshire	?	500+ x 90	60
Springfield, Essex	Bi	680 x 40-50	65
Stratford St Mary, Suffolk	Bi	295 x 65	126
Cardington, Bedfordshire	Bi	180 x 60	136
Biggleswade, Bedfordshire	Bi	380+ x 75	104
Charlecote, Warwickshire	?	200+ x 28	5
Barford, Warwickshire	Bi	185 x 35-40	20
Longbridge, Warwickshire	Bi	270 x 32	10
Hasting Hill, Tyne & Wear	B	410 x 40-45	8
Walton, Powys	B	660 x 60	70
Hindwell, Powys	?	474+ x 54	62
Holywood N., Dumfriesshire	A	400 x 32	26
Holywood S., Dumfriesshire	B	300 x 30-40	156
Balneaves, Angus	B (PD)	450+ x 25	35
Milton of Guthrie, Angus	B (PD)	600 x 25	100
Inchbare A, Angus	B (PD)	240+ x 23-30	55
Inchbare B, Angus	? (PD)	240+ x 25	65
Kinalty, Angus	A (PD)	200 x 30	175
Woodhill, Angus	A (PD)	100 x 50	NE-SW
Bennybeg, Perthshire	B (PD)	110 x 30-35	10
Broich, Perthshire	?	?900+ x 80	N-S
Blairhall, Perthshire	B	190 x 25	70
Bannockburn 1, Stirling	A (PD)	40+ x 35	105
Bannockburn 2, Stirling	B (PD)	89 + x 27	120

Cursiform

Martin's Down, Dorset	B	100+ x 25	100
Buscot, Wiltshire	B	150+ x 20	47
North Stoke, Oxfordshire	B?	200 x 12	10
Feering, Essex	A	95+ x 25	20
Bures St Mary, Suffolk	B	190+ x 22	115
Stratford St Mary, Suffolk	A	110 x 25	90
Cardington/Cople, Bedfordshire	A	125 x 15	60
Barnack, Cambridgeshire	Bi	120 x 25	45
Grendon, Northamptonshire	B	116 x 27	175
Maesyn Ridware, Staffordshire	A?	130+ x 15	75
Sarn-y-bryn Caled, Powys	B	370 x 12	45
Llandegai, Gwynedd	A	170 x 12	110
Kilmany, Fife	A	180 x 10	NE-SW

Bank barrows

Maiden Castle, Dorset		545 x 13	95-115
Long Bredy, Martin's Down, Dorset		197 x 19	45
Broadmayne, Dorset		182 x 16	110
Pentridge 2a/b, Dorset		150 x 20	145
Long Low, Wetton, Staffordshire		201 x 14	25

Auchenlaich, Stirling	342 x 15	170
Eskmuirdale, Dumfriesshire	255 + 650 x 6	0 & 20
Cleaven Dyke, Perthshire	2000 x 40	115

SITES TO VISIT

There is very little of any cursus that is still visible. Those in the river valleys have been completely ploughed flat and are only visible from the air as cropmarks. The following represent fragments of chalkland sites or associated monuments.

The Dorset Cursus

ST 969124	The southern terminal on Thickthorn Down is the only preserved cursus terminal in the country. It and the adjacent long barrows are on Public Access Land.
ST 994138	The Gussage Hill long barrow is well preserved and can be viewed from the Jubilee Trail path but the cursus and all other earthworks have been flattened by ploughing.
SU 008149	The Wyke Down henges are preserved and accessible on a Countryside Stewardship Trail that also takes in the location of the seasonal lake.
SU 017160	The eastern bank of the cursus, preserved as a field boundary, runs up to the south-western side of the B3081.
SU 041191	The bank barrow that lies beside the northern terminal of the Pentridge arm of the cursus can be seen from the footpath by Bokerley Ditch.
SU 024103	The Knowlton Circles henge monuments and great barrow. The 'Church henge' is well preserved and protected by English Heritage.

The Greater Stonehenge Cursus

National Trust information boards make it possible for the visitor to obtain a clear grasp of the size of the cursus and to walk its length. Its bank and ditch survive fairly well just beyond the barrows on the western side of the track leading north from Stonehenge. Its width can be gauged by the gap cut in Fargo Plantation, on the other side of which lies the partially cleared western terminal ditch. The eastern half of the site and the long barrow have been effectively flattened.

Thornborough

The three great henges are preserved. The central one (SE 285795) overlies the cursus. It is invisible but its course can be gauged from the road from Thornborough to West Tansfield that runs parallel to it.

Rudston

The standing stone is impressively visible in the churchyard but the cursuses are invisible. An impression of the course of Rudston D can be gained by looking north from here along the valley. Cursus A ended on the Wold Gate to the south (TA 099658) where the last vestiges of the terminal bank are visible in the field to the west of the road junction.

Cleaven Dyke, Perthshire

Impressively visible and accessible west of the A93 north of Meikleour (NO 167403). Note the ditches set c.25m either side of the mound.

Long Low, Wetton, Staffordshire (Sk 124539)

The bank barrow has been made accessible by the farmer from an adjacent footpath.

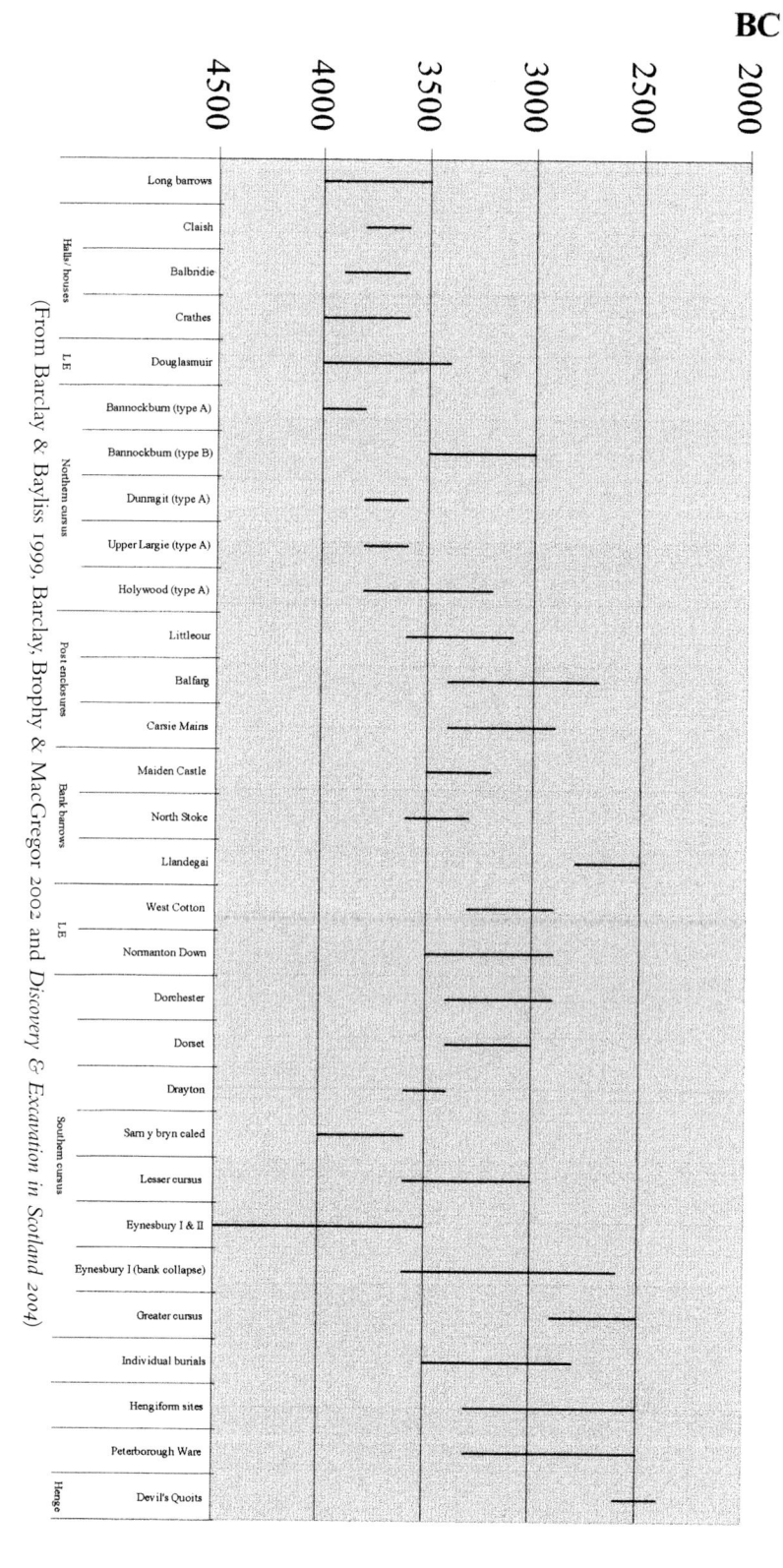

DATE RANGE OF CURSUSES AND RELATED SITES

(From Barclay & Bayliss 1999, Barclay, Brophy & MacGregor 2002 and *Discovery & Excavation in Scotland* 2004)

FURTHER INFORMATION

A Landscape Revealed. 10,000 Years on a Chalkland Farm. Martin Green. Tempus 2000
The Cursus Monuments of Scotland. Kenneth Brophy and RCHM 2006
The Monumental Cemeteries of Prehistoric Europe. Magdalena Midgeley. Tempus 2005
From Carnac to Callanish. Aubrey Burl. 1993
Pathways and Ceremonies. The Cursus Monuments of Britain and Ireland. Alistair Barclay and Jan Harding. 1999
Loveday 1985 PhD corpus of cursus and related sites. Archaeological Data Services
http://ads.ahds.ac.uk/catalogue/resources.html?cursus_phd_2006

ENDNOTES

Chapter 2
1. Piggott, S. 1985, 93
2. Stukeley, W. 1740, 43
3. Colt Hoare 1812, *Ancient Wiltshire* I, 158; 1819, *Ancient Wiltshire* II, 33
4. Heywood Sumner 1913 (1988, 34-5); Greenwell 1877, 253-7
5. Leeds 1934, 414-6
6. Crawford 1935, 77-8
7. RCHM 1960, 27; Webster & Hobley 1964; Maxwell 1978; Loveday 1985; Barclay & Harding 1999; RCHM Scot & Brophy forthcoming
8. RCHME Annual Review 1987

Chapter 3
1. Last 1999
2. Thomas 2004
3. Ford & Loveday 2003
4. Marsac, Scarre & Riley 1982; Loveday & Petchey 1982
5. Pryor *et al.* 1985
6. Kendrick 1995; Rideout 1997; Thomas 1999; Brophy 1999
7. Pryor 1993; Hey 1997; Buckley *et al.* 2001; Reaney 1968: Barclay *et al.* 2003
8. Whittle *et al.* 1992; Loveday 1999; Pryor *et al.* 1985; St Joseph 1964
9. Richards 1990, 93-6; Riley 1988; Stoertz 1997; RCHM 1975, 24-6; Barrett *et al.* 1991

Chapter 4
1. Pryor *et al.* 1985, 59-62; Simpson 1985, 249; Barclay *et al.* 2003, 68-80; Rideout 1997; Stone 1947; Richards 1990
2. Piggott 1974
3. Cornwall 1953 & 1955
4. Entwhistle 1990, 88-93, 105-8; Entwhistle & Bowden 1991
5. Robinson 2003, 163-70
6. Richards 1990, 72-81; Topping 1982; Thomas 1999; Abrahamson 2000
7. Simpson 1985; Pryor *et al.* 1985
8. Barclay *et al.* 2003, 196-7; Gibson & Loveday 1989, 37-8; Guilbert 1996

ENDNOTES

9 Thomas 1999
10 Topping 1982; Lewis 2004; Case 1982
11 Barclay *et al.* 2003, 104-117
12 Gibson & Loveday 1989
13 Buckley *et al.* 2001
14 Ellis 2004, 34-6
15 Stoertz 1997, fig. 38; Entwhistle 1990; RCHM 1975, 24-6

Chapter 5

1 Atkinson *et al.* 1951
2 Kinnes 1992, fig. 2.4.5; Vatcher 1961
3 Pitt-Rivers 1898; Vatcher 1961, 167
4 Ashbee *et al.* 1979, 240-1
5 Barrett *et al.* 1991, 38-43
6 Ashbee 1970
7 Phillips 1936, 49
8 Manby 1976
9 Kinnes 1992, 48-50; Saville 1990
10 Webster & Hobley 1964; Ford 1971; Ford & Loveday 2003; Erith 1971
11 Williamson & Loveday 1988
12 Grinsell 1953, fig. 3; Fasham 1975

Chapter 6

1 Case 1982
2 Loveday 1989
3 Bradley 1992; Brewster 1984
4 Hey 1997
5 Loveday 1989
6 Windell 1989
7 Hogg 1940; Phillips 1935a
8 Keevil 1992
9 Ellis 2004; McKinley 2004
10 Malim 2000, 66-70
11 Richards 1990, 96-9
12 Jones 1998
13 Powell 1969, 11
14 Ellis 2004, 61-5
15 Barclay & Maxwell 1991
16 Ford & Loveday 2003
17 Cook & Dunbar 2004
18 Fraser & Murray 2005
19 Barclay & Russell-White 1993; Hogg 1993
20 Barclay & Maxwell 1998
21 Brophy & Barclay 2004
22 Barclay *et al.* 2003
23 Fairweather & Ralston 1993
24 Mogg 2002, 111-14
25 Piggot 1936
26 Smith 1834; Fussell 1949
27 Kendrick 1995; Barclay and Brophy 2002, 121

Chapter 7

1. Newbiggin 1936
2. Ashbee 1970
3. Wheeler 1943; Bradley 1984; Sharples 1991
4. St Joseph 1964; Topping 1982; Newman 1976
5. Dixon 1988; Williamson & Loveday 1989
6. Case 1982; Brophy 1998; Gibson 1994; Lynch & Musson 2004
7. Carrington 1865; Foster & Stevenson 2002, 114-19; RCHM Scot 1997, 107
8. O'Connell 1990, 19-35; Lewis & Welsh 2004
9. Richmond 1940; Barclay & Maxwell 1998
10. Midgley 2005
11. Madsen 1979
12. Liversage 1992
13. Crawford 1938; Midgley 1985, figs 19-20
14. Hodder 1990, 143-5
15. Kinnes 1999; Midgely 2005

Chapter 8

1. Burl 1993
2. Kinnes 1992, 200-1
3. Thomas 1998
4. Vatcher, L. & F. 1973; Cleal *et al.* 1995, 55-6
5. Burl 1993
6. Gilling & Pollard
7. Smith 1965; Burl 1993, 72-4; Gillings & Pollard 2004
8. Cleal *et al.* 1995
9. Harding 1981
10. Burl 1993, 58-9
11. Burl 1993, 63-5
12. Clare 1978; Burl 1993, 47-8
13. Loveday 1998
14. Harding 1981
15. Burl 1993; Case 1952; Green 2000, 113-7

Chapter 9

1. Ashbee *et al.* 1979, 259; Hogg 1940; Kinnes 1992
2. Hogg 2002; Ashbee 1966
3. Barclay *et al.* 2003; Atkinson *et al.* 1951, fig. 2
4. Buckley *et al.* 2001, 155
5. Gibson & Loveday 1989
6. Vatcher 1960
7. Loveday 1999
8. Richards 1990, 72-81; Brophy 1998
9. Case 2004; Hogg 2002
10. Barclay & Maxwell 1998, 301
11. Drury 1979
12. Warrick 1996
13. Hodder 1990; Richards 1993

Chapter 10

1. Pryor 1985; RCHM 1960; Loveday 1985
2. Ainslie & Wallis 1987; Barclay 2003
3. Loveday 2004; Howard & Garton 1996
4. Brophy 2000
5. Penny & Wood 1973
6. Barrett *et al.* 1991, 56
7. Burl 1987, 43-4
8. Bradley & Chambers 1988
9. Loveday 1999
10. Ammarell 1996; Relke & Ernest 2003, 67
11. www.starrynight.com
12. Ibid.

Chapter 11

1. Atkinson *et al.* 1951
2. Ibid. 55; Loveday 2002, 141.
3. Harding 2003
4. Headlam 1925
5. Tilley 1994, 58; O'Kelly 1967; Gelling 1974, 428
6. Ovsyannikov & Terebikhin 1994, 57-8
7. Conant 1993
8. Silverman 1994
9. Barclay *et al.* 2003, 142; Buckley *et al.* 2001; Barrett *et al.* 1991; Thomas 1999; Rideout
10. Gibson & Kinnes 1997; Cleal 1995, 193; Gibson 1995
11. Gibson 1989
12. Dincauze & Hasenstab 1989
13. Burger 1992, 180
14. Ashbee 1978
15. Manby 1972; Harding & Lee 1987
16. Case 1986, 30-1; Holgate 1988
17. Greenwell 1877, 253-7; Barclay *et al.* 2003, 18 & 22; Brann 2003; Chapman 2005
18. Cleal 1991, 135; Hinman & Malim 1999.
19. Renfrew & Bahn 2004, 406

Chapter 12

1. Scutling & Wysocki 2005
2. Healy 2004; Case 1986, 30-1; Barclay *et al.* 1999, 278-9, 320-2
3. Earle 1991
4. Busia 1954, 202
5. Mair 1977, 41
6. Ibid. 24
7. Manby 1979
8. Thorpe & Richards 1984
9. Harding 1999; Mackey 2000
10. Earnshaw 1973; Manby 1988, 39
11. Defoe 1927, 246
12. Lewin 1969, 51
13. Edmonds 1995, 53; Manby 1979, fig. 7; McK Clough and Cummins 1988, 265-81
14. Kristiansen 1987; Spencer 1990

15 Bruce Mitford 1974, 84-90
16 Burger 1992, 203
17 Durden 1995
18 Stupecki 1997
19 Stoertz 1997
20 Earle 1991, 7 & 78
21 Piggott 1954
22 Spunzar 1987; Saville 1999; Sheridan 1992, 209; Manby 1974, 98
23 Shennan 1993
24 Helms 1993; Kristiansen & Larsson 2005,18
25 Earle 1991,7
26 Kinnes *et al.* 1983
27 Loveday 2002
28 Childe 1954; Parker Pearson 1999, 18
29 Sheridan 1992, 206-7
30 Charles-Edwards 1989

Chapter 13

1 Barclay & Halpin 1999, 320-5
2 Bradley & Edmonds 1993
3 Sharples 1991, 230-1
4 Barrett *et al.* 1991, 51
5 Ibid. 52-5
6 Ashbee 1970, 23-4
7 Barrett *et al.* 1991, 84-7
8 Green 2000
9 Barrett *et al.* 1991, 70-5
10 Entwhistle & Richards 1987
11 Green 2000, 61
12 Barrett *et al.* 1991, 47-58
13 Ibid. fig. 3 4
14 Green 2000, 77-84

Chapter 14

1 Wainwright 1979; Wainwright & Longworth 1971
2 Green 2000, 85
3 Barclay *et al.* 2003; Buckley *et al.* 2001
4 Manby 1974; Harding 2006
5 Richards 1990, 273-4; Loveday 2006
6 Richards 1990, 96; Burl 1987, 45
7 Lynch & Musson 2001
8 Newman 1991
9 Gibson 2000
10 Barclay *et al.* 2003, 241
11 Loveday 2006
12 Piggott 1974, 37
13 Loveday & Petchey 1982
14 Richards 1990, 81-92; RCHM 1975, 24-5; Ellis 2004
15 Stoertz 1997; RCHM 1975, 24-5
16 Blair 1995

BIBLIOGRAPHY

Abramson, P. 2000 Excavations at Pits Plantation, Rudston, for Perenco UK Ltd. *East Riding Archaeologist* 10.
Ainslie, R. & Wallis, J. 1987 Excavations on the cursus at Drayton, Oxon. *Oxoniensia* 52, 1-10.
Ammarell, G. 2005 The Planetarium and the Plough: Interpreting Star Calendars of Rural Java. In Chamberlain, V.D., Carlson, J.B. & Young, M.J. *Songs From the Sky. Indigenous Astronomical and Cosmological Traditions of the World,* 320-35. Bognor: Ocarina.
Ashbee, P. 1966 The Fussells Lodge Long Barrow Excavations 1957. *Archaeologia* 100, 1-80.
Ashbee, P. 1970 *The Earthen Long Barrow in Britain.* Dent: London.
Ashbee, P. 1978 Amesbury Barrow 51: Excavations in 1960. *Wiltshire Archaeological Magazine* 70-1, 1-60.
Ashbee, P., Smith, I.F. & Evans, J.G. 1979 Excavation of Three Long Barrows near Avebury, Wiltshire. *Proceedings of the Prehistoric Society* 45, 207-300.
Atkinson, R.J.C., Piggott, C.M. and Sandars, N. 1951 *Excavations at Dorchester, Oxon.* Oxford: Ashmolean.
Barclay, A. & Bayliss, A. 1999 Cursus Monuments and the Radiocarbon Problem. In Barclay, A. & Harding, J. *Pathways and Ceremonies. The cursus monuments of Britain and Ireland,* 11 - 29. Oxford: Oxbow.
Barclay, A., & Halpin, C. 1999 *Excavations at Barrow Hills, Radley, Oxfordshire.* Oxford Archaeological Unit.
Barclay, A., Lambrick, G., Moore, J. & Robinson, M. 2003 *Lines in the Landscape. Cursus Monuments in the Upper Thames Valley.* Oxford Archaeological Unit.
Barclay, G.J. & Maxwell, G.S. 1991 Excavation of a long mortuary enclosure within the legionary fortress at Inchtuthill, Perthshire. *Proceedings of the Society of Antiquaries of Scotland* 121, 27-44.
Barclay, G.J. & Russell White, C.J. 1993 Excavations in the ceremonial complex of the fourth to second millennium BC at Balfarg/Balbirnie, Glenrothes, Fife. *Proceedings of the Society of Antiquaries of Scotland* 123, 43-10
Barclay, G.J. & Maxwell, G.S. (eds) 1998 *The Cleaven Dyke and Littleour: monuments in the Neolithic of Tayside.* Society of Antiquaries Scotland Mono 13. Edinburgh.
Barclay, G.J., Brophy, K. & MacGregor, G. 2002 Claish, Stirling: an early Neolithic structure in its context. *Proceedings of the Society of Antiquaries of Scotland* 132, 65-137.
Barrett, J., Bradley, R. & Green, M. 1991 *Landscape, Monuments and Society. The prehistory of Cranbourne Chase.* Cambridge: University Press.
Blair, J. 1995 Anglo Saxon Pagan Shrines and their Prototypes. *Anglo Saxon Studies in Archaeology and History* 8, 1-28.

Bradley, R. 1983 The bank barrow and related monuments of Dorset in the light of recent research. *Proceedings of the Dorset Natural History and Archaeological Society*, 105, 15-20.

Bradley, R. 1992 The excavation of an oval barrow beside the Abingdon causewayed enclosure, Oxfordshire. *Proceedings of the Prehistoric Society* 58, 127-42.

Bradley, R. & Chambers, R. 1988 A New Study of the Cursus complex at Dorchester upon Thames. *Oxford Journal of Archaeology* 7, 271-89.

Bradley, R. & Edmonds, M. 1993 *Interpreting the Axe Trade: Production and Exchange in Neolithic Britain*. Cambridge: University Press.

Brann, M. 2003 *Curriestanes Cursus, Dumfries. A Report to Morgan Est plc*.

Brewster, T.C.M. 1984 *The Excavation of Whitegrounds Barrow 1, Burythorpe, North Yorkshire*. Malton: East Riding Research Committee Publications.

Brophy, K 1998. Cursus Monuments and Bank Barrows of Tayside and Fife. In Barclay, G.J. & Maxwell, G.S. (eds) 1998 *The Cleaven Dyke and Littleour: monuments in the Neolithic of Tayside*, 93-108. Edinburgh: Society of Antiquaries Scotland Mono 13.

Brophy, K. 1999 The Cursus Monuments of Scotland. In Barclay, A. & Harding, J. *Pathways and Ceremonies. The cursus monuments of Britain and Ireland*, 119-29. Oxford: Oxbow.

Brophy, K. 2000 Water Coincidence? Cursus Monuments and Rivers. In Ritchie, A. (ed.) *Neolithic Orkney in its European Context*. Cambridge: Macdonald Institute.

Brophy, K. & Barclay, G.J. 2004 A rectilinear timber structure and post ring at Carsie Mains, Meikleour, Perthshire, *Tayside and Fife Archaeological Journal* 10, 1-22.

Bruce-Mitford, R. 1974 *Aspects of Anglo-Saxon Archaeology*. London: Gollancz.

Buckley, D.G., Hedges, J.D. & Brown, N. 2001 Excavations at a Neolithic Cursus, Springfield, Essex, 1979-85. *Proceedings of the Prehistoric Society* 67, 101-62.

Burger, R.L. 1995 *Chavin and the Origins of Andean Civilisation*. London: Thames & Hudson.

Burl, A. 1969 Henges: Internal Features and Regional Groups. *Archaeological Journal* 126, 1-28.

Burl, A. 1987 *The Stonehenge People*. London: Dent

Burl, A. 1993 *From Carnac to Callnish. The Prehistoric Stone Rows and Avenues of Britain, Ireland and Brittany*. London: Yale University Press.

Busia, K.A. 1954 The Ashanti of the Gold Coast. In Forde, D. (ed.) *African Worlds*, 190-209. Oxford: University Press.

Carrington, S. 1865 Some Account of Long Low, near Wetton, Staffs. *Reliquary* 5, 26-30.

Case, H.J. 1955 Excavation of Two Round Barrows at Poole, Dorset. *Proceedings of the Prehistoric Society* 18, 148-54.

Case, H.J. 1982 The Linear ditches and Southern Enclosure, North Stoke. In Case, H.J. & Whittle, A.W.R. *Settlement Patterns in the Oxford Region: Excavation at the Abingdon Causewayed enclosure and Other Sites*, 60-75. London: CBA.

Case, H.J. 1986 The Mesolithic and Neolithic in the Oxford Region. In Briggs, G., Cook, J. & Rowley, T. *The Archaeology of the Oxford Region*, 18-37. Oxford: Department of Extra Mural Studies.

Case, H.J. 2004 Circles, Triangles, Squares and Hexagons. In Cleal, R. & Pollard, J. *Monuments and Material Culture*, 109-19. East Knoyle, Salisbury: Hobnob.

Chapman, H.P. 2005 Rethinking the 'Cursus Problem' – Investigating the Neolithic Landscape Archaeology of Rudston, East Yorkshire, UK using GIS. *Proceedings of the Prehistoric Society* 71, 159-70.

Charles-Edwards, T. 1989 Early Medieval kingships in the British Isles. In Bassett, S. *The Origins of Anglo Saxon Kingdoms*, 28-39. Leicester: University Press.

Childe, V.G. 1945 Directional Changes in Funerary Practices during 50,000 years. *Man* 4, 13-19.

Clare, T. 1978 Recent Work on the Shap 'Avenue' *Transactions of the Cumberland and Westmoreland Antiquarian and Archaeological Society* 78, 5-15.

Cleal, R. 1991 Cranborne Chase – The Earlier Prehistoric Pottery. In Barrett, J.C. (ed.) *Papers on the Prehistoric archaeology of Cranborne Chase*. Oxford: Oxbow.

Cleal, R., Walker, K. & Montague, R. 1995 *Stonehenge in its landscape*. English Heritage Archaeological Report 10.

Colt Hoare, R. 1812 & 1819 *Ancient Wiltshire* I & II

Conant, K.J. 1993 *Carolingian and Romanesque Architecture 800–1200*. London: Yale University Press.

Cook, M. & Dunbar, L. 2004 Kintore. *Current Archaeology* 194, 84-89.

Cornwall, I.W. 1953 Soil science and Archaeology with Illustrations from some British Bronze Age Monuments. *Proceedings of the Prehistoric Society* 19, 129-47.

Cornwall, I.W. 1955 Report on the Soil Samples. In N. Thomas The Thornborough Circles near Ripon, North Riding. *Yorkshire Archaeological Journal* 40, 180-1.

Crawford, O.G.S. 1935 Rectangular Enclosures: a note on Mr. Leeds' paper. *Antiquaries Journal* 15, 77-8.

Crawford, O.G.S. 1938 Bank Barrows *Antiquity* 12, 228-32.

Defoe, D. 1927 *A Tour Through England and Wales II*. London: Everyman, Dutton.

Dincauze, D.F. & Hasenstab, R.J. 1989 Explaining the Iroquois: tribalization on a prehistoric periphery. In Champion, T.C. *Centre and Periphery: Comparative Studies in Archaeology*, 67-87. London: Unwin Hyman.

Dixon, P 1988 Crickley Hill *Current Archaeology* 110.

Drury, C. 1979 *The Houses of Mankind*. London: Thames & Hudson.

Durden, T. 1995 The production of specialised flintwork in the later Neolithic: a case study from the Yorkshire Wolds. *P.P.S.* 409-32.

Earle, T. (ed.) 1991 *Chiefdoms: Power, Economy and Ideology*. Cambridge: University Press.

Earnshaw, J.R. 1973 The Site of a Medieval Post Mill and Prehistoric Site at Bridlington. *Yorkshire Archaeological Journal* 45, 19-40.

Edmonds, M. 1995 *Stone Tools and Society. Working Stone in Neolithic and Bronze Age Britain*. London: Batsford.

Elaide, M. 1954 *The Myth of the Eternal return*. London: Arkana.

Ellis, C.J. 2004 *A Prehistoric Ritual Complex at Eynesbury, Cambridgeshire*. East Anglian Archaeology Report 17.

Entwhistle, R. 1990 Land Mollusca. In Richards, J. *The Stonehenge Environs Project*, 88-93 & 105-8. London: English Heritage Archaeological Report 16.

Entwhistle, R. & Richards, J. 1987 The Geochemical and Geophysical Properties of Lithic Scatters. In Brown, A.G. & Edmonds, M.R. (eds) *Lithic Analysis and Later Prehistory*, 19-38. Oxford: BAR British Series 162.

Entwhistle, R. & Bowden, M. 1991 Cranborne Chase: The Molluscan Evidence. In Barrett, J.C. (ed.) *Papers on the prehistoric archaelogy of Cranborne Chase*. Oxford: Oxbow.

Erith, F.H. 1971 The Levelled Long Barrows *Colchester Archaeological Group Annual Bulletin* 14, 35-6.

Fairweather, A.D. & Ralston, I.B.M. 1993 The Neolithic timber hall at Balbridie, Grampian region, Scotland: the building, the date the plant macrofossils. *Antiquity* 67, 313-23.

Fasham, P.J. 1978 The excavation of a triple barrow in Micheldever Wood, Hants (MARC3, site R4). *Proceedings of the Hampshire Field Club and Archaeological Society* 35, 5-40.

Ford W.J. 1971 Charlecote *Annual Report of Excavations 1970, Dept. of Environment,* 52-3.

Ford, W.J. & Loveday R.E. 2003 'The Neolithic complex at Charlecote, Warwickshire' & 'Charlecote 71: an evaluation in the light of recent research'. *Birmingham and Warwickshire Archaeological Society Transactions* 107, 3-38.

Foster, S.M. & Stevenson, J.B. 2002 The Auchenlaich Long Cairn. In Barclay, G.J., Brophy, K. & MacGregor, G. Claish, Stirling: an early Neolithic structure in its context. *Proceedings of the Society of Antiquaries of Scotland* 132, 114-19.

Fraser, S. & Murray, H. 2005 Ower-by the river: new evidence for the earliest Neolithic on Deeside. *Scottish Archaeological News* 47, 1-2.

Fussell, G.E. 1949 *The English Rural Labourer*. London: The Batchworth Press.

Gelling, M. 1974 *The Place Names of Berkshire II*. English Place Name Society 50.

Gibson, A.M. 1989 The Prehistoric Pottery from Barford. In Gibson, A.M. (ed.) *Midlands Prehistory*, 77-80. Oxford: BAR British Series 204.

Gibson, A.M. 1994 Excavations at the Sarn-y-bryn-caled cursus complex, Welshpool, Powys, and the timber circles of Great Britain and Ireland. *Proceedings of the Prehistoric Society* 60, 143-223.

Gibson, A.M. 1995 First Impressions: a review of Peterborough ware in Wales. In Kinnes, I. & Varndell, G. (eds) *Unbaked urns of Rudely Shape. Essays on British and Irish Pottery for Ian Longworth.* Oxford: Oxbow.

Gibson, A.M. 1999 Cursus monuments and possible cursus monuments in Wales: avenues for research (or roads to nowhere?). In Barclay, A. & Harding, J. *Pathways and Ceremonies. The cursus monuments of Britain and Ireland.* 130-40. Oxford: Oxbow.

Gibson, A.M. 2000 *Stonehenge and the Timber Circles.* Stroud: Tempus.

Gibson, A.M. and Loveday, R.E. 1989 Excavations at the cursus monument of Aston Upon Trent, Derbyshire. In Gibson, A.M. *Midlands Prehistory: Some Recent and Current Researches into the Prehistory of Central England* 27-50. Oxford: BAR Series 204.

Gibson, A.M. & Kinnes, I. 1997 On the urns of a dilemma: radiocarbon and the Peterborough problem, *Oxford Journal of Archaeology* 16, 65-72.

Gillings, M, & Pollard, J, //2004 *Avebury* London: Duckworth.

Green, M. 2000 *A Landscape Revealed. 10,000 Years on a Chalkland Farm.* Stroud: Tempus.

Greenwell, W. 1877 *British Barrows.* Oxford.

Grinsell, L.V. 1953 *The Ancient Burial Mounds of England.* London.

Guilbert, G 1996 Findern is dead, long live Potlock – the story of a cursus on the Trent Gravels. *Past* 24, 10-2.

Harding, A.F. 1981 Excavations in the Prehistoric Ritual Complex near Milfield, Northumberland. *Proceedings of the Prehistoric Society* 47, 87-136.

Harding, A.F. & Lee, G.E. 1987 *Henge Monuments and Related Sites of Great Britain.* Oxford: BAR British Series 175.

Harding, J. 1999 Pathways to new realms: cursus monuments and symbolic territories. In Barclay, A. & Harding, J. *Pathways and Ceremonies. The cursus monuments of Britain and Ireland,* 30-8. Oxford: Oxbow.

Harding, J. 2003 *Henge Monuments of the British Isles.* Stroud: Tempus.

Harding, J. 2006 Pit-digging, Occupation and Structured Deposition on Rudston Wold, Eastern Yorkshire. *Oxford Journal of Archaeology* 25, 109-26.

Headlam, C. 1925 *Oxford and Neighbouring Churches.* London.

Healy, F. 2004 Hambledon hill and its Implications. In Cleal, R & Pollard, J. *Monuments and Material Culture,* 15-38. East Knoyle, Salisbury: Hobnob.

Helms, M. 1993 *Craft and the Kingly Ideal: Art, Trade and Power.* Austin, Texas.

Hey, G. 1997 Neolithic Settlement at Yarnton, Oxfordshire. In P. Topping (ed.) *Neolithic Landscapes,* 99-111. Oxford: Oxbow

Heywood Sumner 1913 *The Ancient Earthworks of Cranborne Chase* (1988 Gloucester: Alan Sutton).

Hinman, M. & Malim, T. 1999 Ritual Activity at the foot of the Gog Magog Hills, Cambridge. *Past* 13, 1-2.

Hodder, I. 1990 *The Domestication of Europe. Structure and Contingency in Neolithic Societies.* Oxford: Blackwell

Hogg, A.H.A. 1940 The Earthen Long Barrow at West Rudham – Final Report. *Norfolk Archaeology* 27, 315-31.

Hogg, D.J. Analysis of the Timber Structures. In Barclay, G.J., & Russell White, C.J. 1993 Excavations in the ceremonial complex of the fourth to second millennium BC at Balfarg/Balbirnie, Glenrothes, Fife. *Proceedings of the Society of Antiquaries of Scotland* 123, 169-75.

Hogg, D.J. 2002 Aspects of the Claish Structure. In Barclay, G.J., Brophy, K. & MacGregor, G. 2002 Claish, Stirling: an early Neolithic structure in its context. *Proceedings of the Society of Antiquaries of Scotland* 132, 111-4.

Holgate, R. 1988 *Neolithic Settlement of the Thames Basin.* Oxford: BAR 194.

Howard, A. & Garton, D. 1996 Prehistoric Human Occupation in the Trent valley in Nottinghamshire. *Past* 22, 1-2.

Jones, D. 1998 Long Barrows and Neolithic Elongated Enclosures in Lincolnshire: An Analysis of the Air Photographic Evidence. *Proceedings of the Prehistoric Society* 64, 83-114.

Keevil, G.D. 1992 Life on the Edge: archaeology and alluvium at Redlands Farm, Stanwick, Northants. In Needham, S. & Mackling, N. *Alluvial archaeology in Britain*, 177-84. Oxford: Oxbow.

Kendrick, J. 1995 Excavation of a Neolithic enclosure and an Iron age settlement at Douglasmuir, Angus. *Proceedings of the Society of Antiquaries of Scotland*, 125, 29-67.

Kinnes, I., Schadla-Hall, T., Chadwick, P. & Dean, P. 1983 Duggleby Howe Reconsidered. *Archaeological Journal* 140, 83-108.

Kinnes, I. 1992 *Non-Megalithic Long Barrows and Allied Structures in the British Neolithic*. London: British Museum.

Kinnes, I. 1999 Longtemps ignores: Passy-Rots, linear monuments in northern France. In Barclay, A. & Harding, J. *Pathways and Ceremonies. The cursus monuments of Britain and Ireland*, 148-54. Oxford: Oxbow.

Kristiansen, K. 1987 From stone to bronze: the evolution of social complexity in northern Europe 2300-1200 BC. In Brumfiel, E.M. & Earle, T. *Specialisation, Exchange, and Complex Societies*, 30-52. Cambridge: University Press.

Kristiansen, K. & Larsson, T.B. 2005 *The Rise of Bronze Age Society. Travels, Transmissions and Transformations*. Cambridge: University Press.

Last, J. 1999 Out of Line: cursuses and monument typology in eastern England. In Barclay, A. & Harding, J. *Pathways and Ceremonies. The cursus monuments of Britain and Ireland*. 86-97. Oxford: Oxbow.

Leeds, E.T. 1934 Rectangular Enclosures of the Bronze Age in the Upper Thames Valley. *Antiquaries Journal* 14, 414-6.

Lewin, J. 1969 *The Yorkshire Wolds. A Study in Geomorphology*. University of Hull Occasional Papers in Geography No. 11. Hull.

Lewis J.S.C. & Welsh, K. 2004 Perry Oaks – Neolithic inhabitation of a west London landscape. In Cotton, J. & Field, D. (eds) *Towards a New Stone Age – aspects of the Neolithic in south-east England*. CBA Research Report 137.

Liversage, D. 1992 Barkaer. Long barrows and Settlement, *Arkaeologiske Studier IX*, Akademisk Forlag, Universitetsforlaget I København.

Loveday, R.E. 1985 Cursus and Related Monuments of the British Neolithic. PhD thesis Leicester University.

Loveday, R.E. 1989 The Barford Ritual Complex: Further Excavations (1972) and a Regional Perspective. In Gibson, A.M. (ed) *Midlands Prehistory*, 27-50. Oxford: BAR British Series 204.

Loveday, R.E. 1998 Double Entrance Henges – Routes to the Past? In Gibson, A. & Simpson, D. *Prehistoric Ritual and Religion*. Stroud: Sutton.

Loveday, R. 1999 Dorchester-on-Thames – Ritual Complex or Ritual Landscape? In Barclay, A. & Harding, J. (eds) *Pathways & Ceremonies. The cursus monuments of Britain and Ireland*, 49-66, Neolithic Studies Group Seminar Papers 4. Oxbow: Oxford.

Loveday, R.E. 2002 Duggleby Howe Revisited. *Oxford Journal of Archaeology* 21, 135-46.

Loveday R.E. 2004 Contextualising Monuments. The Exceptional Potential of the Middle Trent Valley. *Derbyshire Archaeological Journal* 124, 1-12.

Loveday, R.E. 2006 The Valley of the Grand. *British Archaeology* 88, 22-3.

Loveday, R.E. and Petchey, M. 1982 Oblong ditches: a discussion and some new evidence. *Aerial Archaeology* 8, 17-24.

Lynch, F. & Musson, C. 2001 A prehistoric and early medieval complex at Llandegai, near Bangor, North Wales. *Archaeologia Cambrensis* 150, 17-142.

Makey, P. 2000 The flint assemblage In Abramson, P. Excavations at Pits Plantation, Rudston, for Perenco UK Ltd. *East Riding Archaeologist* 10.

Madsen, T. 1979 Earthen Long Barrows and Timber structures: Aspects of the Early Neolithic Mortuary Practices in Denmark. *Proceedings of the Prehistoric Society* 45, 301-20.

Mair, L. 1977 *African Kingdoms*. Oxford: Clarendon Press.
Malim, T. 2000 The ritual landscape of the Neolithic and Bronze Age along the middle and lower Ouse Valley. In Dawson, M. (ed.) *Prehistoric, Roman, and post-Roman landscapes of the Great Ouse Valley*, 57-86. London: CBA Research Report 119.
Manby, T.G. 1974 *Grooved Ware sites in Yorkshire and the North of England*. Oxford: BAR 9.
Manby, T.G. 1975 Neolithic occupation sites on the Yorkshire Wolds. *Yorkshire Archaeological Journal* 48, 23-60.
Manby, T.G. 1976 The Kilham Long Barrow, East Riding of Yorkshire. *Proceedings of the Prehistoric Society* 42, 111-59
Manby, T.G. 1979 Typology, materials and distribution of flint and stone axes in Yorkshire. In McKlough, T.H. & Cummins, W.A. *Stone Axe Studies*, 65-81. London: CBA Research Report 23.
Manby, T.G. 1988 *Archaeology in Eastern Yorkshire. Essays in Honour of T.C.M. Brewster*. Dept. Archaeology & Prehistory, University of Sheffield.
Marsac, M., Scarre, C. & Riley D. 1983 Recent Discoveries of Possible Neolithic Long Mounds in Western France and their British Parallels *Aerial Archaeology* 8, 1-16.
Maxwell, G. 1978 Air Photography and the Work of the Ancient and Historic Monuments Commission of Scotland, *Aerial Archaeology* 2, 37-44.
McKinley, J 2004 Human Remains. In Ellis, C.J. 2004 *A Prehistoric Ritual Complex at Eynesbury, Cambridgeshire*, 95-8. East Anglian Archaeology Report 17.
McK Clough, T.H. & Cummins, W.A. 1988 *Stone Axe Studies Volume 2. The petrology of prehistoric stone implements from the British Isles*. London: CBA Research Report 67: London.
Midgley, M 1985 *The Origin and function of the Earthen Long Barrows of Northern Europe*. Oxford: BAR International Series 259.
Midgley, M 2005 *The Monumental Cemeteries of Prehistoric Europe*. Stroud; Tempus
Newman, T.G. 1976 A crop mark site at Hasting Hill, Tyne and Wear *Archaeologia Aeliana* (5th series) 4, 183-4.
Newman, C. 1999 Notes on Four cursus-like monuments in County Meath, Ireland. In Barclay, A. & Harding, J. (eds) *Pathways & Ceremonies. The cursus monuments of Britain and Ireland*, 141-7, Neolithic Studies Group Seminar Papers 4. Oxbow: Oxford.
O'Connell, M. 1990 Excavations during 1979-85 of a multi-period site at Stanwell. *Surrey Archaeological Collections* 80, 1-62.
O'Kelly, C. 1967 *An Illustrated Guide to Newgrange and other Boyne monuments*.
Osyannikov, O.V. & Terebikhin, N.M. 1994 Sacred space in the culture of the Arctic regions. In Carmichael, D.L., Hubert, J., Reeves, B. & Schanche, A. (eds) *Sacred Sites, Sacred Places*, 44-81. London: Routledge.
Parker Pearson, M. 1999 *The Archaeology of Death and Burial*. Stroud: Sutton.
Penny, A & Wood, J.E. 1973 The Dorset Cursus Complex: A Neolithic Astronomical Observatory, *Archaeological Journal* 129, 22-55.
Phillips, C.W. 1935 A re-examination of the Therfield Heath Long Barrow, Royston. *Proceedings of the Prehistoric Society* 1, 101-7.
Phillips, C.W. 1936 The Excavation of the Giants Hills Long barrow, Skendleby, Lincolnshire. *Archaeologia* 85, 37-106.
Piggott, S. 1937 The excavation of a Long Barrow in Holdenhurst Parish, near Christchurch. *Proceedings of the Prehistoric Society* 3, 1-14.
Piggott, S. 1954 *The Neolithic Cultures of the British Isles*. Cambridge.
Piggott, S. 1974 *The Druids*. Harmondsworth: Penguin.
Piggott, S. 1985 *William Stukeley. An Eighteenth-century Antiquary* London: Thames & Hudson.
Pitt-Rivers 1898 *Excavations in Cranborne Chase IV.*
Powell, T.G.E. 1969 *Megalithic Enquiries in the West of Britain*. Liverpool: University Press.
Pryor, F., French, C., Crowther, D., Gurney, D., Simpson, G. & Taylor, M. 1985 *The Fenland Project 1 Archaeology and Environment in the Lower Welland Valley 1*. East Anglian Archaeology Report 27, vol. 1.

Pryor, F. 1993 Excavations at Site 11, Fengate, Peterborough, 1969. In W.G. Simpson, D.A. Gurney, J. Neve & F. Pryor *The Fenland Project: excavation in Peterborough and the Lower Welland Valley 1960 – 1961*, 127-40. East Anglian Archaeology Report 61.

Reaney, D. 1968 Beaker burials in South Derbyshire. *Derbyshire Archaeological Journal* 88, 68-81.

Relke, J. & Ernest, A. 2003 Ancient Egyptian Astronomy: Ursa Major-Symbol of Rejuvenation, *Archaeastronomy* 17, 64-79.

Renfrew, C. & Bahn, P. 2004, *Archaeology: Theories, Methods and Practice*. London: Thames & Hudson.

Richards, C. 1993 Monumental choreography: architecture and spatial representation in late Neolithic Orkney. In Tilley, C. (ed.) *Interpretative Archaeology*, 143-78.

Richards, J. 1990 *The Stonehenge Environs Project*. English Heritage Archaeological Report 16.

Richmond, I.A. Excavations on the Estate of Meikleour, Perthshire 1939. *Proceedings of the Society of Antiquaries of Scotland* 74, 37-48.

Rideout, J.S. 1997 Excavation of Neolithic Enclosures at Cowie Road, Bannockburn, Stirling 1984-5. *Proceedings of the Society of Antiquaries of Scotland* 127, 29-68.

Riley, D.N. Air Survey of Neolithic Sites on the Yorkshire Wolds. In Manby, T.G. *Archaeology in Eastern Yorkshire. Essays in Honour of T.C.M. Brewster*, 89-93. Dept. Archaeology & Prehistory, University of Sheffield.

Robinson, M. 2003 Palaeoenvironmental Studies. In Barclay, A., Lambrick, G. Moore, J. & Robinson, M. *Lines in the Landscape. Cursus Monuments in the Upper Thames Valley*, 163-70. Oxford Archaeological Unit.

Royal Commission on Historical Monuments 1960 *A Matter of Time: an archaeological survey of the river gravels of England*. London: HMSO.

Royal Commission on Historical Monuments (England) 1975 *County of Dorset V.* London: HMSO.

Royal Commission on Historical Monuments (England) 1987 *Annual Review 1986*.

Royal Commission on Historical Monuments (Scotland) 1997 *Eastern Dumfriesshire an archaeological landscape*.

Royal Commission on Historical Monuments (Scotland) and Brophy, K. forthcoming *The Cursus Monuments of Scotland*.

Saville 1990 *Hazleton North. The excavation of a Neolithic long cairn of the Cotswold-Severn group*. English Heritage Archaeological Report 13.

Saville, A. 1999 An exceptional polished flint axe-head from Bolshan Hill, near Montrose. *Tayside and Fife Archaeological Journal* 5, 1-6.

Schutling, R.J. & Wysocki, M. 2005 'In this Chambered Tumulus were Found Cleft skulls …': an Assessment of the Evidence for Cranial Trauma in the British Neolithic. *Proceedings of the Prehistoric Society* 71, 107-138.

Sharples, N.M. 1991 *Maiden Castle: Excavations and field survey 1985-6*. English Heritage Archaeological Report 19.

Shennan, S. 1993 Commodities, transactions, and growth in the Central European Early Bronze Age. *Journal of European Archaeology* 1.2, 59-72.

Sheridan, A. 1992 Scottish stone axeheads: some new work and recent discoveries. In Sharples, N. & Sheridan, A. (eds) *Vessels for the Ancestors: Essays on the Neolithic of Britain and Ireland in Honour of Audrey Henshall*, 194-212. Edinburgh: University Press.

Silverman, H. 1994 The archaeological identification of an ancient Peruvian pilgrimage center, *World Archaeology* 26 (1), 1-18.

Simpson, W.G. 1985 Excavations at Maxey, Bardyke Field 1962-63. In Pryor, F., French,C. Crowther,D., Gurney, D., Simpson, G., & Taylor,M. *The Fenland Project 1 Archaeology and Environment in the Lower Welland Valley 1* East Anglian Archaeology Report 27, vol. 2, 245-262.

Smith, G. 1834 *Essay on the Construction of Cottages*.

Smith, I.F. 1965 *Windmill Hill and Avebury. Excavations by Alexander Keiller 1925-1939*. Oxford: Clarendon Press.

Spencer, C.S. 1990 Tempo and Mode in State Formation: Neo evolutionism reconsidered. *Journal of Anthropological Archaeology* 9, 1-30.

Szpunar, A. 1987 Die Beile in Polen I (Flachbeile, Randleistenbeile, Randeistenmeisel). *Prahistorische Bronzefunde Abteilung* IX, 16.

St Joseph 1964 Aerial Reconniassance: Recent Results 2, *Antiquity* 38, 290-92.

Stoertz, C. 1997 *Ancient Landscapes of the Yorkshire Wolds. Aerial photographic transcription and analysis.* RCHM (England).

Startin, B. 1982 Prehistoric earthmoving. In Case, H. & Whittle, A. (eds) *Settlement Patterns in the Oxford Region*, 153-6. London: CBA.

Stone, J.F.S. The Stonehenge Cursus and its Affinities. *Archaeological Journal* 104, 7-19

Stukeley, W. 1740 *A Temple Restor'd to the British Druids.*

Stupecki, L.P. 1997 Sacred space in the Cultural Landscape of Slavic Peoples in the Pre-Christian Period. In Chapman, J. & Dolukhanov, P. *Landscapes in Flux. Central and Eastern Europe in Antiquity*, 59-76. Oxford: Oxbow.

Thomas, J. 1998 Pict's Knowe, Holywood and Holm: prehistoric sites in the Dumfries area. *Current Archaeology* 14 (4), 149-54.

Thomas, J. 1999 The Holywood cursus complex, Dumfries: an interim account 1997. In Barclay, A. & Harding, J. (eds) *Pathways & Ceremonies. The cursus monuments of Britain and Ireland,* 49-66. Neolithic Studies Group Seminar Papers 4. Oxbow: Oxford.

Thomas, J. 2004 The Later Neolithic Architectural Repertoire: the case of the Dunragit complex. In Cleal, R. & Pollard, J. *Monuments and Material Culture,* 109-19. East Knoyle, Salisbury: Hobnob.

Thorpe, I.J. & Richards, R. 1984 The Decline of Ritual Authority and the Introduction of Beakers into Britain. In Bradley, R. & Gardiner, J. *Neolithic studies. A Review of Some Current Research. Reading Studies in Archaeology No. 1*, 67-86. Oxford: BAR British Series 133.

Tilley, C. 1994 *The Phenomenology of Landscape: Places, Paths and Monuments.* Oxford: Berg.

Topping, P. 1982 Excavation at the cursus at Scorton, north Yorkshire, 1978. *Yorkshire Archaeological Journal* 54, 7-21.

Vatcher, F. de M. 1960 Thornborough Cursus, Yorkshire. *Yorkshire Archaeological Journal* 38, 425-45.

Vatcher, F. de M. 1961 The excavation of the Long Mortuary Enclosure on Normanton Down, Wiltshire. *Proceedings of the Prehistoric Society* 27, 160-73.

Vatcher, L. & F. 1973 Excavation of Three Post Holes in Stonehenge Car Park. *Wiltshire Archaeological and Natural History Magazine* 68, 57-63.

Wainwright, G.J. 1979 Mount Pleasant, Dorset: Excavations 1970 – 1971. *Reports of the Research Committee of the Society of Antiquaries 37.*

Wainwright, G.J. & Longworth, I.H. 1971 Durrington Walls: Excavations 1966 – 1968. *Reports of the Research Committee of the Society of Antiquaries 29.*

Warrick, G. 1996 The Evolution of the Iroquoian Longhouse. In G.Coupland & E.B. Bunning *Archaeological Perspectives on Larger Domestic Structures,* 11-26. Madison Wisconsin: Prehistoric Press.

Webster, G. & Hobley, B. 1964 Aerial reconnaissance over the Warwickshire Avon. *Archaeological Journal* 121, 1-22.

Wheeler, R.E.M. 1943 Maiden Castle, Dorset. *Reports of the Research Committee of the Society of Antiquaries 12.*

Whittle, A., Atkinson, R.J.C., Chambers, R. and Thomas, N. 1992 Excavations in the Neolithic and Bronze Age Complex at Dorchester-on-Thames, Oxfordshire, 1947-1952 and 1981. *Proceedings of the Prehistoric Society* 58, 143-201.

Williamson, T. & Loveday, R.E. Rabbits or ritual? Artificial warrens and the Neolithic long mound tradition. *Archaeological Journal* 145, 290-313.

Windell, D. 1989 A late Neolithic 'Ritual Focus' at West Cotton, Northamptonshire. In Gibson, A.M. (ed.) *Midlands Prehistory*, 85-94. Oxford: BAR British Series 204.

Wilson, D.R. 2000 *Air Photo Interpretation for Archaeologists* Stroud: Tempus.

INDEX

Allen, Major 18, 202
Aston on Trent cursus 39, 42-3, 118, 119, 124, 127-8, 134-5
Auchenlaich bank barrow 95-7
Avenues 13, 103-113
Axes 164-5, 168-9, 172, 172-6, 183

Baerkar long mound, Jutland 100-1
Balfarg 76-7, 80-1
Bank barrows 89-113
Bannockburn 28, 82-3
Barford 59, 157
Barford-like complexes 66-7, 148, 197
Beakers 160
Bellshiel Law 88
Biggar 179-80
Bracketing ditches 72-3
Brampton 72-3
Broomend of Crichie 108
Buscot-Lechlade complex 116

Callanish 109-10
Carsie Mains 77-8, 81
Celtic sanctuary sites 119-201
Centralising tendency 102, 197-9
Charlecote 54, 56, 92-5, 141
Chavin 155, 170
Chiefdoms 162-4, 197
Claish 78-80, 185
Cleaven Dyke 98-9
Colt Hoare 16-7, 110-1
Cremation deposits 147-8, 177-9
Crickley hill long mound 91-2

Curriestanes 85, 121
Cursuses
   and rivers 133-6
   astronomical alignment 137-42
   areas enclosed 131-2
   carbonised material 127-8
   classification 20-7
   dating 165-6, 194-5, 203
   definition 25
   distribution 34
   ditch recutting 37-8
   ditch size 35
   dog leg courses 107, 158-61
   form and purpose 124-30
   geometry 114-6
   grouping of sites 140-5
   incorporation of long mounds 183-5
   labour estimates 145
   layout procedures 114-24
   mega sites 157-61
   origin of name 14
   post circles 128-9
   post settings 38-40
   survival as landscape features 40-4, 201
   terminal layout 120-4
   woodland environment 36-7

Dorchester upon Thames complex 31, 37, 45-7, 65, 121-2, 138, 140, 141, 144, 146-53, 156-7, 188, 193, 197
Dorset Cursus 11-12, 33, 37, 113, 136-7, 158-61, 183-92
Douglasmuir 82

Drayton North 37, 40-2, 153
Drayton South 115, 193
Duggleby Howe 177-9

Elaborate artefacts 172-8
Eskdalemuir bank barrows 97
Eynesbury
    cursuses 43, 74, 84
    long barrow 70-1

Fussell's Lodge long barrow 51

Giants Hills I long barrow 51, 53
Greater Stonehenge Cursus 13-17, 32, 194-5
Grooved Ware 192-4, 196-7

Haddenham long barrow 68-9
'Halls' 78-82, 85-6, 128
Henges 35, 84-5, 105-9, 148, 192-9
Hengiform sites 46, 146-7, 156-7, 192
Holm alignments 104
Holywood 21, 22, 37, 39, 128, 142, 154

Inchtuthill 75
Individual burials 176-80, 182, 186

Kennet avenue 105-7
Kilham long barrow 51-3, 103
Kintore long mound 75-6
Knowlton henge complex 193

Lechlade 140, 197
Lesser Stonehenge Cursus 17, 37-8
Liff's Low 180-1
Llandegai 94, 95, 195
Long barrow avenues 103-4
Long enclosure dimensions 62-3, 72-3
Long enclosure dating 59, 62, 74-8, 82, 84, 199-201, 203
Long houses 99-102, 126-30
Long Low 95-6

Maiden Castle bank barrow 89-90
Maxey 31, 37, 38-9, 136, 138, 141, 144, 146, 152-3, 156-7
Micheldever Wood 58
Mildenhall Ware 67, 69, 74

Milfield 108
Monkton Up Wimborne 191

Normanton Down 47-8
North Stoke 39, 59, 93-4
Newgrange 195

Paramount kingship 163-4, 169-72
Passy, Burgundy 101-2
Pen Hill, Wells 92
Peterborough Ware 45, 106-7, 153-7, 186
Pilgrimage centres 148-52
Pillow mounds 57-8, 92
Pit avenues 111-2

Radley 59-62
Romano-Celtic temples 36
Rots, Normandy 102
Rudston complex 31, 33, 158-61, 164-9, 172-3, 193

Sanctuary sites 148-53
Scorton 37, 39, 98
Shap avenue 110-1
Sinodun Hills 149, 150
Springfield 28, 37, 43, 118, 128, 154, 188, 202
Stanwell (Heathrow) 39, 97
Stanwick 69-70
Stonehenge avenue 13, 107
Stonehenge post alignment 104
Stonehenge landscape 198-9
Stukeley, William 14-7, 105, 110

Tara, Ireland 195
Thornborough 36-7, 120-1
Turf-built barrows 67-9
Turf-built houses 80-1

Upper Largie 104

West Cotton 67-8
Whitegrounds burial 62
Wor Barrow 48-51

Yarnton 64

If you are interested in purchasing other books published by Tempus,
or in case you have difficulty finding any Tempus books in your local bookshop,
you can also place orders directly through our website

www.tempus-publishing.com